Enduring What Cannot Be Endured

Dorothy Dore (Grant) Dowlen in Manila, ca. 1949 or 1950

Enduring What Cannot Be Endured

Memoir of a Woman Medical Aide in the Philippines in World War II

by DOROTHY DORE DOWLEN

EDITED BY THERESA KAMINSKI

McFarland & Company, Inc., Publishers
Jefferson, North Carolina, and London

Library of Congress Online Catalog Data

Dowlen, Dorothy Dore, 1925–
Enduring what cannot be endured : memoir of a woman medical aide
in the Philippines in World War II / by Dorothy Dore Dowlen ;
edited by Theresa Kaminski.
p.   cm.
Includes index.
ISBN 0-7864-0851-0 (softcover : 50# alkaline paper)
1. Dowlen, Dorothy Dore, 1925–   .   2. World War, 1939–1945—
Personal narratives, American.   3. Nurses—Philippines—Biography.
4. World War, 1939–1945—Underground movements—Philippines.
5. Philippines—History—Japanese occupation, 1942–1945.
I. Kaminski, Theresa, 1958–   .   II. Title.
D811.5.D644   2001   940.54'8173'092—dc21   00-51134

British Library cataloguing data are available

Cover images: (top) the author ca. 1949 or 1950; (bottom) the author,
third from left, as a child, standing in a banca outrigger boat.

Manufactured in the United States of America

McFarland & Company, Inc., Publishers
Box 611, Jefferson, North Carolina 28640
www.mcfarlandpub.com

Contents

Editor's Introduction

For many Americans today the quintessential image of World War II comes from the Hollywood blockbuster *Saving Private Ryan*, which begins with an unflinching re-creation of the Normandy Invasion on D-Day then follows a small group of men on a special mission. This movie depicts war through combat and soldiers (war as men's business), and in doing so it would seem to have little relation to the memoir you are about to read. But in fact, *Saving Private Ryan* illustrates why Dorothy Dore Dowlen's story, which takes place in the Pacific Theater, helps us to understand the many complexities involved in any military conflict, complexities usually absent in popular war films.

In *Saving Private Ryan* American soldiers fought their way up through the Normandy beaches and into French towns, with death and destruction evident everywhere. Largely absent, however, were the civilians who were caught up in the massive invasion. What happened to them as these fierce battles between the Allies and the Germans raged through the streets of their hometowns? Did civilians simply disappear, inconsequential characters in this life-and-death drama? In Dorothy's memoir the answer is certainly no, that civilians and soldiers are inextricably linked in wartime, that the stories of both must be clearly understood to make sense of war experiences. But for Dorothy the civilians (including her own family) on her home island of Mindanao in the Philippines took precedence, yet she knew

1

that their safety was tied to the successes of the United States Armed Forces Far East (USAFFE). The daughter of a Caucasian father and a Filipina mestiza mother, Dorothy was a teenager when the Japanese attacked the Philippines in December 1941, and her national loyalties compelled her to learn nursing so that she could support the USAFFE, which initially took a beating from the enemy.

Dorothy's book therefore broadens our understanding of the far-ranging impact of war, particularly on women and families in occupied and combat zones, an awareness initially stimulated in the post–World War II years by the publication of Anne Frank's diary. Later, in the shadows of Vietnam, which brought the horrors of war into American homes through television, and of the 1960s women's movement, which sparked the creation of women's studies programs and a reinvigorated interest in women's history, scholars turned their attention to women's varied roles in wartime. The 1987 book *Behind the Lines: Gender and the Two World Wars*, for instance, contains articles about American and European women as civilians and as military personnel. This renewed attention to women's activities in military conflicts also paved the way for the publication of memoirs, including Dorothy Still Danner's *What a Way to Spend a War: Navy Nurse POWs in the Philippines* and Margaret Sams's *Forbidden Family: A Wartime Memoir of the Philippines*.

But unlike those two women, Dorothy Dore Dowlen spent the war years on the run. This made her experiences more comparable to those of Abby R. Jacobs, who wrote of her years in hiding with other Americans on the Philippine island of Negros in the privately published (and hard-to-locate) *We Did Not Surrender*. Also, as a biracial woman, Dorothy provides a unique perspective on what happened to civilians during the Japanese occupation of Mindanao. A young, attractive mestiza, she had many reasons to worry about what would happen if she were captured because she knew that Japanese soldiers routinely raped Asian women, a worry compounded by the fact that because she was part Caucasian the enemy would likely treat her even more cruelly. Never self-centered enough to worry exclusively about her well-being, Dorothy acted many times to preserve the lives of her parents and those USAFFE soldiers under her care. Although she clearly understood battle strategies and the military hierarchy, for her the war was about much more: it was about home and family. And to safeguard home and family Dorothy willingly crossed the line between civilian and military, working for the USAFFE when she could but abandoning those duties when her family was in need. She shows her readers the very immediate consequences of war, as well as the reasons for it.

In *Saving Private Ryan* much was made of President Abraham Lincoln's

1864 letter to a mother who had lost five sons to the Union cause, a letter also pertinent to the importance of Dorothy's book, which is steeped in memory. Her memoir is not committed to recounting battle maneuvers and military personnel rosters but to preserving, as Lincoln wrote in that 1864 letter, the "cherished memory of the loved and lost." Dorothy is a survivor, not a scholar. Because her memories are colored by terrible personal losses, these recollections are by turns both sentimental and harsh: Dorothy cannot abide cruelty, selfishness, egotism, or prejudice from anyone. She recalls the self-sacrificing goodness of her family, the unnecessarily brutal treatment of civilians by the Japanese, and the vainglorious actions of some of the USAFFE guerrilla leaders. Although Dorothy is plain about her opinions, she leaves ultimate judgments to God. Readers familiar with guerrilla warfare in the Philippines during World War II may take issue with her interpretation of the way the war was conducted, but Dorothy clearly writes about the war as *she* experienced it.

Those who want to broaden their understanding of the military aspects of the Pacific war should consult Ronald Spector's *Eagle Against the Sun: The American War with Japan* and John Dower's *War Without Mercy: Race and Power in the Pacific War*. Narrowing the field even further, to Dorothy's home of the Philippine Islands, are stories of American and Filipino guerrilla activity, both horrifying and heroic: Jesus A. Villamor's *They Never Surrendered*, Charles Willoughby's *The Guerrilla Resistance Movement in the Philippines, 1941–1945*, and John Keats's *They Fought Alone*. All of these books provide their own viewpoints and serve as interesting companion pieces to Dorothy's memoir, ultimately highlighting the reality that no one fought alone.

What follows is Dorothy's story. As her editor I helped her straighten out some grammar and punctuation, and I encouraged her to tell more, to fill in details so that readers unfamiliar with the Philippine Islands would see them more clearly. What has emerged is a compelling story of love, family, courage, and survival during an especially horrifying time.

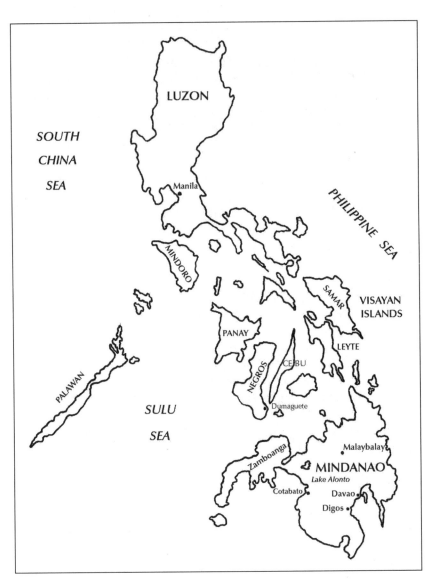

The Philippine Islands.

Introduction

Whenever I hear that old saying, "All's fair in love and war," my immediate, forceful reaction is, "No way!" There are certain realities to both love and war that have little to do with any rational sense of fairness. I ought to know: I was a teenager when World War II broke out in the Pacific Theater, when the Japanese attacked and occupied most of the Philippine Islands, the home of my birth, the home of my heart. I was 15 years old when my entire family decided to oppose the Japanese, to work with the guerrillas to drive the enemy off our island of Mindanao. I was 15 when I first donned a khaki uniform and matching cap with a medical insignia pinned on it and began, under the direction of a USAFFE doctor, nursing wounded and sick civilians and soldiers. I saw things no one should have to see, much less a young woman who had led a rather sheltered life in and around the city of Davao on Mindanao, later at Silliman University on the island of Negros. I also endured the unendurable—the deaths of my parents and my youngest brother and the savage murder of the love of my young life, Captain John "Jack" Grant, an American guerrilla who became my husband for too short a time.

I suffered but survived, and for many years after the war experienced what is now known as "survivor's guilt." If it had not been for my daughter, Jean Louise, born in a corn shed in the jungles of Mindanao not long after Jack's death, and for the religious faith my mother had instilled in me, I do not know that I could have gone on. There was nothing fair about any of this—nothing fair about the devastation wreaked by the Japanese on the beautiful island of Mindanao, nothing fair about the senseless deaths of my beloved family members, nothing fair about a young man's life being snuffed out before he ever knew he was going to be a father.

I was born in the Philippines, a group of over seven thousand islands off the southeast coast of Asia in the Pacific Ocean. The Philippines, nestled between Taiwan and Borneo, stretch about 688 miles east and west and almost 1,152 miles north and south. Luzon is one of the major islands, and Manila, its capital city, is probably the best known of all the cities in the Philippines. Mindanao, my home island, is the largest and southern most of the Philippines, and like the other islands it is divided into provinces, each of which governs itself. Mindanao is also home to the Moros, fierce tribes of Muslims who since before the seventeenth century have violently resisted any intruders. The Spanish, who colonized the Philippines in the 1400s, never quite succeeded in subduing the Moros, a problem passed along to the Americans when they took over at the beginning of the twentieth century. Between 1904 and 1907 General John "Black Jack" Pershing led the United States Cavalry in Lanao Province to try and pacify the Moros. Victor Alexander Dore, a member of the 15th Cavalry, my father, lost his left arm during one of these pacification battles.

Although my dad understandably bore some ill will against the Moro band responsible for his injury, he was already hopelessly in love with the Philippines when he was mustered out of the army in 1907. He lived on Leyte for a time and then during a trip to Cebu City he caught sight of a beautiful young Filipina schoolteacher, Pauline Cueva. He quickly courted and married her in 1918, when he was forty, she twenty. In 1920 my dad moved my mom to Davao City on Mindanao because he had met up with a World War I veteran there who owned a coconut plantation just outside the city, and my dad took over its management. I was born in Davao in 1925, after two of my brothers and about 18 months before my youngest brother. My mom sent all of us to the Davao elementary school, where we learned the "Three R's" and I was schooled in home economics to prepare me for marriage. I also picked up a lifelong love for music there. Although I started high school in Davao, my mom decided that her children should have the very best education available in the islands. In 1939 my older brothers, Samuel and George, and I journeyed hundreds of miles, accompanied by our mom, to the island of Negros to attend Silliman University, which had its own high school. Although I found it difficult to be away from home, I discovered many interesting things to do at Silliman, just loving my brief time there. My

I am seated here between my parents. My brothers are seated in front, Sam on the left, Philip in the center, and George on the right.

studies were challenging. There were plenty of extracurricular activities, including band, and I made wonderful friends.

I planned to finish high school at Silliman and perhaps even talk my parents into letting me attend the university as well. I was 15 years old in late 1941, full of the usual teenaged hopes and dreams, all of which collapsed on December 8, 1941, Pearl Harbor Day for those of us on the other side of the International Dateline. War came to the Philippines, and there was nothing I could do to avoid it. So I did the only thing I could do: I joined the fight against the Japanese by working with the USAFFE guerrillas. This is the story of my family, how it came to be, how we lived happily together on Mindanao, and how the war pulled us apart. But it is also a story of the endurance and regeneration of family because even as I lost the family of my childhood during the war, I began to create a new one that would sustain me in my time of loss and help me build for the future. None of this was fair, but I believe that because it was what God intended for me, I must accept and be grateful for all the good things that I have.

1

A Family Born of War

Whether a conflict is called a war or a revolution, innocent people find their lives irrevocably torn apart, something my family knows well. The irony of the experience of the modern Dore family is that it parallels that of the early Dore family, which fled the horrors of the French Revolution in the late 1700s. My Dore generation struggled through violence and death in the Philippine Islands from 1941 to 1945, during the Japanese invasion and occupation. In 1976 I stood on the same square in Paris where revolutionaries beheaded Marie Antoinette and many others, and for a moment that day I felt shivers run up my spine. If my ancestors had remained in France they would have been slaughtered, and I would not be around to tell my part of the family's story; but to tell my story I had to survive the horrors of the Japanese occupation of the country of my birth, the Philippines. The experience of standing on that square that day in 1976 was monumental for me. My husband, Jim, from Ukiah, California, our 12-year-old grandson, Kelly, and I were on a pleasure trip visiting seven European countries during the bicentennial year of my adopted home country, the United States. Considering my heritage, I felt truly multinational that day.

As a child I learned that my roots may have sprung from the French painter Paul Gustave Doré, born on January 6, 1833, in Strasbourg, Alsace-Lorraine, on the border of France and Germany. Gustave Doré, who always felt more French than German, painted some 190 biblical illustrations for

Don Quixote in 1863. After that his main illustration project centered on the Bible, producing a version that became known within three generations as the Doré Bible. Because of the fabulous reception he received in England in 1866, when his illustrated Bible appeared, Gustave himself fell in love with everything English and settled in London in 1868, establishing a home and studio on Bond Street. From that point on, every respectable Victorian parlor boasted a Doré illustrated Bible. Other notable illustrations followed, including Tennyson's *Idylls of the King*, Milton's *Paradise Lost*, and Edgar Allan Poe's poem "The Raven." Gustave Doré remained an influential member of London's artistic community until his death in 1883 at the age of 50.

It is also possible that my Dore line began even before Gustave Doré: it may have originated with the persecuted Protestant French Huguenots, who came from Finland, Denmark, and Holland. Somehow some of them reached France; a number of them became aristocrats and in the late 1700s fled to England because of the revolution. To hide their ties with France and with the revolution, they changed the pronunciation of their name from Doré, as in "Dor-ay," to Dore, as in "door." Thus our family name took on an Anglo-Saxon sound that blended in with the language of the English spoken in that century.

In the year that my father was born, 1878, Queen Victoria ruled England with her beloved husband, Prince Albert, whom she had married in 1840, three years after she ascended the throne. On May 9, 1878, my father, Victor Alexander Dore, was born to Samuel Dore and Mary Taylor Augusta Dore (nee Young), who registered his birth in the subdistrict of Ripley in the County of Derby. My grandfather was a successful farmer who lived in Plaistow Green in Crich, Derbyshire; he and my grandmother had four sons and one daughter. Charles supposedly migrated to Australia alone after an unsuccessful attempt to live with a disagreeable wife and was never heard from again. My dad, Victor, the second oldest, infused with wanderlust, left England at an early age. The third son, George, like his father, worked on the farm at Castlegate Stud Farm, Eyam, Derbyshire, where he bred Shire horses, a special breed of horse often presented in shows prior to sale. Uncle George married his first cousin Jessie Dore in 1906, and they had two children: Elizabeth, whom we lovingly called Cousin Betty, and her brother, Jack. Betty, born on January 21, 1907, was only 2 years old when her father died at the young age of 25 from diabetes. I knew Cousin Betty for a brief time, a bittersweet time when I first became aware of racial prejudice in the Philippines. My grandparents' fourth child was a girl named Eliza Hill, nicknamed Diddy. She died at the age of 12 from consumption (today called tuberculosis), a very infectious, fatal disease at the time, but fortunately other members of the family did not succumb. My grandmother Mary conceived once more, delivering a healthy son they named Samuel, who followed in his father's footsteps by working the family farm and providing food supplies when the war with Germany began in 1939. Uncle Samuel married and had nine children; they all remained in England.

My grandfather Samuel was considered a successful farm owner, but his whole family helped tend to all the duties on the farm. Milking cows was a daily chore, and because my dad was next to the oldest he had this responsibility each morning before walking to school five days a week. Wintertime was the most difficult because of the heavy snow and bone-chilling cold. In time my dad came to hate being tied down to the farm because, as he later told my brothers and me, milking cows was a woman's job. Soon he began to neglect his work on the farm, often wandering off to a nearby loft to daydream about far away places, his mind bursting with fantasies of exotic lands that beckoned him. Eventually my grandmother Mary recognized the restless spirit in this beloved son of hers, the spitting image of herself. This knowledge made her sad because she believed the outside world was not always a safe place for a young man, and she considered him

The home in England where my dad was born and raised. Here he is flanked by my grandmother, Mary Taylor Augusta Young Dore, and my grandfather, Samuel Dore. The identity of the gentleman on the far left is not known.

unprepared for the pitfalls that surely awaited him should he venture into the world on his own.

At the age of 16 my dad confirmed his mother's fear, running away from home to Liverpool, where he lied about his age to get work as a shipmate on one of the large steamships disembarking from that city. My dad was big for his age and strong as well from working on the farm, so he looked older than he really was and had little trouble getting that job. One day in 1894, the steamship loaded all of its cargo and passengers and prepared to cast off, taking my dad away forever from the country of his birth. He was excited that day, and his only thought was that at last he would see the world.

Each day onboard ship proved an adventure coupled with hard work, and my dad, young and strong, loved the crisp sea air and working side by side with seasoned sailors. He was growing up, wanted to be a real man, and was impressed by the sailors' muscles and sweat, which for my dad signified manhood. After many days on the high seas the steamship sighted land—the United States of America—and my dad found himself at long last coming into New York harbor. After guiding the ship toward the wharf and mooring the vessel into place, the captain ordered the anchor cast overboard so the crew could unload passengers and cargo. At nightfall the sailors received their liberty to go ashore, and my dad realized that he had no immigration papers that allowed him permanent residence in America. It never occurred to him that visitors or immigrants from another country needed documents to substantiate their presence in the New World. Filled with panic, my dad turned to his friend from Liverpool and learned to his surprise that the older fellow did not carry any papers either. Realizing that they were in the same fix, the friend suggested they jump ship—and that was how my dad came to the United States.

Once both men made their way off the ship and to the "safety" of New York, life became difficult because although they had money in their pockets they had no friends and no place to stay. My dad later told me that it was very tough trying to survive in a place called Brooklyn. There was no turning back for either man, so they made up their minds that they would find work in the area. Since he knew how to butcher hogs and cows, my dad took work in a meat market, whereas his friend worked as part of a cleanup crew. Because of their outgoing personalities they quickly made many friends.

In a conversation among these newfound friends a few years later, my dad discovered that men were being recruited into the United States Army, and he saw this as a way out of his dilemma. His friends informed him that he would have three hot meals a day, a warm place to bunk at night, free uniforms to wear, and some money for his pocket. But best of all, he would be eligible for United States citizenship. It was this last statement that convinced the two men; no longer would they have to stay hidden from the authorities after they enlisted in the military. Both men gave up their jobs, made their way toward Fort Ethan Allen in Vermont, and joined the army, which did not ask questions about their background. Honorable men from the beginning, they only wanted to prove themselves by serving their adopted country.

Private Victor A. Dore, 23 years old when he signed up for duty in 1901, could not know that his military career would be filled with adventure and excitement beyond his wildest expectations. He was shipped to the Philippine Islands immediately after making the long trip from Vermont to San Francisco, and he realized that his wanderlust for adventure would be fulfilled. As his children, my brothers and I heard about the close encounters with untamed natives, military chivalry, and unexpected hilarious incidents that made us laugh so hard we literally wet our pants. Most of all we felt honored to have such a brave father, who went through so much to become a real man: he was honest and totally disciplined, and he taught us values to live by, such as obedience, respect, and love of God, country, and family.

One exciting adventure that happened in my dad's military service became the defining incident of his career because it became part of his identity for the remainder of his life. He belonged to the 15th Cavalry, C Company, United States Army when it was summoned by the Philippine government to stop a Moro uprising in Dansalan, Lanao Province, on Mindanao sometime between 1903 and 1907. Upon their arrival the soldiers discovered the darkened forest, heavy foliage, and tall cogon grass conducive to hiding the enemy Moros. The

Sgt. Victor Alexander Dore, my dad, who served in the 15th Cavalry, C Company, United States Army, during the Spanish-American War in the Philippines from 1901 until 1907.

cavalrymen were not accustomed to jungle fighting, whereas their enemies were skilled in guerrilla warfare—a tactical operation of hit and run under cover of darkness.

On a dark and moonless night my dad and the rest of the 15th Cavalry bivouacked, settling in for the evening in Marawi, outside Dansalan. They closed ranks because of the unfamiliar territory surrounded by cogon grass, always a danger itself because of the sharply serrated edges on both sides of its narrow leaves. The men were tense, and some of the young soldiers were flat out afraid, so much so that they did not even dare walk to the latrine built under some trees just a short distance away. They had heard of the Moro *horramentado*, a man heavily drugged with a narcotic weed and armed with a double-edged, razor-sharp weapon called a *kampilan*. A horramentado kills his enemies like he would slaughter animals, and not even a six-shooter could stop him in his wild, drug-induced rage. Fear compelled some of the soldiers to use their boots to urinate in.

On the third night, my dad patrolled the area on his horse to see that all the men were accounted for and the sentries were at their posts. As his stallion slowly walked the path a sudden shrieking cry came from the dark: the Moros were on the offensive. One of them jumped in front of my dad's horse, raised his kampilan, and with a mighty force struck down the fine stallion. My dad tumbled into the cogon grass, which he thought would hide him, but the Moro would not give up on his prey.

When he caught sight of my dad on the ground, the Moro lifted his kampilan in the air once more with the intention of beheading his enemy, but somehow he missed my dad's head, instead cutting a large wound on his elbow when my dad raised his arm to protect himself. The mighty cavalry then began its charge, complete with bayonets and bullets, chasing the marauders back into the jungles. The Moros' steel-sharp weapons could not match the flying bullets from the soldiers' rifles and machine guns; thus my dad's life was spared.

Once the skirmish ended, the dead and wounded Moros had to be accounted for, and the injured cavalrymen had to be treated. When medics arrived to assist those severely hurt, my dad insisted that others be treated first; as a result of the delay in treatment, lack of antibiotic, and festering humidity, infection quickly set in, gangrene spreading from his elbow to the upper left side of his arm. He had to be taken to the military hospital in Zamboanga—a long, slow trip by steamboat—and by the time he arrived, his left arm was so severely infected that amputation was performed to save my dad's life. After a time doctors fitted him with an artificial arm shipped from the United States, but it gave him great pain because it did not fit right, so he quit wearing it.

Years later, when I was a little girl, I saw where he kept that arm in a trunk under our home. He was never ashamed of his handicap; instead, he used to play tricks on the neighborhood children with me helping him. On one nice sunny day when I was young he told me to go round them up so we could scare the living daylights out of them. I went along with him, as I knew what he was about to do, and the secret was ours to enjoy. When the children arrived, we gathered them around the trunk under the house and my dad asked them if they knew what happened to his arm. After the curious, wide-eyed children shook their little heads, he told them that the *As-wang* (evil one) came one night and cut off his arm; then he asked if they knew where it was now. Before they could answer, he opened the trunk and pointed at the object lying in the bottom of the trunk, announcing in a loud voice that there it was. The children screamed at the sight of what was really his artificial arm and ran home as fast they could, leaving my dad and me laughing so hard our midriffs hurt.

Toward the end of 1907 my dad was mustered out of the U.S. Army, and he retired in the Philippines, believing in his heart that at last he had found his Shangri-La, his hidden paradise. Very little of his life is fully known to me during the period of 1907 to 1919. When I was a child I overheard that my dad lived on Leyte with a wife, but because of cultural differences she had to leave town when she discovered she was pregnant with his child, leading me to believe that no legal marriage had taken place. Although my dad was willing to marry her, the woman left or was sent away, disgraced and possibly disowned by her family, disappearing without a trace. Many years after my parents were married in 1920, stories surfaced that the woman bore a son and that she named him Delfin Dore before she died in childbirth. Being an honorable and honest man in his dealings with his wife, Pauline, my mother—a loving, caring, and forgiving woman—my dad sought to find his son. Every effort he made turned out to be a dead end, but the boy in turn tried to track down his father. Traveling from one province to another the young man finally arrived in Davao City, where my dad occasionally made some business trips from Lawayon Plantation, which he ran, yet somehow their paths never crossed.

Retired Major Frank McGee, an American veteran who fought in France during World War I, established Lawayon Plantation. As the result of a head wound he sustained in the war, he was fitted with a silver plate that covered his skull, and once a year he had to make a long voyage either to Manila or to the United States to have the plate checked and replaced. Because of these annual visits to the hospital the major offered my dad a partnership in his coconut plantation to have someone there to supervise and manage the place in his absence. Both men were compatible, as they were retired U.S. military men who understood discipline, dependability, and trust; furthermore, they admired and respected one another. Besides, the major believed my dad's boyhood farming skills and his wide-ranging military knowledge qualified him for the job of business manager and part owner. The two men remained friends for many years, with World War II bringing them even closer once again when they chose to serve in the USAFFE, an expression of their beliefs in duty, honor, and freedom.

Describing my beloved mother is like visualizing a painting of a beautiful saint or angel. Pauline Cueva Dore was petite, just four feet eleven inches tall, a mestiza of Spanish, Indonesian, Malaysian, and South Pacific Islander heritage. Her sweet disposition added to her beauty from within and without: she was the most kind, generous, and loving person on the face of the earth. My mom was born on June 20, 1898, in the town of Ubay, province of Bohol, in the Visayan Islands. Shortly thereafter my grandfather Gregorio Cueva, a tall mestizo possessing a facial bone structure that indicated a European background, moved his family to the island of Cebu, where his shipping enterprise improved. He owned a medium-sized boat that carried passengers and some cargo from one island to another in the Visayans, and he had a knack for landing his small craft on some islands that had no wharves or where the channel was too shallow to allow larger steamboats to land. Captain of his own boat, he was gone from home most of the time, yet he never failed to provide for his wife, a Filipina tiny in stature but highly spirited; she feared no one. The marriage between my grandparents brought about two daughters: Mary and Paulina, who later changed her name to Pauline.

The majority of the people in the Philippines are highly educated because every parent's priority is to give their children an education, often sacrificing any luxury for themselves. Parents discouraged early marriages because they believed that without a college diploma, their sons and daughters could not support their own families. A college degree became a requirement for the Philippine upper class, for without it one is not accepted in the elite group made up of professionals. My mom completed high school with high honors then decided not to go to college so that she could more immediately serve the children in more remote areas of Cebu. Due to the shortage of teachers in those locations, high school graduates with excellent records could teach, even though they had not gone to college, and my mom qualified for a teaching credential in the public school lower grades.

One fine day after school, my mom was walking home laden with schoolbooks. A tall handsome soldier with sparkling blue eyes happened to be close by, exploring the scenery around him. The moment he set eyes on her he somehow knew she was the right girl for him. After arriving at

Pauline C. Dore, my saintly mother, with my older brother, George William Dore, and me. My mother was executed by the Japanese in 1944 as a civilian POW.

the same spot for several days to watch this beautiful olive-skinned woman walk by, my dad finally made his move to introduce himself. He did not realize that even before coming forward to make her acquaintance she had observed him from the corner of her eyes, and she liked what she saw. Once they met and shook hands, both of them experienced shivers up and down their spines.

Since my dad was wise about the strict Filipino rules regarding courtship, he decided not to pursue the relationship until he figured out how to get on the winning side of his future mother-in-law. He sought the advice of the elders in the community, who told him to find the most suitable gift for the older woman and then approach her with all the charm he could muster. When she extended an invitation to visit, he must greet the mother first then offer salutations to her daughter. If the mother approves and wants a second look, she will extend a follow-up invitation. The elders warned my dad not to underestimate this tiny woman who held the power to give approval to the marriage of her daughter Pauline. The tall, ruddy-complexioned, handsome Prince Charming did exactly what the elders told him, and my grandmother was pleasantly surprised by his behavior. What convinced her most was his sincerity, his polite manners, and his respect for their culture.

A long engagement was not a part of my dad's plan. One day in June 1918 he knelt down and proposed to Pauline; she accepted, and they were married immediately. When my parents wedded, my mom was twenty years old, and my dad was forty; yet in spite of this age difference they were compatible. She was not only a scholar and a religious teacher but also a wonderful and loving wife. He was a retired soldier who provided well for his family, the disciplinarian at home who instructed his children about the practical application of "horse sense" or "common sense," which made a great impact on my own life. My parents believed strongly in their marriage vows. Even though they had their problems, like all couples have, they were faithful to each other.

There were five of us children born to Pauline and Victor Dore. Mary Ellen, the oldest and the prettiest because she alone inherited our dad's outstanding features and his blue eyes, was born in 1920 at Lawayon, the family plantation on Mindanao. Lawayon sat far from the nearest city, Davao, which contained modern hospitals and pharmacies where a variety of medications could be purchased. When my fragile sister was born my mom felt a little heaven in her arms. In the beginning Mary Ellen was healthy; however, at the age of nine months she developed a high fever and pneumonia, a combination that proved too much for her tiny body. Even the fastest speedboat that moved like lightning over the ocean could not save my sister; she died on her arrival at the hospital.

My poor mom almost went out of her mind with grief over the loss of her first child. Her inner strength healed her sorrow, though, and like most women in the country accustomed to death and dying, she recovered. However, she questioned my dad about the wisdom of living in a remote place so far from modern conveniences such as hospitals, stores, and other necessities for their future family. She told him that although Lawayon

Plantation was a wonderful place, she could not bear to lose another child, but my dad still resisted the move.

On March 29, 1922, my oldest brother Samuel came into the world, born in a Davao hospital with my mom surrounded by competent doctors and nurses. My mom's delivery was natural, without drugs, as was common for women at the time. Everything appeared normal with the baby at first, but as Sam began to grow he showed signs of convulsions; he suffered from epilepsy. Sam inherited my dad's height and my mom's beautiful brown eyes and her natural wavy ebony hair. The girls in school considered Sam tall and handsome. I did too, because he was my brother.

On May 5, 1923, another son arrived, and he was given the name of George William after our Uncle George, who died in England at a very young age. He too was born in the hospital where the American doctors took care of our mom and her newborn child. After the arrival of this third baby my mom asked my dad to sell his portion of the plantation back to Major McGee so the family could move to the city of Davao, and he finally agreed. George proved to be an introvert most of the time, but once in a while he would let loose, turning into a comedian and imitating the comic Stan Laurel. Laurel and Hardy silent movies were quite popular in our day and gained even more popularity when the comedians' talking pictures came out. George picked up on some of the funny expressions of Stan Laurel by wiggling both his ears and criss-crossing his legs. He always made us laugh, but around other people he was very shy.

On their third try after my only sister died, my parents were finally blessed with a baby girl—me. I was born on July 25, 1925, and my parents named me Dorothy May. Since my mom claimed that I looked like a little doll when she first saw me in the hospital, she nicknamed me "Dolly." Even though I did not have my dad's beautiful blue eyes, I inherited other things from him, such as my light skin and my physical durability. From my mom's side I inherited brown eyes and dark hair. Beyond the physical, I also adopted the best things from my mom's Filipino heritage: close family ties, hospitality, friendship, strong religious beliefs, and inner strength. My birth filled the void created in my mom's heart from the death of Mary Ellen. Even my brothers adored me because I was different from them—I was a girl! They spoiled me, yet at the same time they loved me. Because I was the only girl, my parents spared no expense in dressing me up in the finest clothes money could buy; most of my best dresses came from Sears, Roebuck, and Company in America.

On December 14, 1926, my mom bore a third son, Philip Alexander. His first name, like my brother Samuel's, came from my mom's family Bible, and his middle name came from my dad. This little brother of mine grew into a handsome lad, with deep dimples on his right cheek and my mom's beautiful brown eyes. His light complexion and his height came from my dad. Philip and Sam were the tall ones, and George and I were the short ones, although we were both over five feet tall. Being the youngest, Philip and I became close because he did not want to rough it with two older brothers who were bigger and stronger; as a result Philip stayed around the house with me, and we teamed up for games and laughter with our neighbor friends. I always liked that this brother of mine appeared so willing to participate in my schemes.

I realize that some people have negative opinions about cross-cultural marriages and the children that they produce, but I considered myself blessed with these roots. The rich Filipino culture of my mom combined with my dad's mixed Anglo heritage gave me the best of many worlds, making me feel truly special, making me unique. Yet even on Mindanao, where my dad was so respected, mixed marriages sparked hatred, which soon touched my family. One of my earliest childhood memories is of Cousin Betty's visit, a time of joy for getting acquainted with an English relative and a time of sadness for the racial prejudice that visit sparked. It all started with my dad's friendship and business association with Major McGee, who was a single man. My dad immediately thought of his favorite maiden niece, the only daughter of his deceased brother, George, as a wife for Major McGee; so in 1927 my dad invited Cousin Betty to visit us in the Philippines, paying her way by steamship. She was elated at the prospect of seeing the beloved uncle she had never met, and she did not suspect that my dad intended to marry her off to a fine wealthy gentleman. This turned out to be her first and only journey abroad.

Arriving safely in Manila Betty was pleased to find her Uncle Victor waiting on the wharf. She had no trouble recognizing the tall, handsome, blue-eyed man dressed in the typical American haciendero (plantation owner's) outfit: a white shirt and suit, dark tie, white shoes, and a native straw hat. The meeting was very emotional between them. After so many years away from his homeland, my dad was reawakened to his English roots through his favorite niece's British accent and her custom of drinking tea. Even more than this, she looked just like grandmother Dore. When I first laid eyes on Cousin Betty, I saw that she was indeed beautiful. I was very young at the time, but I clearly remember her light skin, natural pink cheeks, light hair, and blue eyes. Her face turned red as a lobster when exposed to the sun, and unfortunately Betty suffered from rheumatism and arthritis of the worst kind. Her side of the family claimed that the afflictions were a result of the marriage between her father and his first cousin, but no one really knows for sure. The crippling conditions remained Betty's companions for life, yet in spite of this her inner strength and determination made her strong enough to take on the journey across the world.

After hugs, tears, and kisses they booked passage on a steamship for Davao City, then boarded a smaller boat to Lawayon Plantation, located along the coast of Cotabato Province. Upon setting foot on the plantation Betty filled her lungs with the aroma of wildflowers and alluring blossoms from fruit trees she had never seen before. And when she met my mother, Pauline, and all of us children—I was just two years old, George was four, and Sam was five—Betty was overjoyed to be with such a large, loving family. She found peace, contentment, and happiness for the first time in her life on our plantation, and because she was very beautiful Major McGee fell in love with her and wanted to marry her.

Sadly enough Betty's perfect joy was short-lived because her visit to the plantation sparked racial prejudice among Americans living in Davao. When Betty made a few trips with my dad to Davao, the American high-society women who befriended her began their prejudicial campaign, telling Betty that she did not belong on the plantation, where the natives lived, clearly a slur on my mom. They encouraged her to move to the city, where she could be with her "own kind," where they could take her under their wing and introduce her to the elite in the community. At first Betty did not understand what the fuss was all about because she was content to be with our family on the plantation, and she knew that my dad was happy to have married a kind, loving, caring, devoted, and educated woman.

The pressure, racially motivated, continued and finally reached the point where Betty hated making trips to Davao. Soon those busybody women discovered another avenue for their malicious attacks: they wrote letters and mailed them to her at the plantation, letters full of venomous words that made my cousin cringe and tear up the mail. In time Betty could no longer take it. Rather than hurt my parents by revealing the level of harassment from the American women she decided to shorten her stay and return to England; even Major McGee's proposal of marriage could not persuade her to prolong her visit. When she announced her intention to return home, my parents were crushed by the news and could not understand why she wanted to leave so soon. Betty's agony over the vicious letters was compounded by her inability to share her confusion with my mom. Although Betty harbored no racial prejudice, she feared that her continued presence at the plantation would cause harm to my family. Rather than allow any taint of prejudice to filter into the relationship she had with my mom, she chose to leave, taking with her all the beautiful memories she gathered in the Philippines and leaving the bad ones behind. My dad was hurt the most because he was losing his only human contact from England. Betty kept in touch with my parents when she arrived back in England. The letters were frequent, even after Germany declared war against England in 1939; but when the Japanese Imperial Army occupied the Philippines in 1942, her correspondence came to a halt, and we lost track of each other. Even though I was very young when she visited and I did not understand much of what was happening at the time, I heard enough from snatches of my parents' conversations as I was growing up so that I would always remember Betty. And I would always remember the ugliness of racial prejudice.

Aside from this incident most of my childhood memories are fond ones, especially those of the many informal parties my parents threw. We were all involved in planning, decorating, and even participating in the festivities. My brothers and I cranked up the old upright gramophone and played the records of the early 1900s for the delight of our visitors, who enjoyed dancing the waltz, fox-trot, and tango. Most of all they enjoyed hearing Jeanette MacDonald and Nelson Eddy's rendition of "When I Grow Too Old to Dream," "Oh Rose Marie I Love You," and "Desert Song." My dad had the two special ladies in his life—my mom and me—to waltz with. This tall, handsome man with sparkling blue eyes would walk across the room, stop in front of one of us, bow graciously, and very politely ask to have this dance. On occasions with visiting dignitaries from other countries, my dad summoned my brother Philip and me to sing his favorite songs: "Bonnie Wee Hus" and "Granny's Highland Hem." Wiping the tears with his handkerchief, he would turn to his guests and proudly remind them that we were his children. Philip and I enjoyed being his special troubadours, but we were also thrilled because the visitors gave us American dollars as a reward.

As time went by, my brothers, including Philip, outgrew our children's time together. The boys wanted to play with other fellows in the neighborhood, and they did not want me around simply because I was a girl. This made me angry because I had the idea that since I had grown up with the three of them, I should be considered one of the boys! Each time I challenged them to a fight, clenching my fists together in anticipation, they only laughed at me. I got back at my brothers by becoming a leader among the neighborhood children. My brothers refused to let me ride their bicycles, play with their colored glass marbles, or join their baseball games, so I gathered my own team of playmates. My moment of triumph came in 1932, when I was seven, and I formed two groups of children who played war with me. Naturally I was the leader of one group, and a boy my age was the leader of the other group. Little did our childish minds realize that in less than ten years we would all be facing a real war—World War II—in our own country. Some of us had to live and die fighting; the games had ended by then.

The first afternoon that we staged a war game I did not realize that the British officers my dad invited for lunch were still in our home. My mom had directed the outlay of the usual mashed potatoes, roast beef, gravy, vegetables, bread fresh from the oven, and homemade pies, food that always turned out wonderfully since our maids prepared it on the Sears and Roebuck cast-iron stove with my mom's supervision. After the noon meal our visitors retired to the verandah, smoking pipes filled with Prince Albert tobacco or puffing on good Havana cigars. Adding to their pleasure was the aroma of gardenias and other richly perfumed blossoms from tropical plants growing in our garden. My dad described the feeling as being contented as a cow. The men loved my dad's stories of his military life, especially how he ended up in the Philippines. Of course it was not a difficult task for him to talk about this because he just loved to talk about his lifetime experiences and his career as a soldier.

My dad ushered his guests to the verandah, which overlooked the garden, and they settled down in comfortable rattan chairs and began to smoke, whether it was a pipe, cigarettes, or Havana cigars. The maids brought out coffee and tea for those who wanted liquid refreshments. As the men discussed past and current events they were unaware of what was brewing a short distance from our home: my friends and I were playing soldiers. Suddenly, their attention shifted away from their host when they heard shouts of "Advance, advance, let's go get the enemy!" Hearing a familiar voice coming from below, my dad got up from his chair to see if it was whom he suspected. When he saw me leading a group of kids out of the brush with a make-believe wooden sword in my right hand, he turned red in the face and admitted to his guests that I was a tomboy instead of a refined lady. Sensing his concern, the visitors inquired about my age, and when they learned I was seven, the British captain, who had children of his own, reassured my dad that I would grow out of this phase. In time I did grow up and developed my femininity. I gave up fistfights and playing marbles with boys. I became a young lady interested in music and education, and my dad was very proud of me. But neither of us could know that one day what I learned during my old tomboy days would help ensure my very survival.

We were a happy and contented family up until 1934, when, at the age of nine, I noticed some radical changes taking place in my dad. As he slowly approached the age of fifty he drank more and became jealous of his American friends who came around to visit the family. In his mind he believed them interested in my mother. Even if this was true, my mom ignored the interest and was faithful to him to the end of her life. My brothers and I were shocked, though, when once or twice his heavy drinking caused him to physically abuse our mom. This was not like our dad at all. But the death of his beloved mother in 1939 caused him to give up drinking when he realized that his self-respect and the love of his family meant more to him than the alcohol he consumed. And because his fortune changed with the inheritance he received from his mother, he was his old self again. But that happy time did not last for long, through no fault of my family's.

My dad used his inheritance to invest in the Mindanao Oil Palm Corporation in Kidapawan, Cotabato, on the island of Mindanao. A German national planted the whole idea in my dad's mind, drawing him in hook, line, and sinker. From the beginning my mom opposed the investment because she could sense that the foreigner was a smooth talker and a fraud. Her instincts were right: the man did not have his share of the money, but as a partner in the corporation he lived on our generosity for a time. Once my dad recognized the deception, he dissolved the partnership and had the paperwork transferred to his name by legal means, so the property became his own. My dad sold our large home in the city of Davao and moved us to our new farm. Little did we know that dark clouds were gathering on the horizon in the form of war.

To conclude this account of my childhood I must admit that I did not have a perfect family, but I had a lot of love, security, laughter, and even the inevitable tears. Most important, my brothers and I had a mother and father who cared about our well-being. They instilled in us moral values, respect, acceptance of others, and religion, all of which saw us through difficult times in our lives. And having inherited a combination of two cultures from them enriched our own lives through better understanding, insight, and goodwill toward people of other races, cultures, and creeds. Without a doubt we were blessed by both worlds harvested from the lives of our parents.

My parents also put a high value on education. In 1932, when I was one month short of the age of seven, I began attending the first grade at Davao Elementary School, located less than a mile from where we lived. A very sheltered child, I initially feared being away from home. However, just hearing the excited voices of other children eased my apprehensions about not knowing anyone in that public school. In the Philippines the school year begins in June and ends in the middle of March the following year. In grade school all children learned the three basic Rs: reading, writing, and arithmetic. As each student advanced a higher level the girls could choose to take home economics in place of math. This choice, made in fourth grade, almost always resulted in the girls' moving into home economics to prepare them to be good wives, mothers, and homemakers. I, too, chose the home economics course because I believed it would be less taxing on my brain, for even though I could add, subtract, divide, and multiply, dealing with all the other figures did not appeal to me. My choice was vindicated in my adult years when I found out that algebra had nothing to do with balancing my checkbook, that by knowing simple addition and subtraction I could easily keep track of family income and expenses. In my home economics class I learned to embroider pretty handkerchiefs and pillowcases, sew dresses, and cook simple meals. Even though we had maids to do the cooking at home, it behooved me to learn the basic necessities that might one day come in handy.

My parents also expected me to have some cultural accomplishments, so when I reached the sixth grade, they surprised me with a brand-new German piano. Whereas my mom played religious hymns on the piano, I began to take lessons from a family friend after school, which only lasted until the day I heard different music floating into the living room. The sounds came from the newly organized elementary school band that was practicing on the street below. I felt compelled to look out the window, and my eyes quickly focused on a shiny silver-like object, the E-flat saxophone, and then they dropped to the uniforms that reminded me of my dad's military outfit. I thought this would be one way I could follow in my father's footsteps—by wearing some kind of uniform and marching in a band. The band members wore khaki pants with green and gold stripes on each side of the legs, indicating the school colors. The shirts, also khaki, had short sleeves and pockets. These outfits, unlike any military uniform I ever saw, also sported suspended musical instruments around the band members' necks or carried on their sides like the drums. The overall effect was absolutely dashing; I was hooked. I know I disappointed my Mom when I dropped my piano lessons, but she was glad I learned enough to play church hymns. Because I could already read musical notes when I signed up with the school band, I was allowed to take lessons from one of the teachers, and in no time I learned to play the saxophone really well.

After elementary school I moved up to Davao High School, where I completed one year of scholastic training. Samuel, my oldest brother, was in his third year, and George was a sophomore; so I had the support of my brothers during that first year. It soon became obvious to my parents that I was blossoming like a delicate flower. The boys noticed me more, although I had no real interest in them yet. Although I was a well-bred girl, I cannot deny that the attention and whistle calls flattered me. While I was growing up I lived a very sheltered life under the close supervision of both my parents: I could not go out alone, and I had to be chaperoned by one of my brothers, the maids, or my mom. I could never be alone with boys, and holding hands or any other physical contact with a boy in private was simply not acceptable. Kissing for proper women was only done after marriage and in the privacy of the home. Girls who overstepped their boundaries and went around kissing boys were disgraced, and their families disowned them.

Considering all of these restrictions it was fortunate indeed that all the schools I attended had very strict regulations: only students who obeyed the rules were allowed to remain. The principal of the Davao high school permanently kicked out those who violated the rules, never even giving them a second chance, and with this tough stance only a few students were ever dismissed for bad behavior. The combination of strict rules and teachers who cared about each student added to the quality of life on the campus. While still in high school, though, I realized that girls were still restricted in what they could and could not do. In 1939 my dad took a job with the Elizalde Gold Mining Company across the bay from Davao City, where we lived, in mines located in the hills above Kingking. Whoever discovered the mines probably likened them to a king's ransom and so gave the town that name. The area was so remote that it could only be reached by a single-engine Cessna-type plane flown by well-paid American civilian pilots, and the comings and goings in our home of these tall, handsome men fascinated me. Between my early exposure to my dad's military life as a soldier and now watching these men in action with their airplanes, my zest for adventure increased: I decided I wanted to be a woman pilot. In my imagination I was the first woman pilot in the Philippines. When I returned from my first visit to the airport, I told my mom about the excitement within me, but she just looked stricken after I told her I wanted to be a pilot. She told me I was her only precious daughter, that she had already lost one and did not want to lose another. Tears flowed from her beautiful brown eyes, and my heart melted. The aspirations I had to become another Amelia Earhart vanished as quickly as I had thought of them.

In the latter part of 1938 my mom broached the subject of sending my brothers and me to a private Christian school, Silliman, for the remainder of our high school education. Like other Filipino mothers, she was determined that we receive the very best education, and Silliman had an excellent reputation and distinguished history. One day in 1899 a retired businessman and philanthropist from Cohoes, New York, appeared at the office of the Presbyterian Board of Foreign Missions, carrying a proposal to contribute $10,000 toward the founding of an industrial school in the Philippine Islands. Doctor Horace B. Silliman strongly believed that the

Oldest building in Silliman (courtesy of Yale University Divinity School Library)

Filipino people needed a new kind of education, that everything would be taught to benefit them physically, mentally, and morally. Doctor David Hibbard, the missionary minister who searched for the perfect location, ultimately decided on Dumaguete on the island of Negros, describing it as a "place of health and beauty" with friendly people. Silliman Institute, an elementary school, thus was founded on August 28, 1901, by Protestant missionaries under the Board of Foreign Missions of the Presbyterian Church in the United States. It formally opened on August 28, 1902, with fifteen boys, four ten-foot-long desks, two tables, two chairs, a few *McGuffey's Readers*, and several geography, arithmetic and ninth-grade grammar books. In 1910 the Philippine government recognized the institute's right to grant a degree. The school established the Silliman Bible School (later the Divinity School) in 1921 in cooperation with the American Board of Commissioners for Foreign Missions, and in 1938 Silliman won full recognition as a university. As an institution of faith, the University is committed to provide opportunities for its students to seek truth, justice and love—Christian values that permeate every facet of Silliman campus life.

My dad, however, was not too enthusiastic about it because Silliman was thousands of miles away from our home. My mom sought the wise counsel of our American pastor, the Reverend Walter Tong, and his wife Margaret, who performed missionary work for the United Evangelical

Church, a fundamentalist denomination in Davao City. After several meetings my mom and the Tongs convinced my dad that sending us off to Silliman on the faraway island of Negros was the right thing to do. My mom then sold her most expensive and prized jewelry to pay our tuition, which amounted to approximately $500 U.S. or 1000 Filipino pesos per student. Even though my dad could afford to pay it with money from his monthly military pension and wages from the mines, my mom wanted to make her own sacrifice because she valued our education far above any material luxuries.

Toward the end of May 1939 George, Samuel, and I boarded the inter-island boat at Davao. Philip, still too young, had to stay behind, and he cried when we left. Our mom sailed away with us so that she could make all the arrangements with Silliman for our tuition fees and our living quarters on campus. Our travels took almost four days as the boat sailed on the Celebes Sea, the Sulu Sea, and the Mindanao Sea, stopping at a few major ports along the way to drop off passengers and take on others en route to Manila. After the third day we arrived at the port of Dumaguete, in Negros Oriental. My brothers and I caught a glimpse of Silliman University from the sea, and we were excited. It seemed as if the swaying branches of the coconut palm trees welcomed our arrival.

The excitement intensified as the boat dropped anchor and the captain skillfully guided his ship along the side of the wharf. Once properly moored on the dock, the boat became a window on our new world. We heard the loud voices of vendors attempting to sell their edible goods to the passengers and saw children in the water alongside the ship clamoring for the passengers to throw coins over the side so that they could dive after them. We saw how their agile brown bodies adapted to the salt water and how quickly they swam after the money; they were like little fishes going after food. These coins, which they tucked into their mouths until they had enough, supplemented their poor parents' income.

On the wharf several horse-drawn calesas or buggies, conveyances that were cheaper than a taxi and that could easily fit four passengers in the cab, waited for tourists and other passengers. My mom decided that we should take a calesa, but in fact we needed two of them to accommodate the four of us plus our suitcases. The Silliman campus overlooking the sea covered thirty-three hectares of prime real estate, providing a beautiful setting for the pursuit of education—this is what awaited my seventeen-year-old brother Samuel, sixteen-year-old George, and myself, just fourteen, in 1939. At the Registrar's Office my mom made final arrangements and payments. Samuel and George were assigned to the men's dormitory called Guy Hall, and I moved in to the girls' dormitory, Oriental Hall, which housed both female

Aerial view of Silliman (courtesy of Yale University Divinity School Library)

high school and college students. The three-story building had living quarters, shower stalls, modern toilets, a mezzanine porch on the second floor overlooking the campus, a dining room, and a kitchen. Each girl had her own bunk bed with a mattress and a cupboard to store books and clothing. A hired cook and his helpers prepared our meals, and a middle-aged, single matron and her assistant supervised the dormitory.

I had great difficulty parting from my mom because I had never been separated from her. As she prepared to leave Dumaguete, I cried and begged her to take me back, but she told me to be a good girl, to study hard, and to write home often. As she got on a *caromata* (horse-drawn buggy) to drive away, she reminded George, Samuel, and me that she loved us all, which prompted me to burst out wailing. As I continued my hysteria my two brothers also shed tears because they felt the same anguish. My mom of course did not stop and take me back with her, so the three of us finally dried our faces and headed back to our dormitories. We were at Silliman to stay. I believe it was God's plan that ultimately led us to this private and prestigious Christian school. He certainly knew of the dark cloud that hovered over the Philippines, that many of us were to be sacrificial lambs of that vicious and cruel invasion planned and executed by the Japanese Imperial Army in 1942.

Classes began the week after I arrived, and I adapted amazingly well to the new surroundings, probably because of the genuine friendships among the students, Filipino teachers, and American faculty members on campus who fully understood the transition each new student had to make. Because our Filipino teachers and American professors lived on campus with their families, they made themselves available to the students as an extended family, opening their homes to us for advice, counseling, and family dinners. One such family, whom everyone loved dearly, was the Bells. Edna Bell was a loving, caring person with an outgoing personality as big as her heart. Her husband, Roy, was a professor on campus and had a ham radio at home; he would go on to organize guerrilla resistance on Negros during the war. My brothers and I quickly attached ourselves to Mother Bell, as we fondly called her, and she never failed to give us a big bear hug whenever we came to see her to talk of our troubles or our loneliness.

Courses offered in the second year of high school at Silliman resembled those in the public schools except for one additional subject: the Bible. I enrolled in American history, biology, Bible, English composition, literature, and physical education. I also played the E-flat saxophone in the university band and once, at a single instrument contest in a downtown Dumaguete theater, won first prize for playing "Evening Star." When the university band needed a majorette, I became their first choice because I was the only girl who dared to wear short pants and high boots in public. For me, though, the uniform with the tall hat and bright plume in the center, the braided rope to hold my whistle, and the baton I learned to twirl made the challenge to convention worthwhile. I then performed in the college operetta, based on *The Belle of Barcelona*, taking on the singing and speaking part of an older woman. I had a lot of fun being made up to look like an older woman. I brushed my hair upward and inserted a large comb to hold the beautiful lace material that covered a portion of my head and draped down my back. I wore a red and maroon dress that gave me a distinguished matronly appearance, then placed around my neck a large gold chain with an expensive locket from Spain, and it dropped below my bosom. I also participated in the college symphony orchestra directed by Professor Ramon Tapales, educated in Milan, Italy. At first he wanted me to play the timpani drums but I chose to play the French horn instead, and it was not difficult to learn. The beautiful sound from this instrument blended uniquely with the violins, bass fiddle, oboe, clarinets, bassoon, and flute. The music sounded like magic in the air.

In addition to music I enjoyed outdoor sports. First I tried out for the one hundred–meter hurdles and won; then I went on to play basketball, a favorite sport for most of the students, especially me. Other outdoor sports involved swimming early in the morning or on moonlit nights. A chaperone accompanied six of us girls from our dormitory to the ocean, passing alongside the boys' dormitory. At five o'clock in the morning the boys were still asleep, and at night they were not allowed to go off campus to watch us; yet we still wore bathrobes over our swimsuits so we did not make a spectacle of ourselves. Whenever I decided not to go in swimming, I usually arranged an early morning tennis match. The courts lay behind our girls' dormitory, and our American faculty members who lived across the way came over and played tennis; at times they invited some of us girls to participate in a match.

On Sunday mornings I went to church. Catholic students went to a nearby church for early morning mass accompanied by their chaperones, whereas we Protestants attended church in one of the big university halls until the school endorsed the construction of a regular church. I participated in the choir, so I had to arrive early to rehearse with other members for our special number under the leadership of our choir director. I sang in the soprano or alto section depending on the need to balance the choir's special number. I never had any professional voice training, but I possess a natural singing voice, which I call God's gift to me because I inherited this voice from my mom.

On Sunday afternoons, after church, I had some free time to move about on the campus grounds and even beyond, providing I had a chaperone. Some of my dormitory girlfriends decided to perform missionary work among the poor children in one of the seaside barrios, and I went along to help. We followed a rough road on foot for a half hour under the sweltering sun, carrying all of our educational materials, until we reached the beach where several nipa huts stood. At first the parents of the children seemed suspicious of our presence, but the children, while curious, welcomed us. Once we won them over, the parents accepted our activities.

I spotted a dried-out log washed up on the beach, which came in handy, as we did not have regular chairs, and each child had room enough to sit. My college friends began the lessons and told the story of Jesus doing His ministry here on earth, and stories of David and Goliath or Joseph and his brothers intrigued the children. They had never seen flannel graphs on a board with cutout colored pictures, and it kept their interest focused on the stories. Then I taught them songs in their native dialect like "Jesus Loves the Little Children of the World" and "Jesus Loves Me." They learned quickly, and because of their enthusiastic participation, we rewarded them with cookies and candies. I was rewarded with the satisfaction of watching their smiling faces as I taught them about God's love.

Within our dormitory we formed an exclusive gang of high school and college girls whose parents were of mixed marriages, with one parent white and the other of a Filipino mixture. Most of the girls had American fathers, one had an American mother and a Filipino father, and I was the only one whose dad was of British and French heritage with American citizenship. Initially this gang formed out of friendship, fellowship, and camaraderie; since we had much in common because of our backgrounds, we felt drawn together. The first night that we formed our alliance on the mezzanine floor of our dormitory our gang decided on a name. Munching on peaches and crackers one of the girls suggested we call ourselves the Peach Crack Gang, and we all agreed. Then we decided to have nicknames: the girl who loved pink things became Pinky; another who had ringlets in her hair took the name Ringy; a fast runner wanted to be called Sprinty; and because I believed a day would come when I would see snow, I chose the name Snowy. That night we giggled and laughed like little children; then we crawled under our mattresses that we laid on the concrete of the mezzanine floor, gazed up at the heavenly bodies in the sky, and fell asleep.

Unbeknownst to me, while I attended this prestigious private Christian school, the Master Weaver of my life was preparing me for the greatest challenge I would ever encounter: surviving the Japanese invasion of the Philippine Islands. It was heading my way and would be the greatest battle of my life. In the meantime, however, I believe God allowed me time to laugh, cry, and do all the things I enjoyed the most: music, sports, and drama. Above all I was given time to enjoy the pleasure of living the best years of my life while I attended Silliman University, where I found peace. I cannot erase those precious memories from my mind.

My life really began to change in the latter part of 1941, when I was still just sixteen years old, and the first of these changes that hurried along my maturity came as the result of a birthday party. In October 1941 one of my friends, Mabel, who lived with her parents off of the Silliman campus, convinced her mother to allow a few of her high school friends to take part in her birthday celebration, so she invited the Peach Crack Gang to her party. Penny, Ringy, and I, all best friends from the gang, were on the top of the guest list, and Mabel conveniently scheduled her party for a Sunday afternoon, when the three of us had no other commitments. Best of all, for the first time I received an invitation to a party at a private home off the university grounds with boys my own age.

Ringy, the oldest of the group, decided to ask permission from our head matron to attend Mabel's birthday celebration, which had to be done days in advance because normally several girls from the same dormitory could not leave at the same time. Miss Oliva, a petite unmarried woman, meticulous and business-like, was not difficult to approach as long as the request was within reason, but she became dangerous when crossed. To follow the rules, we needed a college student to chaperone us, and I knew that Sprinty and Pinky, older members of our gang, would not mind going with us; but we found out that they had already left the campus and would not be back in time. Our only other chaperone choice boiled down to one of the college girls from Siam, and I knew that this did not bode well. For some reason the Siamese girls did not mix well with the Filipina students, which fortunately usually resulted in apathy rather than hostility. The Siamese girls especially directed their indifference and ambivalence at those of us living in Oriental Hall because we all had at least one American parent. They disapproved of racial mixing. But the Peach Crack Gang wanted to go to Mabel's party, so we willingly obligated ourselves to one of the Siamese university students.

With Miss Oliva's permission one of the Siamese girls reluctantly accepted this charge. Dressed in her native Sunday best, a slim cotton gown, the girl, with her quiet manner and ever-so-slow footsteps, led the three of us toward the fence beyond the dormitory and on to the home where Mabel's party was already in progress. Although the afternoon was hot and humid I felt no exertion at all as I traipsed rapidly along with Penny and Ringy. From a window in her two-story home Mabel saw us coming and beckoned us to hurry; as we entered the house and ascended the stairway leading to the second floor I heard beautiful music coming from a phonograph. My excitement began to grow, followed by even more exhilaration when I discovered that two boys I knew were present. One, a Silliman faculty member's son, had an interest in me because we had something in common—a love of music. Romeo, the other college student, was smitten with Penny because of her good looks, wit, and American accent, which she never lost. After being ushered into our host's living room, Penny, Ringy, and I sat on one side of the room, and the boys stayed on the opposite side. Keeping in mind that our religion strictly forbade dancing, we simply exchanged greetings and smiles with the boys and remained seated on our long bench next to the wall. Mabel's mother then appeared and, in an attempt to stimulate mixing, told us to help ourselves at the table.

As we all ate and drank, the sweltering heat rose, and the music played on. Romeo, the bold one, finally broke the ice and encouraged everyone to dance. He respectfully approached our chaperone and asked her permission to dance the fox-trot with Penny, but she did not reply to his request; instead, she just turned her head away from him. Penny interpreted this as permission, and she danced with Romeo. After watching that first dance, which seemed like clean fun, the rest of us joined in with our partners, ignoring the presence of our chaperone, who sat in the corner like a wall-flower. At about five o'clock our chaperone suddenly decided she had seen enough and commanded us to leave. After Penny, Ringy, and I made our hasty good-byes, we reluctantly started back to the dormitory; we had been having a good time and did not want it to end. The boys, although clearly smitten, sensed that it was not wise to walk with us, so they made a bee-line in another direction. Our chaperone suddenly changed on the way back to Silliman, walking quickly ahead of us on the path, her narrow dress straining with the exertion of her rapid stride. When the three of us girls finally entered Oriental Hall, I saw our chaperone standing next to the matron, Miss Oliva, who was now fuming with anger and spouting unwarranted accusations at us. Ringy, with her hot-blooded American temper, challenged our accuser until the matron lost her composure and began calling us nasty names. Realizing that she was losing her grip, Miss Oliva picked up the phone and called the president of the university, Dr. Arthur Carson, who summoned us to his office.

Outside of the dormitory Ringy immediately turned to Penny and me and asked if we were all going to stand together. We quickly agreed, so Ringy then generously offered to be our spokesperson with Dr. Carson. Even though I had seen the president on the Silliman campus many times and even greeted him when we were close enough, I had never before encountered him in his office. As young girls familiar with the dominant male authoritarian culture of the Philippines, we did not know how this particular man of authority would deal with us. Surprisingly, given the gravity of our offense, his first questions sounded pleasant and polite, as he asked us how we were and why we had come to his office. While Penny and I sat quietly, Ringy explained what happened at Mabel's party. She began calmly enough, but her voice grew increasingly loud as she recalled our encounter with the matron who unfairly accused us of being bad girls.

Dr. Carson relaxed himself into the back of his padded chair after Ringy ended her outburst, apparently amused at the whole episode. He told us that he knew our school records were clean but that he also knew our matron, Miss Oliva, was an upstanding person who understood her responsibilities well. Dr. Carson told us we could return to the dormitory if we apologized to Miss Oliva for our behavior. The strong-willed Ringy refused to accept the president's terms, so Dr. Carson suggested that all three of us move out of Oriental Hall and live off campus for the remainder of the school year. He seemed saddened by the decision Ringy made for the three of us, and I immediately questioned our willingness to allow Ringy to speak for us. Penny and I could have broken with Ringy and refused to leave the dormitory, which we considered our home away from home, but we had promised we would all stand together. So the three of us left Dr. Carson's office, returned to the dorm to pack our belongings, and called one of our basketball friends whose parents owned a boarding house for students. Mr. Nazaren was a Silliman faculty member, and his wife managed the house. Luckily they had room for us on such short notice, and once we settled in our new surroundings we decided it was not so bad after all.

With this move to off-campus housing I suddenly felt grown-up. Even though I could not do exactly as I pleased because Mrs. Nazaren had certain rules for her boarders, I knew that I had more responsibility for behaving myself. For the next couple of months I kept up with my studies and extracurricular activities and stayed out of trouble. Mrs. Nazaren, the woman who ran the boarding house, proved an excellent cook, so I enjoyed wonderful meals while I lived there. The weeks went by quickly, and soon Thanksgiving peeked around the corner, a holiday that residents of Dumaguete celebrated because of the influence of the American faculty members at Silliman. As soon as Thanksgiving ended, everyone in Dumaguete began planning for Christmas, the most celebrated religious holiday of the year in the Philippines. Children, of course, looked forward to their short vacation from school when they could go home to enjoy the festivities of the holiday. The joy, laughter, exchange of gifts, hugs, and kisses, all made up what families looked forward to at Christmas time.

But there would be no such reunion in my family that Christmas. My brother George and I knew that the Christmas vacation did not allow us enough time to travel from Silliman to our farm in Kidapawan, Cotabato, on Mindanao. Penny, Ringy, and I kept ourselves occupied with our schoolwork; we just could not seem to throw ourselves into the holiday preparations. We still lived in the off-campus boardinghouse where the Nazarens prepared their own family for Christmas, and although they invited me to join them, I chose not to. I could not bear to. Many days, when the humidity was unrelenting, Penny, Ringy, and I took short walks along the boulevard overlooking the sea. These walks, taken just before the sun set in its blaze of glory, exposed us to the cool, gentle breeze as it began to blow away the heat of the day. As we walked back and forth on the boulevard we never discussed Mabel's birthday party, the dancing, or our removal from Oriental Hall. Rather than dwell on what happened, we simply picked up where we left off and carried on the best way we knew, unaware of the more severe trials just around the corner.

December 8, 1941, began with the usual early risers who peddled their bread on foot or on bicycle. "Pandisal! Who wants to buy my freshly baked pandisal?" the peddlers called out. *Pandisal* literally means salt bread but is in fact similar to crunchy French bread except it is shaped in the form of a bun rather than a loaf. Pandisal was one of the most well known bread specialties of the Philippines, and Filipinos loved to eat it for breakfast. The most distinct sound, though, that one heard between four and five o'clock in the morning was the loud crowing of the roosters. Accurate timekeepers, these creatures proved indispensable for those people who could not afford a watch or a clock. The morning of December 8 the sleepy residents of Dumaguete continued to stir from their beds while dogs barked, roosters crowed, and vendors peddled their wares. All of a sudden radios in every home blasted the frightening news that the Japanese had bombed Pearl Harbor in Hawaii. The newspapers quickly hit the streets. Pandemonium broke loose. People jumped out of bed in disbelief. As soon as the Japanese bombed Pearl Harbor, the Philippines was in for very hard times—we all knew that the Japanese were on the move, and the Philippines lay right in their path. People immediately absorbed the reality that the war would come to us, so they hurriedly made plans. Silliman students from other countries as well as from other far off provinces in the Philippines were especially affected by the unexpected turn of events. They wanted to go home. We all felt prepared for natural disasters such as typhoons, earthquakes, and heavy rains. But war? Who would dare make war on our beloved country while we were under the protection of the United States?

As soon as I heard about Pearl Harbor I frantically tried to find my brother George, who remained a resident at Guy Hall on the Silliman campus. We were family, the only family each other had at that point, and any decisions had to be made together. Samuel, already graduated, had taken a teaching job in Cotabato, Mindanao, the previous year, so George and I did not have his wise counsel to rely on. We quickly decided that the best course of action would be to consult with one of the Silliman faculty members. We went to the home of Roy Bell, one of the most popular teachers at Silliman, who suggested that we join his family in their vacation home in the mountains behind Dumaguete, where we would be safe until the war ended. Safety certainly concerned us; however, the urge to make every effort to return to our parents seemed more important to us because we knew that our mom and dad would worry themselves to death if we did not come home. Mr. Bell understood our anxiety and suggested that George and I do all we could to get back home, but he left the door open for us to accept his offer in the event we could not secure passage on an interisland vessel. I could not know then that Roy Bell would become one of the most effective guerrilla leaders on the island of Negros, that his family and other Silliman faculty families would spend the war evading the Japanese forces. And of course I could not know how closely my own experiences would mirror those of Mr. Bell's.

Within a week of Pearl Harbor most of the out-of-town students left the university grounds. It seemed as if my brother George, now seventeen years old, and me, still just fifteen, were the only ones left. We had a long way to get home and had trouble arranging transportation back to Mindanao. Our worst fears about Japanese intentions had been confirmed the very day of Pearl Harbor when we learned that they also bombed Manila and other strategic locations on the island of Luzon. I knew that those attacks would soon spread to other islands. Our anxiety increased as George and I realized that we had to cross one hundred miles of open water patrolled by Japanese aircraft to reach Iligan, located on the northern coast of Mindanao. Then we would have to forge across another hundred miles of land before we reached the family farm, never sure if Japanese foot soldiers or even the fearsome local Moros would threaten us.

During that week following the terrible news of Pearl Harbor, George and I tried to get onboard any vessel heading south, but each time we went down to the docks in Dumaguete we returned to the Silliman campus, downhearted and discouraged. Every ship that arrived and left in haste from the docks was already overloaded with passengers from other big cities. Penny

The wharf facing Silliman (courtesy of Yale University Divinity School Library)

and Ringy already managed to get home. I felt lonely and unconvinced that George and I would ever make it back to Mindanao; although the odds seemed to be against us we continued to make every attempt to stay at the wharf from early morning until dusk. Finally, on December 14, when George and I began our usual walk down toward the dock, we were surprised to see a large ship docked alongside the wharf, and we walked quickly toward it. But when we actually reached it, we saw that the ship was filled to capacity; passengers spilled over everywhere. Our feet glued to the wharf, we kept looking up, scanning the many faces onboard the ship in hopes of finding a familiar one. If we found someone we knew, we could at least send a message to our parents to let them know that we were alive, but we did not see anyone familiar to us. As we turned away from the ship a friendly voice from somewhere on deck called over and asked if we were the Dore children. This question came from the ship's captain himself, a man who knew my dad from earlier boat trips he made to Davao. George and I nodded our heads simultaneously and told him of our plight; then the captain asked us how long it would take for us to get our things and get back to the boat. I told him we would run as fast as our feet would take us, and off we went.

When darkness came that night, the ship finally got underway with George and me onboard, crammed in with hundreds of other people trying to get home or at least to a safer place. We had uneasy thoughts; questions kept nagging at us. What if the boat sank from being overloaded with passengers? Would there be giant man-eating sharks in the water? What if we were spotted from the air by Japanese planes? Would the pilots machine-gun and bomb the ship? These were not baseless fears. Ever since the surprise attack at Pearl Harbor, the territory of the Philippines had become a nightmare to all of its citizens. Japanese airplanes equipped with heavy-gauge machine-gun bullets and bombs made daily flights, delivering destruction throughout the main islands. Ships with their human cargoes were easy targets; after all, the Japanese bombed the *Panay* en route from Manila to Negros, and everyone including the captain perished. Because of the air attacks and the sinking of the *Panay*, other ship captains maneuvered their vessels by night, and by day they hid along island coves.

In the dark of night I heard many sounds onboard the ship: moans, groans, and snoring from the old folks as they slept; the screaming of children who had nightmares; and the rustle of feet as people tried to find a place to relieve themselves. During the second night of our trip I wondered what happened to my close friends from Silliman. Many years later I did meet my old friend Ringy in the United States, and she told me that during the war she met a widower with several small children who served as the mayor of a small town outside of Dumaguete and also owned a sugar-cane plantation. Although she did not love him at first, he pursued her until she agreed to marry him; then after they had several children of their own he died suddenly, leaving Ringy alone to raise two sets of children. Ringy also met up with Dr. Arthur Carson, the president of Silliman, soon after the war. Dr. Carson and his family had spent most of the war evading the Japanese on the island of Negros and had been evacuated by a U.S. submarine in early 1944, but he returned to Negros in the summer of 1945 to resume his duties at Silliman. Ringy met him then. They had a good laugh about what happened to the three girls who appeared in his office that hot Sunday afternoon in October 1941, when the greatest tragedy in our lives had been getting caught dancing.

Because there was nothing much to do on the ship George and I traveled on, I found my thoughts occupied with the family I was trying to reach. My mom, I thought, would be pacing back and forth in the house, wondering what had happened to her two children who were several hundred miles away from home, wondering if she would ever see George and me again. But she would fight off her tears because she knew that whatever happened to us, we loved each other very much; after all, we were a close-knit family, and we cared very much about each other. My mom was our spiritual guide because she adhered to Christian principles in thought and in deed. Little did I know then the unjust fate that awaited her during the war.

After several days at sea dodging enemy planes by hiding in coves, we finally caught sight of Mindanao, and it could not have happened soon enough for me, for I felt scared, tired, and cramped. Within a few hours of that initial sighting we arrived at Iligan in the province of Lanao, our final port, and the passengers rejoiced and prayed out loud in thanks that the ship had not been sunk. George and I, quickly recovering our land legs after we disembarked, timidly approached our friend the captain and admitted that we had very little money to pay for our trip. He was so touched by our honesty that he smiled and told us that God had put us on the wharf that day and that he made the decision to take us onboard because of the friendship he had with our dad. The captain advised us to keep our money to make sure we had enough to pay for our overland transportation; then he dug deep into his back pocket, brought out his wallet, and handed my brother more money, saying that he would never be able to spend it all anyway. With tears in our eyes we thanked him. Then George and I walked down the gangplank and turned around and waved our last good-bye to the kindly captain. We started for home.

2

A Call to Action

Finding our way in Iligan, Lanao, proved easy because my brother George had attended a youth conference in the area during the summer of 1940. He knew his way around, but since Iligan sat about one hundred miles from our farm, I was totally unfamiliar with it, so it really helped having my big brother with me. George flagged down a horse and buggy and informed the driver that we wanted to go to the overland bus station. As the two of us approached the depot we saw how fast people filled up the buses, everyone anxious to get away from the coast of Mindanao, where the Japanese would most likely land and take control. The island's interior surely afforded more safety. Once again George and I were in luck—we got onboard the last bus leaving Iligan the morning of December 21, 1941. The vehicle groaned under the weight of passengers of all shapes, sizes, ages, and gender; plus most of the occupants carried with them their suitcases, trunks, and sleeping mats, and the older folks also brought their pigs, goats, dogs, chickens, and cats. Believe me, this combination of humanity and beast on a crowded bus on a hot December morning in Mindanao did not make for the most pleasant smells in the world. At a time like this, though, George and I did not have any other choice. We simply had to tolerate our surroundings because we were, after all, caught up in a war zone and desperate to get home.

Our bus driver, a seasoned and clever man, began the long trip by following the Sayre Highway, named for the American High Commissioner of the Philippines, Francis Sayre. The highway linked the western part of Mindanao to the eastern, running from the city of Davao east to Iligan, where our journey began. The highway was not the best, nor was it the poorest, and to compound the highway conditions the bus we traveled in was not first-class. The colorless vehicle was open on all sides to allow some ventilation to circulate, and it had an overhead rack where some of the passengers secured caged chickens and other personal belongings with Manila hemp rope. Because of the large number of passengers, some unlucky ones sat on top of the bus and held on for dear life lest they be thrown off as the bus rounded a curve or made an abrupt stop. Worst of all, the bus was not equipped with a lavatory.

Despite these conditions I could not help but notice the breathtakingly beautiful scenic route as the bus traveled through the pine trees in the high mountains of the province of Lanao. Despite the uncertainties of war I thrilled at the idea of going home, so I could not help but recognize the unrelenting splendor of the island. Every variety and hue of wildflowers native to Mindanao, butterflies of brilliant colors, birds soaring and singing, and finally the famous Maria Cristina Falls, complete with lush green ferns and tons of clear water—all of this I saw from the inside of the bus as it chugged along its way, and the sight made my heart swell with pride. This was my home. Yes, Mother Nature kindly allowed such beauty to exist in that part of the world even in wartime. One unfortunate disadvantage of this very beauty, at least from my point of view and sense of personal safety, was that Muslim Moros occupied the whole province of Lanao. Christians have always feared Moros because of their religion, their reputation as fierce fighters, and their insistence on self-government. I think the war caught them by surprise as it did the rest of us, establishing the possibility for cooperation among all Filipinos regardless of tribal affiliation. As our bus traveled through their sacred land the Moros were probably busily planning their own strategy in the event they came face-to-face with the Japanese army. They did not bother to attack our bus, and I thanked God for this. While the Dansalan Moros did not like the Japanese, some possessed no real fondness for Americans either because of the military skirmishes they had had with American soldiers in the early 1900s, and had never forgotten. I would cross paths with the Moros during the course of the war; some were friendly, and others were not.

A few hours after leaving Iligan, the winding road going uphill toward the center of Lanao finally developed into a problem for the overloaded bus, and the driver had to decrease speed. Likewise people repeatedly insisted that the driver stop at regular intervals so they could go into the bushes and relieve themselves. This slowed our travel, making some passengers irritated and argumentative in the afternoon heat as they tried to urge the driver to go faster. When the bus reached the top of the highway where the road leveled out I heard the roaring sound of approaching airplanes. One passenger immediately shouted that they must be Japanese planes. With its brakes screeching and squealing the bus stopped quickly and everyone, including George and me, jumped off and headed for cover in a grove of nearby trees. "Rat-ta-ta-ta," came the noise from the machine guns on the planes as they came down low and strafed the bus. I squinched my eyes tight; my hands turned to ice. Then up the planes flew, circled, and returned again with the same "Rat-ta-ta-ta" with their machine guns. After three passes they finally headed off on their way, probably because they did not see anyone moving on the ground. Perhaps they thought that the bus had been abandoned and did not want to waste any more of their ammunition, but whatever their reasoning, we were safe. The entire attack took no more than five minutes, but I was sure that the world had ended, that my life was finished. When I realized that the air had grown quiet again I felt my heart beating and knew that I was alive. I looked over at George and smiled weakly. We both survived our introduction to warfare.

Someone gave the all-clear signal, and the passengers, none of whom had gotten lost or injured, headed back to the bus. The bus driver urged us to hurry and get settled in, and then we continued our journey as the driver dropped off his passengers when they reached their individual destinations. Soon we crossed the border of Lanao into the province of Cotabato, also occupied by the Moros, but in my home province I did not fear the Moros so much. One of them happened to be a very good friend of my dad's, a well-known leader named Salipada Pendatun, who had been educated at Harvard University. He married a Moro princess and ruled his people with understanding and respect, hence his popularity among his own subjects, as well as the Christians who lived in Cotabato. In time Pendatun became a military leader who guided his people against the Japanese Imperial Army and helped my family in its time of direst need.

George and I were exhausted from the rough roads, the humidity, the overcrowded bus, and the other inconveniences we encountered on our wild ride over mountains and through forests and open meadows. The sudden attack from the air by enemy planes had not helped our situation. Just before the scorching sun began to set the driver announced that we had arrived in Kidapawan, the town closest to our family farm. George and I heaved a big sigh of relief when the driver dropped us off at Kilometer Fourteen, but from there we had to walk another five kilometers through the jungle to reach home. We each carried a suitcase that made every step

especially burdensome, and knowing that this was the last leg of our journey did not make things any easier for me. I still worried.

I asked George what would happen if we reached the farm only to find
that our parents had evacuated further into the jungle? What would we do
then? Before he could respond, I went on and asked what would happen
if the Japanese soldiers had managed to break through the mountains,
reached the farm, and captured mom and dad?

George finally told me to stop thinking of bad things, reminding me
that our dad was a retired military man who would surely know what to
do, that the Japanese wouldn't get a chance to surprise him. Trying my best
not to think about what awaited us at the farm, I let my mind wander back
to the previous summer when we came home for a vacation. That had been
a happier time. Even though we had chores to do, George and I had a lot
of fun swimming in the water hole once we completed our work. With the
help of an American friend, Joe Perkins, who temporarily stayed with the
family, my dad built a dam on the property. He and Joe piled large rocks
all across the stream to hold back some of the mountain-stream water and
created an area of water deep enough for us to swim in. Tall trees with over-
hanging branches stood on both sides of the stream, and birds of all sizes
and shapes sang their fascinating tunes as we swam; then they roosted on
the limbs of the trees when darkness fell. The wild monkeys, initially annoyed
with our intrusion into their territory, gradually accepted our presence
probably because we were young and acted almost as foolishly as they did.
George and I felt like we lived in a magical forest whenever we went swimming in the late afternoons, and the monkeys could only be our friends
in that enchanted place.

Daydreaming about those bygone days on the farm helped me on
December 21 as evening descended, as I wearily lifted one leg after another
while carrying a suitcase that felt as if it were filled with lead. The weight
almost proved too much to bear for someone who had been away from farm
work for so long. Oh how I wished that my parents knew George and I were
coming so they could hitch their cart to the carabao and come and pick
us up! This form of transportation would have made travel much easier for
us, with our suitcases and ourselves resting comfortably in the cart as the
yoked carabao trudged over the rough and muddy road toward the farm.
Finally, with the darkness closing in, we reached the edge of the farm. Our
youngest brother, Philip, still working outside, caught a glimpse of us and
screamed to our parents that George and I had arrived. By the time they
emerged from the house George and I stood, wilted, at the foot of the front
stairs of the long one-story farmhouse. The excitement and anxiety of seeing my parents again gave my weary legs an extra boost, and I flung myself

into their waiting embrace. Their hugs and kisses made me forget my fatigue as I felt such joy that we were all together again.

George and I felt absolutely famished, so our mom prepared a delicious meal for us, the second dinner she cooked that night. Since we had moved to the farm and the war started we no longer had maids working for us; they all went back to their own families and my mom performed all the housework, the rest of us pitching in whenever we came home. She never complained—she just seemed happy when all of her children were around her. Exhausted and unable to keep his eyes open a moment longer, George slumped back in his chair and dozed off as soon as he finished eating. A moment later I followed. My mom and dad carried us to our beds, removed our shoes, and lovingly replaced our stiff sweaty clothes with sweet-smelling freshly laundered pajamas. George and I were home at last with those whom we loved the most. A plaque on the wall in our living room read: "Be it ever so humble, there's no place like home." How true that was.

George and I did not awaken until almost ten o'clock the next morning. When my eyes first eased open that morning I thought I was still in the boardinghouse and that George and I had to hurry down to the Dumaguete docks. As I focused my eyes and saw the familiar furniture of my bedroom I realized with relief that that journey had ended; I was home now, and come what may, I was with my family. I got dressed in a hurry, eager to see my parents and brothers. George and I arrived in the kitchen at the same time and we ate a hearty homemade breakfast of bacon, fried eggs from our own chickens, hot native chocolate made from local cocoa beans, and ripe yellow bananas raised on the farm. My mom and dad watched as we ate, beaming from ear to ear as they gazed on the children whom they had feared they might never see again. It all seemed so perfect, and I carried a very warm feeling in my heart.

After George and I finished eating and helped clear away the table, my dad brought us all together, including young Philip, for a serious conversation. Just like the military man that he was, as well as head of the household, he expected his family to come to an immediate decision about what to do now that the war was on us. The way he stood in the kitchen that morning, alternating brisk pacing with gentle taps on the table for emphasis, I could well imagine how imposing he had looked in his uniform when he had been part of the United States Army. He had a real sense of purpose now, something his civilian work never quite provided. My dad told us that we were caught in the middle of this war, that we were living in a war zone. Our Japanese neighbors and former friends in the city of Davao turned into military officers overnight, and they led their troops, taking over the city without a fight; but our USAFFE troops held them along the Digos front lines. Digos was a small town approximately fifty kilometers from Kidapawan, so the war was indeed very close to our family.

My dad informed us that we had two choices: to surrender to the Japanese when they entered our area or to offer our services to the USAFFE and help them with the fight against the Japanese. Like almost everyone in the Philippines then, he referred to the Japanese as "Japs" or "Nips," and during the war it proved difficult to keep the scorn out of our voices when we used those words. My dad then turned and looked at my mom, his face fixed in the serious military manner so familiar to all of us, and asked her how we should decide. We all remained silent, deep in thought. Then my dad explained that he was well known in Davao for being the only one-armed American who participated in the Fourth of July parades in the city and who marched in full military uniform with the Philippine Scouts and retired American veterans on Memorial Day. He reminded us that the neighbors who once rented the big house across from ours were Japanese men who ran a printing press, so everyone around, friends and enemies, knew that we were American.

I remembered our former Japanese neighbors who had been so polite to us, bowing from the waist whenever they greeted us. Every night they got drunk on saki, their native alcoholic drink, or San Miguel beer, which was made in and distributed throughout the Philippines. I easily heard their loud voices and the clattering of empty bottles because my bedroom faced the large verandah where they congregated every night. As I thought back on this I remembered something else that seemed strange at the time: in addition to all of the sounds from their drunken reveries I also heard regular tapping sounds, which I now realized must have been Morse code. I felt aggravated that none of us grasped what our neighbors were really up to, that they knew when Pearl Harbor was going to be bombed and knew that they would be able to take over Davao without a fight. The men that we knew as printers were really seasoned military officers.

My dad tried to tell us about our current situation without scaring us too much, but the reality was frightening. If we surrendered to the Japanese in Davao, we would all probably be tortured and maybe even executed because of our pro–American sympathies. The Japanese considered people like us their mortal enemies; they had surely already marked us as spies on their hit list. Even without my dad's saying so, I quickly understood that surrender was not a realistic option if we expected to survive the war. That left joining up with the American and Filipino armed forces on the island (and later on the guerrilla outfits) because we believed the war would not last too much longer. By that time the United States would surely have sent major reinforcements and the Japanese would be driven off of Philippine soil. The Japanese may be strong enough for a temporary occupation, but we believed that they could never hang on in the face of additional American troops and weapons—as good and loyal Americans we could not believe otherwise. We were also fully aware that my dad's monthly military pension from the United States could not be delivered during the war, and our family needed money to stay alive. The military here would provide that. So we thought we really had only one choice: we unanimously agreed that we would willingly cast our lot with the Filipino and American soldiers on Mindanao. My dad decided to contact the American military immediately.

Dressed in full uniform, complete with all of his well-earned medals from the Spanish-American War, my dad rode off on one of our best horses that very afternoon. My eyes followed him all the way to our gate, which was about two hundred yards from the house, and once the horse galloped out of the clearing, the forest seemed to swallow both the rider and the beast. I spent a long day waiting for my dad to return, wondering about the news that he would bring. Just before dusk I heard an excited voice coming from the entrance to our property. My dad had returned! After he dismounted from his horse George returned the saddle and bridle to their proper places near the stable while my dad checked that the horse had enough food and water before he joined the rest of us in the house. Each one of us pulled up a chair to the kitchen table, our anxious ears ready to hear the news, good or bad.

My dad addressed my mom, telling her that he had the luck of the Irish because he met with General Vashion, commander of the Davao-Cotabato sector, who was impressed with the sergeant's stripes and medals on my dad's uniform. When he told the general of our family's dilemma, he was sympathetic. My dad went on to explain that he offered the general his services, that he was prepared to fight against the Japanese in exchange for food and protection by the USAFFE for his family. General Vashion quickly recognized the value of having my dad with the USAFFE because of the forty-odd years he had lived and worked with the Philippine people. The general offered him a commission in his outfit with the rank of major but told him it would mean an end to his monthly U.S. pension, and there was no guarantee of any officer's compensation when the war was over. My dad's other option was to come aboard as a civilian working with the quartermaster, assuming the responsibility of taking food supplies to the troops at the Digos front lines and exchanging canned goods for fresh meat, eggs, chickens, vegetables, and fruits with the local people. By doing this he could continue to receive any pension checks that got through and could then claim the accumulated checks in the United States when the war was over. My dad would not suffer financially, and he could still serve his country.

My dad accepted the second option because he believed, like everyone else, that the war would be over in six months. He wanted to continue receiving his veteran's pension checks as long as he lived, even if they were delayed because of the war, and after all, six months was not such a very long time. The idea of venturing to the front lines intrigued him; my dad's adrenaline was revived. He became very excited because his first love, the United States Army, held him in high esteem even though he was retired. Although my dad would be serving as a civilian, he felt like he was back in the army again. Before he left General Vashion's headquarters, where he and the general had regarded each other with mutual admiration, the general commanded one of his aides to gather a few food supplies for my dad to bring back to his family. After receiving his official written order, he and the general saluted each other; then my dad went on his way home to us. My mom, pleased with the arrangement, cooked a huge feast for us that night.

The following day an army jeep, driven by an American soldier accompanied by a second soldier armed with a rifle in case they encountered snipers, roared up to the farmhouse. They came to escort my dad to his first assignment for the quartermaster. Bright-eyed and bushy-tailed, as my dad would have described himself, he readied himself. He did not even seem to be concerned that he was headed to the front lines at Digos, where heavily equipped Japanese soldiers had dug in. No, this old soldier had come alive again, eager to perform his duty, and his family felt extremely proud.

A whole long week passed before I heard the familiar roar of the jeep's engine again, and looking out of the kitchen window I experienced a sense of relief to see a familiar face in the jeep. My dad returned with a few more supplies for us, items basic for our existence. In his absence the farm needed taking care of, so George, Philip, and I pitched in, happy to keep busy even as we heard bombs exploding in the distance. We put aside our chores for a time to greet our dad and to hear about his exploits. As the American soldiers waited politely in the jeep, my dad gathered us around the kitchen table and eagerly told us of his exciting work bringing food supplies to our boys at the front. Then he turned to me and told me there was a need for a nurse's aide at the military dispensary in Kidapawan where a lot of wounded soldiers and civilians really needed help. I could work under a bona fide military doctor who ran the place, and the military would pay wages for my work. My dad asked if I would be interested in doing this. I didn't even have to think; without a hesitation in the world I replied that of course I would. My early exposure to military discipline and training from my dad insured that I could not respond in the negative. I was indeed ready for my call to action to serve the cause of both my countries.

ent with my dad, leaving my mom, George, and Philip to
m and each other. Although only sixteen years old, I felt
...y-five, a mature woman with a responsible and important
job. When I arrived in Kidapawan, the supply clerk issued me a khaki uniform of slacks and a button-down shirt, plus a military cap with a medical
insignia on it. I was then introduced to an American major with the USAFFE,
a doctor, who directed the operations of the dispensary behind the Digos
lines. When he traveled from the field hospital to other points to check
on the wounded and dying, he assigned a Filipino doctor to take charge of
the dispensary. Once I started work with my first supervisor, this Filipino
captain, he made sure that I stood right beside him watching everything
he did to take care of the injured. First I learned how to clean, medicate,
and bandage open wounds, which were the most common injuries I encountered. On my second day the captain taught me how to use a syringe—how
to remove the cover from the needle, insert the point into the medicine
bottle of serum, draw the appropriate amount of liquid in, press the plunger
slowly upward to remove any air, and find the right place on the patient's
arm or buttock for the injection. This doctor also made sure that I knew
about every medicine in the cabinet so that I would not make a mistake
with the injections.

I thrived on this work; I quickly absorbed information and never forgot it. I rarely had to be told more than once how to do something, and
this really pleased the captain that I worked for as he found me both capable and dependable. Most of the patients at the dispensary were civilians
who had crossed over the treacherous mountains to escape the advancing
Japanese soldiers, and many of them had malaria, open sores, and gunshot
wounds. One middle-aged man had an open wound on his neck, and when
he came to the dispensary the only thing I could do for him was clean his
wound and give him sulfa drugs. At that time the dispensary stocked a variety of sulfa drugs, including Sulfanilamide and Sulfathizol, to combat infec-
tions such as this, but within a year those basic drugs would be a luxury,
to be used only on those who stood a good chance of recovering. Unfortunately, this particular man did not get to the dispensary in time; despite
my efforts and the good drugs he eventually died from a gaping wound that
simply refused to heal.

Another one of my strongest memories from the first days of working
at the dispensary involved a large Filipino man who came from the mountains and whom the USAFFE suspected of spying for the Japanese. They
brought him into town yoked like an animal, a pole slipped behind his back
and his arms fastened to either side of it. The man, whose name I never
learned, wore only a pair of tattered pants and badly-worn sandals, his bare

chest filthy from rolling on the ground with the soldiers in a futile attempt to avoid capture. When I first saw him from the window of the dispensary, he was screaming in pain and outrage as his captors marched him into the local jail. Curious bystanders gathered around him, calling him crazy, and as he passed the dispensary he turned toward the window that I was peering out of. Our eyes met. His large soft brown eyes seemed to be pleading for help or mercy, and my heart tugged with the realization that I could do nothing for him. Or so I thought. I returned to my duties, trying to forget what I had seen but found it impossible because the man continued to scream so loudly that I thought that surely his lungs would burst. With the jail right across from the dispensary I continued to hear his cries. As soon as I finished with my current patient I decided that my medical duties dictated that I should aid the helpless, no matter who they were. Besides, I was curious to find out if he was really crazy and if he really had been spying for the Japanese. So I left the dispensary in the care of one of the guards and headed across the street. Once outside I saw that a large crowd had gathered outside of the jail, chanting, "Bu-ang, Bu-ang ka dong" ("Crazy, you are crazy boy").

As I approached the crowd, I addressed the people, asking them why they were standing around shouting at a man who had not done any harm to any of them. A woman from the center of the group responded that although he had not harmed any of them, he was really crazy in the head, with all of his screaming like a lunatic. Ignoring her pronouncement I decided to get closer to the poor man and his cell. The jail guard, glancing at my uniform, which accorded me more importance than I probably deserved, waved me in. The cell, made of heavy bamboo poles, measured about eight feet by ten feet and did not have a toilet, bed, or even a wash bowl. The prisoner sat on the floor with his back against the far wall, moaning.

Using his native Visayan dialect, which I had learned while growing up, I asked him what was wrong. This caught him by surprise; he must have thought that I was one of the regular army nurses everyone had heard about. In my khaki uniform and with my lighter skin I could have been one of the American nurses who had remained with the army in the Philippines. I was anxious to learn as much as I could about his situation so that I could help if possible, and before he even replied to my first question I asked why he was in jail and if he realized that his piercing cry frightened everyone.

He looked at me and finally responded, referring to me as "mom," the Filipino way of saying ma'am. He told me he was accused of being a Japanese spy, which he firmly denied. He said he might look like a "Japon" because of his slanted eyes and large frame but that he was a Filipino all the way. I regarded his form and thought that he did look a bit like a Japon, his way of saying Japanese, and I asked him what his most urgent need was, besides convincing his jailers that he was not a spy. Again addressing me as "mom," he told me that he was thirsty, that he had not been fed or given water since being put in this rotten jail.

I immediately called to the man in charge and asked him to bring me a large cup of water and then told him to open the cell door for me. The jailer stared at me and asked me if I was out of my mind, respectfully adding the "mom" at the end of his question. He stated emphatically that this man would kill me once I was inside. The people outside, who could hear everything, fell silent, as they feared for my safety as well as their own. They believed that the prisoner would overpower me, that he would escape and would kill them all. But I had made up my mind. I repeated my request to the jailer in a more forceful tone of voice.

Sighing with resignation the man removed the large chain that wrapped around the bamboo cell, opening the door just wide enough for my small frame to slip through. My assurance and bravery slipped and I felt myself beginning to shake. Then I reminded myself to have courage; after all, I had two things going for me. I believed that God was watching out for me on my mission of mercy, and I was the only daughter of a brave military man who risked his own life by traveling back and forth from the front lines. Surely helping a prisoner could not be as dangerous as that. As I moved toward the prisoner I could not help but notice that his eyes followed my every step. He did not say a word.

I finally found my voice and announced that since he asked for a cup of cool water, I had returned to give him what he needed. He gulped the water eagerly, choking a bit, and quickly emptied the cup. He thanked me profusely, calling me one of the angels, and then he pleaded for my help to clear his name. After we finished our quick conversation I retraced my footsteps out of the cell, relieved to be out of the filthy environment—my courage had its limits; it only took me so far. As I walked out, the crowd cheered and clapped their hands in praise of my effort to help the man they had thought of as a lunatic. One lady admitted that he was not "buang" after all and that he should be let go. After an immediate investigation the matter was brought before the provincial high officials, who released the man from jail. I had been traveling between the dispensary and the homes of people too sick or injured to come in for help, so I never got to see him again. But he left a message for me with one of the guards: "Salamat angel, salamat. You saved my life." Although we never crossed paths again this encounter always stayed with me. Although my dad had always admonished me not to take any unnecessary risks, I believed I had no choice in this particular situation. The man in jail could have been crazy; he could have killed me, but he did not. I had faith that he would not; I was able to help him, and I did. This set the pattern for my actions throughout the war.

But at that point I did not have time to dwell on what happened because the battle between the Japanese and the USAFFE still raged just 50 miles away. Civilians by the hundreds streamed into Kidapawan in search of safety, old men and women, young couples with many small children, all confused and angered that these infidels had invaded their country. The Japanese burned their homes to the ground, and they captured, tortured, and shot many helpless civilians. Some of the luckier ones were thrown into dark dungeons to await their fate. The hatred within the young Filipino men swelled until many of them decided to join the USAFFE to fight back, to try and avenge what had been lost. Women contributed what they could by rolling bandages and cooking for the soldiers who traveled from one post to another. The spirits of these women came alive when they realized that they were making a difference, too, that in their own small way they were helping to win the war. They were willing, able, and ready when the call to action came. They wanted freedom from oppression, not the aggression of the Japanese. I knew just how they felt. With my medical work I made my own contribution. I could not know then, at that early point in the war, just how much the Japanese would take from me, what I would never be able to get back. I was only sixteen, but the war made me an adult before my time.

3

Retreat Without Defeat

In early January 1942 the Japanese dug themselves into deep trenches at the Digos front lines outside of Davao City, and our American and Filipino troops did the same thing on the opposite side. Our soldiers were equipped with modern armaments and our C-47 airplanes brought in the supplies. Because I knew this I felt sure the war would be over within six months after its start, and I marked off with an X each day on my 1942 calendar, the last printed one I owned during the war years. Each X signified to me that we only had a few months and or weeks before peace and tranquillity returned to the Philippines. In the midst of conflict brought on by that war, the days passed just like the blowing of the wind. I remembered when I was a child in first or second grade I read a poem that asked, "Who has seen the wind? Neither you nor I, but when the wind begins to blow, we know it's passing by." That was how I felt about each day the war plagued our countryside. Even Christmas and New Year's Eve of 1941 did not hold meaning anymore; we were constantly on the alert as the advancing Japanese army forced people to abandon their homes and flee for their lives. When they tried to return, the Japanese slaughtered them. Civilians who fled to the mountains and forests found other enemies in the forms of wild animals, lack of food, blood-sucking leeches, and half-naked hostile natives. The natives, equipped with bolos, spears, and knives, killed their victims, leaving their bodies behind for the vultures and wild animals to devour. City people who sought refuge in the jungles knew nothing about those hazards, so they discovered the tragedy of facing enemies of a different kind only after they entered the forbidden forest.

Between January and March 1942 American officers and their men traveled to and from the Digos front lines to replace the exhausted soldiers who remained in their trenches fighting the Japanese. Some of the tired soldiers journeyed to Kidapawan for their R and R (rest and recuperation), where they bathed, ate hot meals, and found a nice place to sleep. The Filipino doctor and I treated those with minor medical problems, but sadly enough they often had to cut short their leave when they received orders to transfer to another front line. Filipino soldiers and officers alike enjoyed the same R and R privilege; they all certainly deserved their time off. I found it heartwarming to watch how the American and Filipino soldiers fought side by side for the same cause—freedom—united in their aim to battle and to force the enemy to capitulation. The Philippine army and the Philippine scouts, trained by the American officers, became one in strategy and purpose, and although high-ranking American officers commanded the overall army, Filipino officers exercised leadership over their own men. This reduced and controlled any friction that might develop.

Working with the medical corps made my reputation among Filipino and American soldiers in the province of Cotabato, who also knew me as old man Dore's daughter or the one-armed American's daughter. Because I matured so fast in body and mind, military and civilian personnel believed I was a grown woman, but rather than reveal my true age, which might have gotten me sent home, I convinced everyone that I was older so I would gain respect. After all, being a part of the USAFFE medical team was not child's play—I carried a lot of responsibility. In return I expected respect and acceptance from the men in uniform, as well as deferential acknowledgment of my womanhood. I kept the men at bay, refusing to give out information regarding my real age, and no one ever discovered the truth. In a culture where mothers, sweethearts, and wives remained in the home and subservient to their menfolk for life, I, because of the necessities of war, carved out my own independence. I emerged from the war a full-fledged woman with practical knowledge for surviving life's many harrowing experiences.

Because of my conscientious effort to be a good nurse, I did not notice my transformation from an ugly duckling to an attractive swan. The war rendered vanity frivolous. My work held my interest and I regarded men only as patients. Nursing kept me busy from sunup to sundown; by the time I finished my work at the end of the day I was too exhausted to do anything else. However, I could not help but notice that some Filipino and American officers came around the dispensary with the excuse that they wanted some kind of medical attention. Being naive and unsophisticated, I did not make the connection about their intentions; in fact, I was ignorant of any knowledge regarding boy-girl relations. In my time sex was only to be discovered after marriage and never before. I kept the moral standards I learned at home, school, and church.

Some of the American soldiers who came around found it comforting to talk to me in my spare hours because I possessed a strong command of the English language and was a good listener. This made the men feel at ease in sharing their feelings and their homesickness of missing the people they loved the most back in the United States. More over, they vented their feelings of anger about the war. I felt flattered that they chose to recount to me the pain of their aching hearts for their mothers, wives, and sweethearts. Being a good listener, I also learned about life in the United States, which interested me very much.

My first experience of real courtship happened when a young handsome first lieutenant in the Philippine army, a Spanish mestizo named Estrella, came calling. He claimed that the moment he set eyes on me in my uniform, even from a distance, he fell head over heels in love. At first I could not believe what he said because his visits were short and friendly, not romantic or passionate, but when he came around more often I became convinced of his seriousness. After he performed his daily army duties he took me out for a ride in his jeep. In the early evenings two young, unattached people could find temptation because of the odd combination of an uncertain, war-torn atmosphere and lush surroundings. In spite of the war the aroma of wild flowers, the sweet smell of the Ilang-Ilang tree, and the presence of the moon drew a man and a woman closer together. I cannot deny that we kissed, but we did not go beyond that boundary. Kissing felt daring enough to me. I was a virgin and true to my culture, and I wanted to remain one until I married. I firmly believed in abstinence before marriage, and I refused to dishonor my parents by engaging in premarital sex.

Lieutenant Estrella (his last name meant star) understood all of this and still pressed the courtship. After we went on a few more dates—some local parties and some short rides in his jeep—he proposed marriage. War or no war he did not want to lose me. Knowing Filipino customs so well he decided to approach my parents and ask for my hand in marriage. Estrella did not know about the two problems involved in this matter: first, I was only 16 years old, too young to get married; second, my mom lived a long distance away on the farm, and my dad was off doing his official duty at the front lines. I knew his suit would be refused. Estrella never resolved his marriage plan because in the middle of one night, under cover of darkness, his company commander received orders to move the troops out of the area.

Of course this meant my lieutenant had to leave with them, and Estrella never had the chance to say good-bye to me. Situations such as this were not uncommon; troop movements happened all the time. I understood the rules of war and learned to accept my destiny. I could not have a life with the lieutenant. A few months later I received word that the man I almost married was killed in action—the first devastating blow I had to accept during the course of the war. I had no time to cry. I realized that no matter how painful the tragedy, life had to go on, and I also had a feeling that what happened, my separation from the lieutenant, had been for the best. I knew I was too young to settle down in marriage, anyway. I worked hard at my job to ease the pain of my loss of Estrella, and in time the beautiful relationship became a memory.

Toward the middle of March 1942 the ammunition for our troops dwindled, and company commanders on the front lines tried in vain to requisition more. The only response they received advised them to hold out a little longer, that fresh troops and supplies were on their way from the United States. This never happened. Even more shattering, on April 9, 1942, the radio news announced the fall of Bataan, one of the last strongholds of the USAFFE, where approximately 76,000 Filipino and American soldiers were forced to surrender to the Japanese. The USAFFE had tried valiantly to hold on for five months in the face of repeated enemy attacks, but reinforcements did not arrive to take their places. Their food supplies rapidly diminished, and there were no replacements for the tons of ammunition they used against the Japanese. Capitulation to the enemy was the only way to avoid a wholesale slaughter. A month later Corregidor fell. Because the Japanese military code regarded surrender as an unforgivable offense, they considered their American and Filipino prisoners unworthy of any humane consideration. Japanese soldiers must commit hara-kiri, instant suicide with the use of a dagger to their stomach, rather than be taken alive to be disgraced; surrender was never a part of their military code of honor. Because of this belief, the Japanese treated the American and Filipino soldiers most inhumanely. The infamous Bataan death march exemplified their cruelty to our soldiers: out of some seventy thousand men who began the death march, at least seven thousand died of atrocities at the hands of Japanese soldiers. Those who barely survived the march to Camp O'Donnel looked like walking skeletons because they received no food or water along the way. News of Bataan and Corregidor came as a blow to our Filipino and American forces on Mindanao, but we had our own troubles to deal with, and we were not yet defeated.

Our own medical supplies were running low and Major Orbase, a Filipino officer, realizing the great need for more medical supplies, decided to do something about the situation before we completely ran out. He inducted me into the Philippine army, attached to the USAFFE, with the rank of second lieutenant. I could then use a military staff car, with a chauffeur and a guard to protect me, to travel to every pharmaceutical store in the area, requisition the medicines that the army needed, and sign promissory notes to guarantee that each owner would be repaid for their medical supplies immediately after the war.

After I received my brass bars the orders went out for the motor pool to dispatch a car covered with camouflage paint. The driver showed up at the dispensary with a Filipino soldier, and when they saw my rank, they saluted me and opened the car door. Whenever I questioned either one of the men about our destination they responded quickly with a crisp "Yes, Mom," or "No, Mom," since they knew the exact location of the drugstores on my list. I enjoyed the status of my official rank and did not dare tell the soldiers that I was born and raised in the Philippines. I was not ashamed of my roots, but the customary cultural divisions between the roles of men and women made my position awkward. It was simply more convenient if they thought I was an American nurse. I carried this professionalism off because of the military-style training I received from my dad when I was a child: I walked like a soldier, talked with authority, and kept my head high. How could I ever forget that when I was young, my dad used to order me to stand to attention, with my chest out, stomach in, and then walk like a soldier? I remember how obediently I followed him even though my tiny feet could not keep up with my dad's giant stride. In the staff car that first day I knew I had a lot of responsibility on my hands, and I did not want a dominant male to interfere with what I must accomplish for the good of all concerned.

Every day my driver, my guard, and I made trips to many towns in search of medical supplies, and I basically confiscated the needed supplies by providing a written promissory note. The captain I worked for expressed pleasure at my accomplishments, and he reported all of my work to Major Orbase. Another man became even more proud of my achievement: my dad. Although he came and went to the front lines so quickly, he remained well informed of my work, and he knew that I would not let him down.

April of 1942 arrived with the morale of our troops at low ebb because they had a difficult time accepting the terrible news that Bataan had fallen to the Japanese. In addition to this, none of the promised replacements arrived; fighting and living in foxholes day and night exhausted our young soldiers. These GI Joes became soldiers while still teenagers when they responded to Uncle Sam's call to arms in America, just after the Japanese air force savagely attacked Pearl Harbor. After December 8, 1941, when the war escalated into a true world war, some of those same soldiers found themselves in a distant land—the Philippines—wondering why they were fighting in this God-forsaken land. The Filipino soldiers fighting side by side reminded them the fight was for freedom for all: freedom for Americans and for Filipinos, freedom for everyone's families, freedom that might come with the ultimate price of death. In some instances the American GIs, raised in the land of plenty, did not completely understand what the Filipino soldiers meant about freedom, did not understand how long Filipinos had not been free. On the other hand, the rough experiences in this foreign land and quick, close friendships with Filipinos made some American soldiers realize what freedom meant to their new compatriots. Living in muddy trenches, tolerating mosquitoes and other bugs, suffering in humidity and even heavy rains—soldiers from America had not encountered any of this back home, where their lives were easier, their freedom more taken for granted. Here in the Philippines our Filipino soldiers fought for right on their home soil.

In the beginning of the war the American and Filipino soldiers forged a strong bond, yet much of the respect they had for each other sprang from historical roots. At the turn of the century, during the Spanish-American War in the Philippines, General "Black Jack" Pershing commanded U.S. land forces while Admiral George Dewey commanded the U.S. Navy. Dewey destroyed and sank the Spanish galleons built during the fifteenth and sixteenth centuries, and as the Spaniards got drunk on shore, the American fleet sailed in to Manila Bay, annihilating the Spanish Armada. This destruction helped the Filipinos obtain their freedom from the cruel Spaniards. After that battle the people of the Philippines did not forget what the Americans had done for them. Henceforth, the two countries became close allies, a partnership born of brute force.

The close relationship between the American and Filipino soldiers after Pearl Harbor did little, unfortunately, to repel Japanese forces, which easily reinforced their troops because they controlled the sea-lanes from Japan to the Philippines. They possessed a large cache of armaments and trained their soldiers to be fanatics: as soldiers of the Imperial Army their lives meant only kill or be killed. Many stories filtered through our front lines about how their soldiers continually advanced, just like marching ants. When the first row of casualties fell to the ground from machine-gun bullets, hundreds more automatically followed in columns from the rear until they overpowered their enemy. If they failed in their mission, they preferred to die by their own hand rather than surrender in disgrace. Later in the war kamikaze pilots acted in a similar way by ramming their crippled planes into their targets and perishing in honor. Before crashing their planes they cried out, "Banzai!" Apparently this gave them much satisfaction; they felt like great warriors in sacrificing themselves to the emperor Hirohito.

When the USAFFE soldiers could no longer hold on to the front lines that spring of 1942, General William Sharp, the commander-in-chief of the Mindanao sector, ordered a full retreat. General Vashion complied, and the troops in Digos moved out along the highway leading toward Cotabato and Bukidnon. At that very instant my dad obtained a weapons carrier driven by an American soldier, and he immediately gathered his family so that we could retreat along with the USAFFE. He picked me up at the dispensary first, and we drove to the farm to collect my mom; my younger brother, Philip; and as many of our worldly goods as we could carry. We worked in a frenzy to put together necessary items and sentimental ones as well. During the course of this frantic activity we decided that my brother George would take my dad's horse and provisions of rice, canned goods, jugs of water, and clothing and make his way to the coastline, where our Aunt Mary, my mom's sister, lived with her family. We all agreed that as soon as George reached Kling Plantation, he would send word to us and we would follow to the coast. Aunt Mary lived on a small farm bordering a wealthy American plantation owned by a man named Rhodes, and since her farm sat close to the sea, there was a natural food supply through an abundance of fish. She also had animals and a vegetable garden, so everyone staying there could eat well and remain alive. Because the farm was located in a remote place, outsiders could not locate the access roads—a perfect hiding place! I watched with a mixture of apprehension and fear as my brother George slipped through the thickness of the trees in the forest and disappeared. I never heard from him again during the war years; we all thought he had been killed.

We also buried many of our valuables at the edge of our property before we left the farm since we only had room for a few pieces of clothing, my parents' personal papers, and my mom's expensive jewelry. Then we climbed in back of the weapons carrier and rode off. On our way out of the farm I saw Major Orbase and convinced my dad to stop the carrier for a minute so I could inquire about my status in the army. As soon as the vehicle slowed down, I called out my question to the major, who assured me that I had done a magnificent job at the medical dispensary and was to be commended. However, he warned that the situation was very critical and he feared for my parents and me. He advised me to remove my second lieutenant's bars from my uniform, hide them, and change into civilian clothes. If the Japanese captured me and found me with an officer's insignia, they might torture, rape, and kill me. With my heart in my throat, I promised

I would do as he advised. The major also said he would include my induction papers in the official USAFFE personnel roster so that I might receive recognition and compensation for benefiting the war effort through my work with the medical corps in Kidapawan. Major Orbase perished shortly after the war, and I thought my induction papers were lost forever. However, I found my name listed in a roster after the war with my first name missing, and a copy of this document is in my possession today. Meanwhile, I will always remember that gentle, kind man who praised my work and gave me good advice.

As soon as our carrier reached the highway I saw the Engineer Corps burning and dynamiting all the bridges to slow down the advancing enemy. The large convoy of military equipment—ten-ton trucks, jeeps, and weapons carriers—and men was just about to leave when our vehicle appeared; they signaled our driver to get in line with the rest of them. As we waited, though, Philip, curious about all of the activity, jumped off the back of our carrier and failed to join us when we moved out. We were not to see him again for quite some time, and the uncertainty about his whereabouts caused my mom a great deal of anguish. Still, in the midst of the mighty army of American and Filipino soldiers, I felt jubilation, for although our fighting men retreated, I knew they had not been defeated. Their commitment remained in their hearts, to free the Philippines, and I would help them.

In 1948, three years after the war ended, I managed to make a brief visit back to Kidapawan to find out what was left of our farm. Newcomers who settled in the town quickly warned me not to venture out to the farm because squatters, who kept themselves armed with guns, had taken over our land. These people claimed their squatters' rights, and the government could not do anything for me even though I was one of the remaining heirs to the property. I did not pursue the matter. I survived the war and had many emotional scars, but I lived. I did not feel up to fighting with Filipino squatters. These displaced people found themselves a ready-made farm and had likely tilled the soil during those three years since the end of the war. They believed the land should be rightfully theirs. For me, all that remained on the farm were warm memories of a happy childhood and dashed hopes for what would have been had my family not been victimized by that terrible war. I lost almost everyone I loved and saw no point in fighting over a piece of land for the sake of sentimentality. But I did not lose my faith in God; I knew I had to continue believing.

4

The Infamy
of Capitulation

Miles of military vehicles continued their slow trek on the highway heading toward the border of Cotabato Province. According to my calculations we were moving northeast into the heartland of Mindanao, the military transports moving slowly to buy precious time. Even though everyone believed that the situation was hopeless, we still trusted that at any moment reinforcements might arrive from the United States, and with new supplies of ammunition and modern equipment the men could turn and fight again. Enemy planes had a field day as they followed the highways and repeatedly struck at the retreating American and Filipino army. The Japanese easily crippled their enemy because they controlled every air corridor. Furthermore, they hated the Americans and those who sided with them, even calling the Americans white devils, a derogatory term designed to discredit our soldiers. The Japanese intended to build a Greater East Asia Co-Prosperity Sphere that would incorporate everyone in the Pacific Rim into their vast empire. Naturally this included the Filipinos, whose roots were a mixture of Chinese and other Asian blood, but the Japanese made the big mistake of overlooking the past history of the Filipinos. The Philippines endured bondage under the Spanish for almost four hundred years, and the Americans helped them attain their freedom in the early 1900s, something the Filipinos never forgot. The Japanese had not counted on that.

By day our military commanders ordered the men to bivouac under heavy tree foliage along the highway. The lush camouflage provided by green branches over green canvas made the convoy appear to be a part of the forest—great strategy, as I recall! My family received priority to occupy any vacant house along the way whenever we stopped, and my mom and dad normally chose a house close to the officers' quarters, which was usually located in a tent under the trees. The officers unfamiliar with the terrain and forest consulted my dad, who had experience in fighting in the Philippines, and they welcomed his knowledge. I kept a low profile, as I was the only young woman among those many men. My parents, always close by, impressed their code of ethics on the officers and enlisted men, expecting everyone to act like gentlemen. In fact, they never used bad language when ladies were around, reserving that kind of rough talk exclusively for the men. We all realized that under these stressful conditions it was important to respect one another so that together we would win the war. My dad repeatedly used his trite expressions during those days—"There's a time and place for everything" and "There's a time to live and a time to die"—to encourage his family to support him and cooperate in every way to ensure our survival. Even I, his only beloved daughter, had to be obedient and mindful of his vital work with the USAFFE. The war had uprooted us from our home, our money had been frozen in the bank, and my dad's U.S. pension had stopped. We survived only because the military took us under its wing, giving us jobs and supplies. Now the military took us along to guarantee our protection until we reached safety.

Every day the Japanese army gained ground in its pursuit of USAFFE troops. During this offensive, which was hard enough on everyone, I heard a radio broadcast in a woman's voice from somewhere outside the Philippines. "Tokyo Rose," a Japanese woman educated in the United States before the war, spouted propaganda in fluent English across the air waves, saying things like, "Why don't you give up, Joe? Surrender and you will be treated well. Your loved ones back home don't care about you; they believe you are dead." Each day, Tokyo Rose broadcast a slightly different appeal, designed to demoralize our men, but fortunately only a few fell for the seductive voice of this woman. Most of our soldiers knew better; still, I hated the Japanese for playing on the emotions and psyches of our exhausted soldiers.

By the time the military convoy crossed the border of Cotabato into Bukidnon near the end of April 1942, wild rumors filtered through that General Jonathan Wainwright, United States Commander-in-Chief in the Philippines (after General Douglas MacArthur's departure to Australia), surrendered the entire USAFFE at the island of Corregidor. The news stunned everyone. The company commanders in Mindanao refused to believe what they heard—they knew about the Japanese propaganda machine, and this might be one of those false reports. But it was not. Soon General William Sharp on Mindanao received orders that Mindanao forces must give up their arms and surrender to the Japanese as of May 10, 1942. Each commanding officer had to account for the men on their roster because the Japanese intended to match their dog tags with serial numbers. I saw grown men cry when they heard the surrender order, weeping openly, unashamed, not because of the surrender but because they felt betrayed, abandoned by leaders they trusted. Only two questions came to their minds: "Why?" and "How could this happen to the mightiest army in the world?" Even the emotional feelings and tears that were shed that day affected me. I cried along with the soldiers.

The convoy kept going until it reached Kibawe; then all vehicles abruptly halted so everyone could have one last night and day of freedom. After another hundred kilometers the convoy would reach its destination—Malaybalay, Bukidnon—where the surrender would take place with all military supplies turned over to the conquerors. I heard that the Japanese then intended to place our soldiers in a concentration camp, where they likely would be incarcerated for many months. Knowing that our army had until May 10 to surrender, some of the officers and soldiers decided to celebrate, but others continued their disbelief and anger over the surrender. A number of enlisted men and their officers got drunk, while others formulated plans of their own: these men decided to go over the hill rather than surrender. They approached my dad and asked him to join them in the mountains because it would have been to their advantage if our family agreed to go with them. We spoke the native dialect and the presence of my mom, who had Filipino and Spanish blood, would be the ticket to everyone's safety, as the locals would likely feel comfortable with her around. As it turned out, though, both sides, civilians and military personnel of any background, expressed concern for each other's safety.

The captain of the group that wanted to flee to the hills singled me out and asked my dad if he realized what would happen to his daughter should the Japanese get hold of her? He told my dad I would be raped and made into a geisha (a Japanese woman trained as an entertainer to serve as a hired companion to men—we did not know about the comfort women then). The captain then bluntly reminded my dad that he was a white man, a one-armed white man, working for the USAFFE, and surely the Japanese knew about his activities.

We listened to bona fide and provoking questions that night, and as a family we struggled with our decision: surrender or evasion. As darkness covered the land, the officers and enlisted men heading for the hills loaded jeeps with guns, ammunition, and medical supplies. Some commanders tried in vain to discourage these men from going, but they soon gave in, realizing the small group's determination to leave. The captain approached us one more time, addressing my dad as "old timer," asking if he had decided to go over the hill with him and his men, promising to protect and take care of us until the war was over. My dad truly agonized over the choice of making our escape rather than surrendering to the enemy, but he made up his mind to continue on with the rest of the troops. We would take our chances by giving ourselves up because he believed his family could not withstand the rugged terrain or the high mountains—we were city folks.

My spirits sank. I had hoped to avoid surrender, but I understood the logic of my dad's final decision: he worried that my mom and I would not survive the rigors of hiding out. I watched, dejected, as the group rode off in their jeeps, until the darkness swallowed them up. Several months later our well-known bamboo telegraph system (word of mouth) provided us with an update of their situation. The Japanese, in relentless pursuit of those who refused to surrender, had captured, tortured, and killed some of those men. I felt terribly sad for these men that we had known so well, but their fate convinced me that my dad's decision had been the correct one. I felt glad we did not go with them.

When daylight arrived I found that between 50 and 100 men had left the convoy the night before, so the remaining officers faced a dilemma over whether to list the departed men as AWOL (absent without leave) or as escapees. Even I understood that the commanding officers had to adhere to the articles of war and strict military rule, but the question went unanswered that day because the convoy had to move on. In defiance of the Japanese, who were temporarily victorious, the enlisted men used their spare white underwear as flags of surrender; I watched wide-eyed as they attached a piece of wood to the front of their military vehicles and then tied their underwear on to it. The men got their kicks from this even though they hurt inside over the capitulation of our mighty army. With their mixed emotions that flag of surrender released their anger and frustration toward the Nips. No one could bring himself to say anything remotely nice about the Japanese anymore; to us they were Nips, Japs, or even worse—they were the hated enemy.

I continued to travel with my family in the weapons carrier as it rolled along the highway, keeping up with the military convoy, this time with a Filipino driver accompanying us in hopes of making us less conspicuous. Soon the triumphant Japanese soldiers began patrolling the roadways, but as they remained outnumbered they did not dare bother the convoy carrying thousands of armed American and Filipino soldiers. The Japanese knew enough to avoid confrontation in this uncertain period of transition. As civilians my family kept to the enclosure of our vehicle so that the patrols would not see us. The Japanese did not want civilians mixed in with the military; they had separate plans for dealing with each group. Although the bumps from the potholes on the highway caused a lot of discomfort, we did not complain as we continued to travel until we reached the barrio of Maramag. Here the convoy slowed to a crawl because of civilians who wanted to sell fruits, native cakes, and fried bananas to our soldiers. Kindly Filipinos gave their goods away to the soldiers who had no money because these civilians felt awful about the surrender, too. Some people in the crowd lifted up two fingers, making a victory sign, and shouted words of encouragement like, "Victory, Joe! Victory! We are with you all the way." Then, unashamed of what the Americans might think, their beautiful brown eyes filled with tears and they wept. Because of their past history of oppression and conquest by the Spaniards they knew what it meant to be defeated by an enemy; they understood exactly how the American soldiers felt. Even though morale among the soldiers was at an all-time low, the retreating army drew inspiration from the loyalty of the Filipino people: the smiling faces of old men, women, and children lifted their spirits. The people exhibited courage in coming out from hiding to sell or give away the limited supplies of food they had, and the USAFFE needed this kind of boost just before it began incarceration in the concentration camp.

We could not afford to tarry long; the officers gave the order to move, so we were on the road again, the long convoy crawling under the scorching sun creating quite a sight. Soon I caught a glimpse of the town of Valencia, but its few inhabitants had already deserted the area, fleeing to the jungles. In the next barrio, Mailag, the people heard the roaring sound of many vehicles on the road and came out to see what was going on. Recognizing the American and Filipino troops on their way to surrender, the townspeople lined the crowded highway and cheered encouragements such as, "Hey Joe! We are not giving up the fight. You might be in the prison camp but we are still out here. We will do our best to fight again and get you free." When the convoy came to a full stop the Filipino civilians reached out to shake the hands of as many of our officers and men as they could grasp. That exuberant greeting was the best thing I had seen all day. Each side felt a special bonding with the other. As the convoy rolled away, again many voices from the roadside shouted, "Victory, Joe! Victory! Down with the Japs." Then I heard one of the men in the trucks remark that these people were great: despite the USAFFE defeat they still cheered the troops. But another soldier told him to shut up, that he knew better the reality of the situation. That tart response ruined the mood. Except for the rumble of the vehicles there was silence as the long line of military vehicles continued on.

Timing was an important factor in the surrender of our troops. The Japanese commander set May 10, 1942, as the official date of surrender, and he remained adamant about this deadline. Anyone who dared report after that day would be shot without question, and he meant it too! For this reason the convoy picked up speed on the highway leading to Malaybalay. Just outside of a small barrio named Linabo we received the signal to move out of the long line of vehicles. A member of General Vashion's staff, an American officer, approached our carrier and told my dad that he would have our driver take us two miles down the road into Linabo, where he would have to remain with his family as a civilian. The officer believed that this was the best time for my dad to disassociate himself from the USAFFE, and hopefully the Japanese would leave us all alone. My dad fully agreed and understood the instructions. He told the officer that it had been a pleasure to work for the U.S. Army again, that he would never forget this day. Then we parted company at the fork of the road, not knowing what lay ahead of us, but on our own, without the mighty army to protect us, we still possessed the courage to go on.

The barrio of Linabo was desolate, deserted because its former occupants packed everything they had and left to avoid the Japanese. Their chosen path toward those rugged mountains represented their hope for survival of the Japanese occupation. Having heard too many horror stories from civilians who escaped the Japanese, living testimonies of torture and decapitation of fellow prisoners, the untamed jungles and mountain areas had to be a better place for them. An example of one such torture happened to the father of Lily, one of my friends from Silliman. Her father was a retired Spanish-American War veteran like my dad and a plantation owner in Kiamba, Cotabato, along the coast. One of their disgruntled workers betrayed the location of the family hideout, and the Japanese captured the American, took the old man to the beach, mocked him, and told him to bow before their flag of the Rising Sun. When he refused, they forced him to kneel on the sand, and using a samurai sword, one of the soldiers decapitated him. As the poor man's torso jerked on the sand, the small group of Japanese military men laughed and drank their saki.

The Japanese also abused their prisoners with water torture. A prisoner was bound, hand and foot, with a hose placed in his mouth, and then the torturer forced gallons of water into the stomach of the victim. The power of the excessive water expanded the body like a balloon and when the soldiers took turns bouncing up and down on the stomach, blood and water choked

the life out of the prisoner. Still another form of abuse was the bamboo treatment in which pieces of bamboo two or three inches long were sharpened
at the tip and forced under each fingernail or toenail with a hammer or a
hard object. The excruciating pain killed any prisoner with a weak heart. The
very worst tortures were the application of an electric probe to the genitals
and the bayoneting of helpless women and children. Being shot in a firing
line was more merciful because such forms of torture unconscionably administered by Japanese soldiers caused prisoners to go out of their mind; they
were never the same again if they survived their ordeal. Whoever devised
these methods of inhuman degradation and death must be so evil in their
hearts. Only God can bring judgment to this kind of wickedness.

I believed that I would not see our military friends again after we separated in Linabo. As our vehicle pulled alongside the fork in the road it
stopped briefly so we could all wave our last good-byes. The convoy continued on until it reached its final destination: Casisang Concentration Camp
in Malaybalay, Bukidnon. The camp contained several huts, some small, some
large, already occupied by the American and Filipino soldiers who came from
the coastline north of Mindanao. The commanding general, General William Sharp, stood in one of the huts waiting for the rest of his troops to
arrive from the south, the group my family and I had traveled with. Again
our bamboo telegraph system had informed us of the general's whereabouts
after the surrender, so I knew of his presence at the Casisang camp.

We had to move on while we still had daylight on our side. Two or three
miles from the fork in the road, we found an abandoned hut that stood alone,
fifty feet from the main passageway. The hut was built on stilts, common in
most structures to keep flood waters, insects, and animals from entering the
house. By all appearances it had belonged to a family of four: the hut possessed
two bedrooms measuring about eight by ten, each with a large window that
allowed the breeze to flow through the entire house for proper ventilation.
The very small kitchen, which still contained a native stove made of red clay
that was used for cooking everything, including rice, vegetables, and meat,
and for boiling water for coffee, was attached to the living room. The former
owners left behind a small, worn-out rattan bed, an old table, and a chair.
We felt lucky to have them. Everything else had been removed so that the
Japanese would have no reason to occupy the house. Since the bona fide
owners fled from their property, any family wanting shelter could occupy
the home for as long as they felt safe. Transient families did not pay any rent,
but they did take care of the place in the owners' absence. Unfortunately,
not everyone respected this honorable arrangement because in some homes
where furniture remained, transients helped themselves and hauled these
items away. They sold them for extra money, bartered for edible goods, or

simply destroyed the furniture to use it as firewood. Some folks called this "the rule of the jungle"—take what you can, run with it, or use it. My family, though, used such houses in an honorable way.

Exhausted from our long journey with the military convoy, we decided to occupy the empty hut rather than search for something else. Hunger gnawed at my stomach, and I felt grateful for the supply of canned goods and GI rations the USAFFE gave my family; so we immediately decided to take care of the persistent hunger pangs, leaving household organization for the next day. My tired body could no longer stay awake once my stomach was full; my eyes simply dropped shut, and I dozed off to the sounds of gunfire in the distance. The following morning I woke up to the crowing of young roosters. Most people do not know that you can almost tell a fowl's maturity from the pitch of its voice: the younger ones have a high pitch and the older ones have a deeper pitch. Regardless of their age, the sound of a crowing rooster is music to the ears of a Filipino who is used to hearing them. These fowl-feathered friends were our timekeepers in the absence of modern watches, and it was simply a great relief to hear such a familiar sound.

After the roosters woke us up that first morning in our borrowed hut, my mom decided to take our dirty clothes to the nearby stream and do a little washing. We planned on staying put a few more days to give ourselves a chance to clean up and rest; and having worn the same clothing for a few days, now soaked with perspiration, we all smelled like billy goats. We had no deodorant or powder to disguise the offensive smell, and while we were on the run, we took little time for such things as changing and washing our clothes. Fortunately, most everyone who came near us had the same problem, so no one was singled out as smelling like a skunk; we simply learned to tolerate each other, hardly noticing the offensive aromas. This is one of the things that war does to people normally conscious of cleanliness. Living in a house made us all feel normal again, causing us to make the mistake of letting our guard down.

After lunch my mom gathered all the soiled clothes, tied them in a bundle, picked up a bar of army soap, and made her way to a stream behind a clump of banana trees. Shortly after she left my dad cleaned out his favorite pipe, filled it with some of his special tobacco, and enjoyed a quiet smoke, his first in a long time. I shall never forget that aroma because it reminded me of the happy home and family I once had as a child, just a few short years ago, fond memories that cannot be relived but can be recounted and enjoyed. After my dad finished smoking his pipe he felt like a contented cow and settled in for a siesta, something the Spanish introduced during their four hundred–year occupation. They did not believe in rushing about like the Americans do today: if something could not be done in a day, they believed there is always mañana (tomorrow). My dad did not believe in putting things off, but he did enjoy a good rest in the afternoon.

I knew my dad had fallen asleep when I heard the rattan bed stretch and groan from the weight of his large frame. I knew that the siesta would help his old body recover from the strain brought on by the war, and realizing he was content, I too decided to have a catnap on the bamboo floor in the kitchen because I was still exhausted from our hasty retreat. My eyelids felt like heavy lead, they quickly closed, and I fell into a deep slumber. Soon I dreamed that someone was trying to force me to awaken, I could feel a masculine arm pulling me upward. I woke up in a daze. Then I saw them— two uniformed Japanese soldiers, one holding a rifle, the other pointing a Colt .45 pistol at me. The soldier with the rifle stood at my feet grinning like a Cheshire cat, the other had a strong grip on my right arm as he pointed the revolver at me with his right hand. Without a doubt they had one thought in mind: rape. Gathering my wits I took hold of the gun barrel with my left hand and asked rather unintelligently what was going on as I pushed the pointed pistol away from me.

It was a dumb remark, but my brain raced trying to come up with my next move. In spite of being overpowered by these two Japanese, I would fight for my honor even if it meant death because I had always been taught that a lady chooses death over dishonor. The commotion awakened my dad from his siesta in the next room, and he rushed toward the kitchen to defend me, only getting halfway out the bedroom door before a third Japanese soldier stopped him with a rifle pointed at his head. My dad shouted at them, calling them SOBs, insisting that they leave me alone, but the two soldiers continued to force me out of the kitchen, leading me toward the stairway.

All of a sudden, the soldier with the rifle aimed at my dad's head glanced beyond the front window in the living room and saw a convertible car flying a small flag bearing the symbol of the Rising Sun with a Japanese officer sitting in the back seat. He quickly raised a warning sound to his two other companions, and in a flash they fled the house, leaving their intended victims behind them. I always believed that the soldiers knew they were doing something wrong and were scared to death that one of their officers would find out. Now my dad and I needed just a split second to get out of the house. My dad urged me to hurry, to get the hell out of the hut while the getting was good. He understood that those SOBs might come back to finish what they came for, so he told me to run.

Like two jackrabbits we split out of that hut, running toward the stream to warn my mom, arriving just in time. She had just finished her wash and was heading back to the house. As we approached, I put my finger to my lips to indicate silence. My mom kept her voice in a whisper as she asked what was happening and where we were going. I quickly told her that three Japanese soldiers entered the house while we were taking a nap, and they tried to rape me and that my dad and I were lucky to get out when an officer appeared in a convertible and the soldiers left in a hurry. Trembling like a leaf on top of a running motor, my mom almost dropped the clothes basket. She told us she knew this would happen the moment she left the house, that while she was down by the stream alone she had a premonition that something was wrong. Turning to my dad, who was still out of breath, she asked him what we should do now. In silent response he nervously guided us toward the banana trees so that we could hide until darkness came.

When the clouds darkened in the sky the crickets began their usual chirping, telling us it was night. Having had a bad experience that day we decided not to spend another night in the house; instead, we agreed to remain in our hiding place. Not having any bedding, we cautiously approached the house in the dark, carefully listening for any human voices or footsteps and when we heard nothing we dashed into the building, grabbing everything and anything we could put our hands on, including our food. After returning to the clump of trees we spread our native mats, ate our cold meal, and drank cold water from the stream. We could not build a fire for our coffee or to keep us warm for fear of having unwanted visitors discover our hiding place.

Restless from lying on rough ground for the first time since the war broke out, our tired bodies eventually adjusted, and we fell asleep huddled close to each other. The following day the old reliable rooster woke us up, and we decided it was safe enough to boil some water for coffee. My mom did not think that the Japanese prowled around that early, so she urged us to take advantage of a hot meal and some good old java. My dad and I welcomed the idea, and we all enjoyed a scrumptious breakfast of hot rice and canned corn beef.

Shortly after breakfast my dad decided to make a trip to Casisang Concentration Camp. We learned that the lenient Japanese commander in Malaybalay did not surround the camp with barbed wire, and he allowed the prisoners to be governed by their own commanding officers, at least in the beginning. While my mom and I remained in our hiding place, my dad visited General Vashion, his former boss, for one last piece of advice. It was a risky but necessary trip for my dad, a former American soldier free in enemy-occupied territory, but he hitched a ride with a civilian driving in the same direction and managed to slip into the camp. The general was taken by surprise to see the one-armed American again; they talked quickly, and my dad slipped out of the camp again. He returned to us with good news and with a weapons carrier to help us move to a place across the road from the camp, where we would be among some Filipinos.

For about a month, maybe two, after the surrender on May 10, 1942, the Japanese High Command stationed in Malaybalay permitted the camp to remain open. This allowed the prisoners to visit one another's huts and to go across the road to buy and sell their last possessions to the civilians. At that time the Japanese felt confident that the naturally isolated camp, nestled between high mountains and forests, would keep the prisoners of war from escaping, so they were not in a rush to string a bunch of barbed wire around the camp. Although Filipinos could easily make contact with the prisoners, we faced more difficulties. As a British-born American, my dad could be picked up at any time; plus my own background and loyalties could be questioned. Most of all, though, regardless of nationality, my parents worried that as a young girl, I was in the most danger from the Japanese.

Across the highway from the camp, near where the civilians lived, flowed a river laden with rocks, some of which looked rough whereas others were so big and smooth that the cascading waters appeared to bounce over them with effervescent grace. The river was a beautiful sight to behold, even in such a gloomy atmosphere as a prisoner-of-war camp. Other natural beauties lay across and beyond the river: lush green ferns, giant trees, and wildflowers swayed in the breeze, and this natural habitat brought wildlife near the river as long as they remained undisturbed by the presence of man. Evacuees heading for Malaybalay temporarily occupied the native huts beside the road leading to the river, staying just long enough to earn money to sustain their families. As long as the soldiers had money to buy their goods, they stayed. The presence of civilians also added to the morale of the prisoners, keeping them in good spirits despite their internment.

Realizing that we had very little money left, my mom and I decided to take in laundry for the officers and men across the way. In times like these one's pride had to be relinquished in order to survive; we never would have done someone else's laundry otherwise. Rich people lost all their material goods, the middle class had lost just as much, and the poor had nothing to lose. What was left in everyone's mind was basic survival. Fortunately, since the Japanese tried to push their Co-Prosperity Sphere among the Filipinos, they allowed those in the native huts across from the camp to stay a short period of time. Despite their generosity we were never under the illusion that the Japanese could be trusted at their word because they flip-flopped on their decisions each day, so we had to take advantage of the time they gave us to make a living for ourselves. The prisoners seemed happy to have us as their neighbors, especially because we could do their laundry for them. They provided us with soap for their uniforms, and my mom and I did the rest; when we returned the clean clothes, they paid us with money, American cigarettes, or canned goods. The items could then be sold to those who smoked or wanted certain kinds of food, and since I did not smoke, I bartered ours for fresh meat and poultry. Because some of the Americans and Filipino soldiers had no money, we did their work for free. My mom and I believed they had sacrificed much for the cause of our freedom so surely we could do something for them in return. They were always thankful.

Civilians and prisoners alike shared the big river across from the concentration camp. Everyone understood that when the men came down to bathe, the civilian women remained in their thatched-roof nipa huts with the windows and doors closed up tight while the soldiers dipped in the clear running water naked as jaybirds, a sight inappropriate for women. Even though some of the large boulders served as a makeshift screen for their nakedness, others bathed in the open where the rocks were smaller. The prisoners could not tarry any time they took a bath since their officers had to account for them when they left the camp and when they returned. If one of the men stayed out for too long, he might have to be counted as missing, which would infuriate the Japanese.

Once the men gave the all clear and removed themselves from their bathing area, the women gathered up the dirty uniforms to wash at the river. The process of doing laundry was simple but time-consuming. First my mom and I found a flat rock; then we soaked the clothing in water and applied a thick layer of soap. As the soap built up, we each used both hands to rub the soil out of the uniform, going back and forth until the dirt came out. If difficult stains remained, and they usually did on socks, underwear, and undershirts, we laid the soapy material on a smooth rock and applied a flat paddle to the clothing, hitting several times until the stubborn dirt loosened. Then we rinsed the clothes in the river, squeezed out the excess water, and hung the clothing to dry on a line strung behind the huts. Filipino women usually carry baskets of wet laundry on their heads, and I found it fascinating to watch them balancing their loads. I never mastered that task.

I sometimes watched the women coming from the river with their loads of wash: they appeared like marching ants, moving in a straight line, heading toward the clotheslines. Had they included the song, "The ants go marching one by one. Hurrah, hurrah! The ants go marching one by one. Hurrah, hurrah!" the music would have lifted our morale. Of course no one on Mindanao knew this song at the time; I learned it in one of the YMCA camps in the United States where I worked as an office secretary to the camp director. As soon as I heard it I saw those washing women in my mind and remembered their daily trudge. Even with the absence of music, though, these women knew how to laugh and giggle like little children while doing their work. They enjoyed working for others—pay or no pay—and like my mom and I, they felt grateful to the USAFFE soldiers. The nicest thing about our association with them is that we all accepted one another in our struggle for survival. Problems arose only when outsiders, or maybe even family members, stole somebody else's laundry from the clothesline. After we found the culprit we ended up showing compassion for the person because we understood why people took things in wartime: it was not their normal behavior; it was fear derived from the war.

Although most of the civilians living in the huts across from the camp struggled for subsistence, there were a few wealthy ones among us, but they were not really any better off. One rich woman stands out in my mind because of her many golden earrings, gold bracelets, and diamond rings. She remained in her hut all the time for fear others would notice her jewelry and rob and kill her for it. She only trusted our family to enter her hut because she knew us personally, and I shall never forget the constant fear in her eyes, how she clutched her jewelry box to her bosom. After she moved on we never heard from her again. I felt very sad because all of her wealth did not do her much good—she and her husband lived in constant fear.

War definitely does strange things to everyone caught up in its insanity. Even the rich and the powerful were not in a good position in their struggle for survival, but the middle class and the poor knew better how to adjust to their circumstances. Of course there is always the exception to the rule. Some of the wealthy ones survived because they bought their way out of their dilemma; others worked as collaborators and spies to insure the safety of their possessions and their lives. The question is, Did the rich learn the true value of sacrifice in the midst of war? I doubt it! Then again, I cannot tell their stories, only my own. I sacrificed enough during the war. It is my hope and prayer that none of my family members will have to go through any war that may possibly destroy all humankind. God knows war is not the answer to any problem.

5

House Arrest

A month or two after the surrender of the entire USAFFE on Mindanao, a sudden change occurred. I watched from across the road as a truck full of Filipino civilian workers, guarded by Japanese soldiers, appeared at the entrance of Casisang Concentration Camp. They carried with them many rolls of barbed wire, posts, and shovels. The officer in command, with his limited knowledge of the Filipino dialect, barked out his order, "Sigi-na! Sigi-na!" (Hurry now! Hurry now!) His soldiers carried their rifles with fixed bayonets pointed at the Filipinos. The threatened laborers jumped off the parked vehicles and began their backbreaking task of digging holes in the ground. Once they placed the poles in the ground they nailed barbed wire to the post, permanently enclosing the whole camp. The prisoners of war panicked at the sight of their quickly vanishing freedom: no more bathing in the river or going back and forth to see the civilians in the huts to do their laundry. Those of us who lived in the huts became nervous as well because we all knew the Japanese could not be trusted despite all their propaganda about the Co-Prosperity Sphere. It was nothing but a bunch of lies; they broke their promises. They did not know how to live honorably and well among the Filipinos.

It took the Filipino workers many days to complete the job of surrounding the whole camp with barbed wire. Judging from the many huts spread across the compound, the camp must have been a thousand hectares, or about ten thousand square meters, and the scorching sun that kept the temperature at more than one hundred degrees did not help the hard-working men. In normal times men had sense enough to find shelter under shady trees to cool themselves off; however, the Japanese guards, wearing sun-shading hats, did not allow any rest. Whenever a worker fell to the ground exhausted from the heat, a guard poked his bayonet at the man, forcing him to get back to work. If the man became too weak or ill, the soldier, without a conscience, bayoneted the worker to death, then the guards laughed over the anguish and misery of the remaining laborers. The Japanese simply left the lifeless body for the buzzards and other wild animals to devour.

While some freedom still existed because the barbed wire could not be completed in just a few days, some soldiers took chances in coming across the road to see us about their laundry. Gone were their laughter, smiles, and the happy times we shared as friends. They even stopped believing that the one man who could save them, General Douglas MacArthur, would return and get them out of their hellish situation. The barbed wire crushed their spirits and filled their future with anxiety: they realized they were going to be confined within the perimeter of the camp, left to the mercy of their Japanese guards. The worry turned young soldiers into old men; even the baby-faced doughboys developed wrinkles on their foreheads. I felt sad to see them like this.

After the installation of the dangerous barbed wire, well-seasoned Japanese guards were posted at the one-way entrance of the camp and at other strategic areas. These guards wore baggy uniforms that made them look like Arctic penguins, especially when they walked, and their mismatched shirts and hats gave them an unkempt appearance. The officers looked no better, but each wore a large samurai sword dangling from the waist. They reminded me of the slapstick comedians I saw in the American movies before the war. Other Japanese officers wore oversized uniforms formerly belonging to the Americans, making them look even funnier. How could a short, fat Japanese soldier fit into a tall American soldier's shirt, pants, and boots? Impossible, yes? Yet the Japanese, who touted their own superiority, wanted what our men had. They not only confiscated uniforms—they even had over a dozen good wristwatches, taken from our soldiers, strapped on both sides of their arms. Filipinos likened the Japanese soldiers to sea lions, penguins, or even old walruses.

In spite of the hilarious appearance of the Japanese soldiers, I knew that their fanatic training in military discipline made them very dangerous. Their first loyalty was to their emperor, their second to their country. Dying in battle for their country's leader was more than a great sacrifice; it was honor in the first degree. But their brutality, their methods of torture, decapitation of prisoners, killing of women and children, provoked no remorse, guilt, or feeling of shame. I often wondered if all this was part of a religious ritual, as well as military training.

All of us civilians living in the nearby huts realized that the enemy's new brutish behavior with our prisoners meant that our time here was at an end, especially since we no longer felt safe living across the way from those barbed wires. My parents and I left first, and the rest followed. A large empty truck happened our way, so we stopped the driver and offered him money to take us to the town of Malaybalay, which was about six to eight kilometers away from the concentration camp in Casisang, on a high elevation, nestled close to the mountains. Far enough to feel safe, we thought. Those people not lucky enough to get on the truck traveled on a cart pulled by a carabao, an animal with horns and about the size of a large bull. The carabao walks almost like a turtle: every so often it has to stop and wallow in watery mud to cool off its hide; otherwise, the beast would become debilitated, and it would die. We piled in the truck with what little belongings we owned, and off we went. The soldiers and officers we knew felt sorry to see us go, but even without an explanation they understood why we had to leave. Standing close to the fence line they waved their last good-byes, not knowing whether they would see us again; a few shed tears because we had been like family to them.

Slowly the truck moved in the direction of Malaybalay. As we pulled away we shouted as loud as we could, "Victory! Long live America! We love you." Then everyone on the truck gave a victory sign to all our men. We wanted to leave behind one final lasting bit of inspiration, to let our soldiers know that we were still on their side. But the Japanese guards were not sympathetic—they suddenly appeared and ordered us to move on without delay. They knew how to frighten us with their rifles and their fixed bayonets. In silence we moved on.

Just below Malaybalay, about three hundred feet before reaching the plateau where the level ground began in the town, my family spotted a deserted two-story building on the right-hand side of the road. For some strange reason we were drawn to this place, so we asked the driver to stop and drop us alongside the road with our things. We tried to find the owner at the neighboring house, but the people living there were evacuees, just like us, so they did not know anything. Peering in from the outside, I figured that the owner must have occupied the upstairs and used the downstairs as a bodega or storehouse for buying and selling sacks of corn or rice. Farmers often brought their stock of dried corn to a place like this to have it weighed and sold to the bodega owner, and in turn the owner sold the accumulated bulk to big companies in far away places like Davao, Cebu, or Manila.

After exploring the first floor of the building we decided to check out the upstairs part, where we planned to stay for as long as we could. I immediately noticed a large door at the bottom of the stairs, obviously placed there to keep trespassers out. While walking up I noticed my dad struggled with his breathing. On his birthday, May 9, 1942, the day before the surrender, he turned 64 years of age. The capitulation of the USAFFE, however, hastened his aging process, while his spirit, his will to live out the war, and his determination to protect his family motivated him to go on.

By now our family had a single addition: besides my dad, mom, and me, there was a pet monkey named Cheeta that I inherited. Its previous owner, an American friend in the prison camp, turned Cheeta over to me for safe keeping since the Japanese did not allow pets in camp and the American soldier feared the Japanese would destroy his animal just out of meanness. Also, with a scarcity of food they might have killed and eaten the monkey. Having the monkey around was a delightful experience because he was very entertaining, and we really needed Cheeta to cheer us up. Monkeys are playful, but they can also be dangerous. According to Filipino legend, when a monkey is kept without a string tied to its neck, it heads right for the burning firewood in the open kitchen stove where it will grab hold of a burning ember, jump from place to place, and set the house on fire. The homes made of bamboo and nipa roof were easily ignited because they become brittle with wear; therefore, a spark from burning wood can easily bring on a bonfire. For this very reason some people believed that having a monkey for a pet is "malas" or bad luck because of the destruction they might bring to a family residence. Conveniently enough Cheeta had a collar and a leash around his neck, so I kept him tied to the outhouse. Legend or not, at least we were safe from monkey mischief.

The upstairs of the building we occupied for several months contained three large bedrooms, a living room, and a kitchen; the toilet, built ten or fifteen feet away from the house, was really an outhouse. A sturdy, narrow platform connected the house to the toilet, with railings on both sides to hang on to for safety since an accidental fall from the platform meant instant death because of the large rocks below. The toilet, surrounded by a nipa roof and siding to keep the rain out, had a one-hole seat with wooden shafts to guide the waste matter as it dropped down into a hole in the ground. Although sanitary, I considered it primitive.

Each of the bedrooms had large windows to allow proper ventilation on very hot days, with the largest window located in front overlooking the road below. From here I watched anything passing by: people, animals, or vehicles. The hill on the other side contained no homes but was overgrown with shrubs and trees. The kitchen held a few items including a table and two chairs, causing me to wonder why the previous owner left a wide opening where walls should have enclosed the kitchen area. Either he had not completed the construction before the war broke out or he wanted it open to be able to see into the back wooded area of the house. I did not concern myself with anything else about the house's structure. I was simply thankful we found a safe place, if only for a little while.

My parents occupied the front bedroom on the left side of the house facing the street, next to the stairway. Concerned for my safety, they wanted to be able to hear every footstep coming up those stairs, especially if they were Japanese. The room I stayed in was located on the right side, closer to the open-ended kitchen. I tied my monkey, Cheeta, to the railing, giving him the freedom to go back and forth from the edge of the kitchen to the outhouse, but he preferred being on the tree next to the toilet. My dad amused himself with Cheeta by singing, "Oh the monk, the monk, the monk, he climbed the elephant's trunk. The elephant sneezed and fell on his knees and that was the end of the monk, the monk, the monk." I was happy that my dad retained his sense of humor in the midst of adversity, and I learned from him that humor is a valuable quality.

Shortly after we settled in our new dwelling place, my dad and I paid a visit to the Japanese commander in Malaybalay because my dad believed that it would be to our advantage to let the Japanese know where we were rather than to have them stumble on us. He also wanted to show them that this young woman, me, was a pure and obedient daughter living under the protection of her parents. The commander's headquarters were located in the Bethany Home, where an American missionary lady had lived prior to the war. She had fled for her life, and the members of her congregation protected her in the mountains, where the Japanese could not find her. Today she is alive and well and although in her nineties, she heads the Bethany Children's Home for Children in Talakag, Bukidnon. Many years after the war, when my husband, Jim, and I applied to help a child at the home, little did I know that the woman in charge was the same person I met many years ago in Malaybalay during the war. I feel very privileged to have known this saintly missionary, who dedicated her whole life to taking care of abandoned and abused children in that remote part of the world. She is truly one of God's angels here on earth.

When we arrived at the Japanese headquarters, a soldier carrying his rifle with a fixed bayonet escorted my dad and me to the office of the commander. I looked around at the changes that had been made and found myself hating that this lovely building was being used for purposes of war.

My dad sat down in one of the office chairs and introduced himself to the Japanese officer, telling him that he was Mr. Dore, of French-English descent, just as General Vashion had encouraged him to do. Our last name came from the French, and besides, the Germans, allies of the Japanese, had occupied France. The wise general felt we might have more luck dealing with the Japanese if they believed we were French. My dad then requested permission to take his family back to our farm in Kidapawan, Cotabato, because as civilians we needed to work the land to survive.

The commander's suspicious, penetrating eyes scrutinized us throughout my dad's brief speech. I felt my heart pounding in my chest; I believed that this Japanese officer knew exactly who we were. Then he zeroed in on my dad's missing left arm, his long thinning white hair, his unshaven face, and his aging frame. Through an interpreter the commander asked my dad that if he was French, then where were his papers? My dad quickly responded that our home was burned to the ground, the municipal building burnt down as well, and all our records were destroyed, so we had no papers.

The commander considered this for a moment and then spoke again through his interpreter, addressing my dad as Mr. Doré, using the French pronunciation of our name. He acknowledged that my dad might be a Frenchman as he claimed, but he would not allow my dad to return to his farm because he was still a white man. The commander claimed it was too dangerous for my dad and his family to go back to Kidapawan because of the bandits and the Moros in that place; then he insisted that we all remain under Japanese protection because France was a country allied with Japan. Moreover, the Filipino rebels would not be able to touch us as long as we were in the care of the Japanese.

My dad and I knew this was double-talk because when the commander mentioned "white man" in his admonition we recognized we were in fact prisoners of the Japanese. We all knew that Filipino rebels would not harm us; more likely they would try to recruit us for anti–Japanese work. Even the Moros were more worried about the Japanese than rival Filipino tribes, and bandits targeted everyone, Caucasian and Asian alike. No, the commander told us through his various insistences that the Japanese suspected us simply because we were white people. To leave the area now without permission would be as good as signing our death warrants because the Japanese would hunt us down and execute us as spies or traitors. I knew my dad had not expected this response, but he kept his tone and his temper even, politely thanking the commander for his time and for his concern for our welfare. We hastily excused ourselves, and I felt tremendous relief once we got outside because I had been afraid that the Japanese would take me away for God knows what evil purposes.

When we left Japanese headquarters, soldiers followed us all the way to the house, making it understood that they intended to keep us under surveillance. We felt trapped but could do nothing except keep a low profile and stay indoors, as it would be unwise for my dad especially to be seen in public because of his obvious white skin. Without a doubt we knew we were under house arrest from that moment on; the house that had seemed so perfect just the day before was now little more than a prison. We had to abide by the instructions of the Japanese commander because he and his army possessed the weapons and the authority to regulate our lives, but I took comfort in the knowledge that they did not have the power to control our destiny. Only God could do that.

As soon as my dad and I returned to the relative safety of our home, we sat down with my mom to discuss our options. My biggest concern was for my dad's safety: I knew that a white man with blue eyes could not disguise himself in any way to blend in with the locals. To avoid his arrest on any false charges we all agreed he must stay inside the house. My mom's physical appearance would have allowed her to trade freely in town, but the war had already taken a toll on her health; by this time she was too fragile to engage in any buying or selling of goods to help us survive. Besides, someone had to stay in the house to make sure that my dad did as well, so I had to take the initiative to go out and learn how to buy and sell in order to make a living, to survive. This could be a risky business for me. I knew that many of the local Filipinos would recognize that I was not a full-blooded Filipino and any one of them might turn me in to the Japanese, or the Japanese themselves might pick me up off the streets and use me for their own dire purposes. If I did not go out and start trading, though, our family would not survive. I had to take the risks.

With the small cache of canned goods given to us by our friends in the prison camp, I had enough to get started in trading with other civilians for goods and cash. My mom, overly protective, continued to resist my solo trade career because she did not want me exposed to any danger. She worried incessantly about our safety—my dad and I represented all the family she had left—and would have preferred to make the sacrifice in order to protect us, but her health simply did not permit that. Little did any of us know then that her impulse toward self-sacrifice would eventually cause her to make the ultimate sacrifice so that I might live.

Despite these unpredictable and dangerous circumstances I did find some amusement in the way the Japanese army dealt with the civilian population after the surrender. The Japanese formed a puppet government to conduct business as usual, to have full control of the Filipino people through their handpicked government officials who were so corrupt. They printed money we called "Mickey Mouse" money because it was worthless; the Japanese had no way of backing up the money they printed, and everyone knew it. Civilians continued to trade with pesos and dollars as long as they were able because they believed in the value of those currencies. To stimulate cash flow for the emergency money, the Japanese commander came up with a brilliant idea: he issued passes to civilians so they could take the long trip on foot to Casisang Concentration Camp to sell edible goods to the soldiers and officers who still had some American money in their possession. Since the Japanese took away the younger Filipino men to work on their airfields and other construction places, only old men, women, and young girls could apply for the vendor's pass to the camp.

I was fortunate enough to be granted a pass through the influence of a woman friend who rubbed elbows with the Japanese high officials. When she applied for herself, she requested an extra pass and without any questions, they gave it to her. This woman did not mind helping me because I did not condemn her for her association with the Japanese—I recognized the fine line between collaboration and survival, and all of us vendors were just trying to survive. In our trading and buying of each other's goods, I told jokes to make her laugh, and she enjoyed this immensely. She wanted the American cigarettes I had because she smoked and sold some of them to the Japanese officers at a high price. I knew all along that she worked with black-market contraband, but that was she, not me; I drew my line there. I kept my business with her strictly buying and selling goods so that I could make some profit to support the three of us at home. I also knew she was an agent for the Japanese, so I was very careful around her because I did not want to get turned in, nor did I want people to think that I was an agent as well.

At first I decided to sell lemonade because of the abundance of lemons in our backyard. I gathered all the empty bottles I could find and bought some more from my friends so that I had containers for the juice, then I sterilized the bottles so any remaining germs would not contaminate the drinks. I had to do all of this the night before I sold the lemonade to avoid delays in joining the vendors in the morning. I remember the first time I picked the lemons, laid them on the table, squeezed each one by hand, and then added sugar to sweeten the juice. My dad watched me at work and let out a hearty laugh, telling me that I reminded him of the bootleggers in America who made their own dynamite juice out of corn. I primly reminded him that my concoction was nonalcoholic so there was no danger of getting our troops drunk. I was too young to know how much the soldiers would have appreciated alcoholic beverages, especially in their current situation.

The bottled lemonade was heavy; because of its weight I could only carry two dozen bottles at a time, but later I switched to items lighter and more plentiful to make the long trip worthwhile: cakes, cookies, tropical fruits or fried bananas that did not weigh as much as the bottles of lemonade. In our struggle for survival we vendors had to work together. Whenever someone bought large quantities of fruits or vegetables through wholesale or "pak-yao," as they said, we divided up the goods so that no one would be left with much spoilage. Local farmers harvested fruits like lanzones, mangoes, guavas, papayas, and many others each season; as the fruits ripened, we actually had an oversupply of them.

Each day about fifteen or twenty women, including myself, congregated at the bend of the road with our fresh-baked goods, patiently waiting for each other because we believed there was safety in numbers. To protect each other we only knew each other's first names; that way Japanese collaborators who often wormed their way into a group like ours could not get much information about us. Still, by using first names only we were able to count heads and to keep track of one another easily. Since I was the youngest in the bunch, I kept myself in the center of the group, the older men and women understood why and they willingly gave me their protection.

After walking the eight kilometers we went to the guardhouse located next to the Japanese post commander's own little hut. The post commander gave orders to the civilian vendors, and the guard made all of us stand in a straight line while he checked our passes. When the commander was ready to make his own inspection, each of us had to make a fifteen-degree bow, without looking up at the face of our enemy. If we glanced up at any time during this review the commander slapped our faces and embarrassed us in front of everyone. We had no rights as people; we had to act like obedient coolies, unskilled laborers in India or China also subjugated to our new Japanese masters. Right after the ritual of bowing to the Japanese officer, the guard inspected our baskets for hidden weapons or information, and if he found nothing he allowed us to march in single file guarded by soldiers who kept an eye on every move we made.

At first the Japanese soldiers did not abuse the civilian vendors only because they did not come from the hard-core military whose members tried to make points with their superiors by showing off their power. However, when Japanese soldiers from the front lines replaced the mild, less-professional ones, I learned what terror was all about because these soldiers did not hide their arrogance of authority. I shall not forget the time when the Japanese discovered that three women had brought in American magazines and newspapers for our soldiers to read. The Japanese soldiers were furious: they screamed like a bunch of banshees, ordering the women to step out of the inspection line. Then they shouted questions at them, asking why they had brought magazines to American soldiers, and accused them of being spies who could now be shot. They each took turns slapping the women's faces. Back and forth went their hands until the hysterical and trembling women's faces became cut and swollen, blood came out of their mouths, and their eyes swelled red. The soldiers then struck the women's bodies with such force that they fell to the ground sobbing.

Crying out loud, one woman pleaded that they were not spies, that the magazines contained nothing more suspicious than pictures and leisure reading material. The Japanese officer ordered her to be silent, telling her that the Japanese were the masters now, that she and everyone else must follow their orders. This was how the Japanese treated the Filipino women who innocently thought their harmless magazines meant nothing to them or the Japanese.

Despite the brutality of the Japanese soldiers and some of their officers, some of us civilians continued to risk bringing in vital information to our friends in the camp. It was true cloak and dagger because of the deadly consequence if caught. In my case I thought at first that I was doing my part to help our prisoners because they were Americans, the same ones who helped us when we needed them early in the war. Now it was my turn to bring them tidings of good news from the outside, although even my presence in the camp appeared to lift their morale since I spoke fluent English and was a girl.

Casisang Concentration Camp had one Japanese commander who stood out from the rest, a stubby fellow clad in baggy pants, leggings, a soiled shirt, and a samurai sword attached to his big fat belly. He wore a pair of old-fashioned eyeglasses with black rims and a funny-looking dirty old painter's style cap. What made him different from the rest was the bushy mustache that gave him the look of an old bull walrus. He enjoyed being flattered by the women vendors, but when they disobeyed the strict rules or were caught smuggling contraband goods in the camp, he turned mean and wretched with his authority. I cannot forget the day when I was delivering very important contraband to the camp. When I arrived with the rest of the vendors at the guardhouse for inspection, this ugly-looking officer picked me out of the group of women, sitting on his chair, beckoning me to come forward so he might speak to me. "Kora, kora" was the usual way of calling someone; it meant "come here, come here." At first I pretended that I did not hear him, but he repeated the call, then he spoke a little English, first addressing me as "hey you," then as "dalaga" (young lady). This time I knew I could not ignore his beck and call. I felt like a rat caught in a trap; my adrenaline began to soar so that I could almost hear my heart pounding against my chest, and my mind raced for some type of strategy. I knew I had to muster up all my inner courage, and I told myself to keep my nerves steady, that everything would be all right.

On this day that the Japanese officer singled me out I was trying to smuggle in a navigator's compass plus two radio messages to the prisoners in the camp. I had to be cool, calm, and collected; I had to believe that the Japanese firing line was not quite ready to claim me as one of its victims. An American officer by the name of Captain Richardson gave me the compass for temporary safekeeping before the barbed wires went up around the prison camp, and I cared for that compass for many months until he asked me to bring it back to him. He and a few of the men wanted to make an escape from Casisang because they were tired of the food that consisted of nothing more than rice and floating worms, and they had seen too much of the bad treatment of the prisoners. The captain decided he was ready to take his chances in the mountains with his men. To hide this rather large object, I wore my brother's short pants underneath my dress, which had a large flared skirt, and I hid the instrument in one of the pockets. As for the radio messages, I rolled one of them up in one of the curls on my head and sewed the other into the hem of my dress. My biggest challenge was to outwit the old walrus so that my hidden objects could get through—and this would be the last time I smuggled.

Picking up my basket, I rushed over to the commander with a big smile and asked him if he would like to try some of my cookies. I told him that I had made them myself and assured him that they are very good. Before he could respond I reached into my basket, pulled out a cookie, and handed it over to him. As he munched on the cookie, I kept talking, telling him how good the cookies were and asking him if he wanted more, using this as a diversion to keep him from searching my person. It worked! He kept on eating, occasionally muttering between swallows that the cookie was indeed very good, very good. But the next thing the old walrus said concerned me very much: he asked me where I lived because he would very much like to visit me. This really threw me because I thought that I had out-smarted the old boy with a cookie, believing him dim-witted, yet he turned around and asked where I lived. The hot items I carried were my biggest concern, so rather than having them discovered, I gave the old walrus my address, and he appeared satisfied; but I was still worried. Although the other vendors had to pass inspection while I was talking to the officer, I did not, so I simply got back in line and marched into the camp, unsearched, with the others.

While our marching group continued its way through the camp I spotted Captain Richardson and his men waiting for me. My eyes met the captain's, and I blinked once or twice to give him the signal that I had the compass. As soon as I arrived at the designated area for selling goods the guards busied themselves with the other vendors, the captain's men surrounded me, and I quickly reached underneath my skirt, retrieved the compass, and handed it over to them. When I removed the radio news reports from my hair and my hem, I felt a great burden of relief lifted. I told Captain Richardson to please not ask me to do anything more for him because I almost got caught out there, and I thought it was getting too risky for me. He and his men understood, so that marked the end of my bringing in messages or items of importance to any of them. As for the captain and his men, I did not hear anything about what happened to them, and I did not want to know because they were my friends. I prefer to remember them as they were that day: alive, relatively healthy, and hopeful.

I realized that the soldiers in the camp needed money; the little they brought in with them had just about vanished. Some of the men hung around the open building where the vendors sold their goods, even if they had no money, and I cringed when I watched the American soldiers fight it out to pick up food that had been dropped on the ground. They acted like hungry dogs—the food from the ground was full of dirt but they simply brushed this off and ate it. Whenever this happened I felt so sorry for our soldiers that I ended up giving away much of the food I made the night before to sell. When I returned home, my mom, who thought me very foolish to just give away things when we badly needed money to live on, scolded me for not bringing back enough money from selling my goods. My mom also reminded me about the distance I traveled every day and how tired I was when I returned from each trip. But I gently reminded her that she was the one who taught me that it was better to give than to receive, that that was the Christian way to live, and she just smiled, knowing I was right.

The night I returned from my smuggling expedition started out just like any other. When the sun began to set, we all sat down to a nice hot meal at the table, and following the meal my dad took out his tobacco, filled up his pipe, lighted it, and started smoking. He eagerly questioned me about what went on during the day. As my mom washed the dishes, I told them about Old Walrus, describing his appearance and his manners until my parents burst out laughing, a release we all needed because we did not know much about our future under the Japanese. As soon as my parents calmed down I told them of the more serious danger I had put myself in that morning with transporting a compass and two radio messages inside the camp. I had kept this a secret from them until it was over because I did not want them to panic or give me any negative thoughts—it was bad enough that I took the life-and-death risk on my own. I wanted it to succeed without hearing any doubts or hysteria from my mom. My dad understood my actions and said he was proud of me; my mom, on the other hand, was afraid for me, especially when I admitted I gave Old Walrus our address. I told her I had no choice in the matter, but I had an uneasy feeling that Walrus was indeed planning to drop in on us.

Worn out from the day's events and this emotional exchange with my parents, I retired to my room, changed into my long nightgown, crawled under the mosquito net, and promptly fell asleep. Knowing their daughter was safe in bed my parents locked the door to the upstairs and withdrew to their own room. At about nine o'clock a loud noise came from the bottom of the stairway, startling us awake. That part of the house was pitch dark because it had no electricity; we used a lighted petromax or a coal oil lantern that we turned down low after we went to bed at night. I heard heavy footsteps followed by grunts, the sounds of a drunken man, and a flashback to the day's events reminded me of my likely visitor, although I never expected him to be drunk. I cried out in a whisper to my parents that it must be the Old Walrus and that I thought he was drunk. If he asked for me, they had to tell him that I was not there. Before exiting my room to hide, I picked up a leather shoe to use as a weapon just in case, and I walked down the gangplank toward the outhouse, wagering that no drunken man would dare think that I would hide in the toilet. Plus I knew he would not be foolish enough to walk the plank in pitch darkness because falling off the plank and hitting the big rocks below meant instant death. I held the shoe in one hand and remained quiet as a mouse but ready to do battle with Walrus if he came my way.

My guess was right; it was the old fool Walrus who came looking for me. As soon as he reached the top floor my parents greeted him in an attempt to divert his attention, but he drunkenly brushed them aside as he headed for my bedroom. I watched from my hiding place as his ugly hands reached underneath my mosquito net, no doubt hoping to find a warm young body shaking with fright. He could not know I was not the kind of girl who froze or shook in the midst of danger. Walrus became very angry when he realized the bed was empty. He bolted out of the bedroom and started to yell, but when he came face-to-face with my dad, his voice became soft and pleading, telling my dad that his baby was a very nice girl, that he would like to marry her. Drunk on saki, he repeated that he liked me very much and wanted to marry me. My dad calmly replied that there was no "baby" here, that I had gone away and he did not know where. The Old Walrus did not believe him, though, and in his drunken stupor he swayed back and forth while looking through the house for me. He growled like a wounded bear as he came toward the kitchen; then he stopped in

front of the gangplank trying to decide whether he should venture out in
pitch darkness. No doubt his drunkenness caused him to change his mind
about checking the toilet, especially when he heard the sound of my pet
monkey—he must have thought the outhouse was part of the jungle. Dis-
gusted and angry, Walrus stamped out of the house. I rushed to my parents,
and we came together in triumph, hugging each other with relief, but I
understood that my reprieve was likely short-lived.

Early the next day I awoke to loud voices coming from a group of civilians who lived a short way from our house. They marched up our street,
angry and protesting; some cursed the Japanese soldiers in their native
tongue, and I understood every word they said. My parents and I went out
on our porch and asked them what was going on. One of the women told
us that a Japanese officer and his men raped three dalagas (virgin women)
the night before. They had been drunk, and they caught the women by surprise. The civilians were now on their way to the headquarters of the Japanese commander to report the disgraceful incident to him; they were so
angry that they expected the culprits who raped their women to be punished
for their crimes. The Filipino families knew that their single women would
never be the same again after they had been robbed of their virginity. When
my parents and I heard this, we all looked at each other with the same
thought. I quietly asked my mom and dad if it could have possibly been
Old Walrus and his men who raped those poor innocent girls.

I did not get a direct answer to that question, but Walrus seemed to
just disappear after that incident, so we believed it was he. That night while
the parents of the girls slept, all three of them committed suicide rather
than become pregnant with Japanese bastard children—they felt dirty and
ugly over their misfortune, and they did not want to be the talk of the town.
The next day I heard wailing, screaming, and crying, which went on for
many days. It was a sad time for those families. Although we shared our
neighbors' grief, I could not help but feel thankful that I had not become
a victim that night when Walrus came to our home. In reconstructing the
events of that evening my parents and I surmised that after Walrus left our
place, he and his men must have gone down the street looking for women.
When drunken men in authority come around, it is not unusual for timid
Filipino women to freeze in their tracks rather than run or jump out the
window. In this case the women were simply too scared.

After this terrible crime the officer and his men were banished from
Malaybalay, and civilians were no longer accosted or threatened with rape.
Meanwhile I continued to sell and sometimes give away edible goods to the
prisoners in the camp. In September 1942 I heard that a small group of
Americans escaped from the camp, but as far as I knew it was not Captain

Richardson or his men. The Japanese hunted down those who got away and brought back four of them. To make an example out of them, the Japanese beat and tortured them, then made them dig their own graves. The Japanese forced everyone in the whole camp to watch. The vendors, including myself, were marched in a single line and made to stop so that we could observe the execution as well. The prisoners' eyes were bound, hands tied behind their backs, and they were forced to kneel in front of the hole that would become their grave. On receiving the order, an officer with his samurai sword hacked the heads off their prisoners and shoved their bodies inside the hole in the ground. It was a horrible sight. Because of the anger of the civilians and remaining prisoners of war over this barbaric act, the Japanese army put itself on alert in case of a reprisal.

Rumors soon filtered through that the guerrilla forces in Cotabato had successfully defeated the small Japanese garrisons on the highway leading toward Malaybalay, striking along the main road that the American convoy had taken during the surrender on May 10, 1942. When the guerrilla leader heard about the brutal execution of the four Americans in the prison camp he became furious. He pushed on with his men in hopes of reaching Casisang Concentration Camp in time to free all of the American and Filipino prisoners of war. This made the Japanese nervous because they knew that if the camp was liberated, the guerrillas would have enough men to fight against them and take back the land that was lost in the early part of the war. Suddenly, the Japanese began loading up their ten-ton trucks with American and Filipino prisoners to move them to other camps located in different parts of the Philippines. My parents and I knew about this transfer of prisoners because each truck loaded with GIs and their officers traveled past the house we occupied. It took the Japanese two to three weeks to empty the whole concentration camp, and when they finished, the place became a ghost town with only the dead and the howling of the wind remaining behind. The many months of the early incarceration of our troops had ended.

Now only the civilians remained. I had to chance wheeling and dealing with Japanese collaborators in Malaybalay because it was the last town in which to try and earn a living so that we might survive. My friends in the camp had given me a bunch of American cigarettes, so I felt fortunate— brand names like Camel, Kool, Chesterfield, Lucky Strike, and Philip Morris brought good prices on the black market. Sugar, coffee, corned beef, and other rations disappeared from most households, but we still had some, so I made sure that each item brought enough money for us to live one day at a time. We used cash for buying rice, eggs, fresh chicken, meats, and vegetables. I often dealt with the most unforgettable character I ever met during my time in Malaybalay, the woman named "Goldie," who helped me with the Japanese vendor's pass. Her name fitted her to a T because when she smiled she revealed gold wrapped around every tooth in her mouth. The Filipinos used to believe that you carried your wealth in every part of your gold teeth, which Goldie knew, so she made it a point to smile every time she met and talked with people. Although Goldie reminded me of an old witch because of her age and her appearance, I had to learn to humor the old girl; after all, she had good connections with the Japanese officers who supplied her with all sorts of merchandise. I had to learn to be her friend without giving myself away as a supporter of the Americans. Whenever I bargained her out of her salable goods, she said to me, addressing me as "Inday" (young girl), that I was worse than a Chinaman because I knew how to bargain more than they do. What she said was true because I learned well about bargaining Chinese-style when I was a child, a skill I practice even today. In spite of Goldie's compliments of how clever I was in wearing her down on her prices, I always mistrusted her. Everyone knew that she worked for the Japanese, and the civilians hated her for this. In my case I felt that as long as she thought I was a mere kid who could humor her and bargain her down on her goods for my benefit, her personal life was her own to deal with. But supplies soon dwindled to nothing, despite Goldie's connections. My parents and I had to ration ourselves while the Japanese kept us under house arrest. I knew that something would change soon.

6

Facing Life and Death

While waiting for something to happen that might free us from our house arrest, my parents and I spent a lot of time talking about my three brothers, Samuel, George, and Philip. Sam signed up with the USAFFE in Cotabato, where he had been teaching, when war broke out. The only time we saw him was when he appeared on one of the military trucks that traveled from Davao to Malaybalay then on to the coastline of Cagayan de Oro. George, we hoped, was with my Aunt Mary at Kling Plantation but we had not heard any news from him. And Philip tarried with the soldiers during our evacuation from Kidapawan, and we lost track of him. I could see the sorrow in my mom's face every day; she worried about her sons. This was what war had done to our family.

Darkness came early during that time of the year, and to conserve our oil we ate our meals early in the evening. The same night we all talked about my brothers after finishing our meal, and my dad smoked his pipe, puffing the smoke into the air. Then he turned to my mom, using the endearing name "kiddo" he had for her, and asked her if she knew why he married her so many years ago. Without giving her a chance to answer he replied that he married her because of her beautiful long black wavy hair, her good looks, and her good cooking. He told her that she was a good woman, that he loved her. My heart swelled in that moment because in all the years I knew my dad, this was the first time he openly expressed his true feelings toward my mom. It was so touching. He was faithful, a good provider, and a wonderful dad to us, but I rarely ever heard him speak of love with my mom. He usually demonstrated his feelings to us through his actions and his commitment. I felt glad that my mom finally received a public expression of love.

Just before we retired that night I heard light footsteps coming up our front stairs. I knew it was not an animal like a cat or dog prowling around; therefore it had to be a human being. At that late hour we were not expecting any visitors. Suddenly a shabbily dressed man, much smaller than the Japanese soldiers, appeared at the upstairs doorway. None of us knew where he came from or who he was, and my dad quickly demanded that he come forward, show his face, and identify himself. As soon as the man thought it safe, he opened his mouth to explain that he was a courier for the Americans hiding above Malaybalay. Addressing my dad as "Sir," the stranger said he knew that my dad was the best friend of Major Frank McGee, that for many years they were partners in Lawayon Plantation in Cotabato, and he now brought an important message from the major.

Responding quickly to this man we did not know, my dad raised his voice in anger, denying that he knew a Major Frank McGee. He accused the man of being a Japanese spy who was trying to trick him and get his family into trouble, and he yelled at him to go away and leave us alone. The Filipino did not budge, despite my dad's hostility. Instead, he nervously responded that he was not a spy, but rather he was Major McGee's personal bodyguard, carrying a written note for my dad from the major. With that he reached in to his pocket, pulled out a piece of paper, and insisted that my dad must read the note before he left. Then my dad could decide whether his words were true or not.

Reaching for his eyeglasses my dad moved into the direction of the light, and my mom and I followed. The note said that Major McGee needed my dad's help badly: his men were ill, and they needed medicines, blankets, and some food. Major McGee signed it; my dad recognized the signature after all those years, and it brought back fond memories. My dad could not help but shed a tear or two before he admitted that this was indeed the major's signature, that he would recognize it anytime, anywhere. Then his mood changed as he turned to my mom and me to ask what he should do because there was no way he could help at a time like this—we had so little ourselves now that we were under house arrest.

I consoled my dad, assuring him that I would take care of the situation myself. I realized then that our father-daughter roles had changed: while the war seemed to drain his life from him, it gave me a sense of strong purpose. I turned to the courier and told him to come back the next night at the same hour of nine o'clock, when I would have something ready for him. Then the nameless man quickly left the room, disappearing in the night. Once again I faced the task of trying to help the Americans in hiding at the risk of my own life. Even though I did not know who the men were with Major McGee, I knew they needed any help our family could provide. I did meet one of the men from that group many years later in the United States, a man named Mills, who had been a radio operator. We met at a World War II reunion in Denver, Colorado, in the 1960s. Mr. Mills thanked me for risking my life in the latter days of 1942 when, in their moment of despair, my parents and I helped to save them.

While the townspeople and the Japanese soldiers still slept the following morning, I woke early enough to visit my good friend Pacita MacFarland Cid. Even though our friendship was just a brief encounter, we had a special type of bond: both our fathers were white men, so our appearance favored our fathers' side, a visual Caucasian heritage that the Japanese could not help but notice. Fortunately for Pacita, she married a Filipino doctor who had a successful practice in Malaybalay before the war. Although the Japanese incarcerated him in Casisang Concentration Camp for being in the USAFFE, in time they released him to return to his wife and family, as well as his medical practice, in Malaybalay. Pacita had another advantage she could rely on: her mother, a Filipina, was very old and because of this and her poor physical condition Pacita had to care for her mother twenty-four hours a day. Besides having the honor of caring for her mother, this situation allowed Pacita to stay out of a Japanese prison as long as she kept herself confined to her home to tend to her mother. But I knew that Pacita would know how to help Major McGee's men.

The back entrance to the Cid home was well sheltered from prying eyes. I quickly followed the pathway, made my way up the stairs, and knocked gently on the back door, hoping someone would hear me. When no one answered, I knocked again, this time a bit harder. The maid, still half asleep, came to the door, and asked me in a surprised voice who I was and what I wanted. I responded that I was Pacita's friend, that I needed to see her about some important business. The maid told me that Pacita was still asleep and that she did not like to wake her up. Then I heard footsteps coming toward the kitchen followed by Pacita's sweet voice greeting me, asking me what I was doing at her house at this hour of the morning. But still she invited me to come in and have a cup of coffee with her. Then she turned to her maid, addressed her as "Inday" (young lady), and instructed her to get us two cups of coffee then leave us alone. We waited in silence until the maid served us and left.

Pacita MacFarland, much older than I, had been educated at one of the universities in the United States before the war. Although she had a good command of the Visayan dialect, she was more proficient with English. Given the kind of education she had, she was soft spoken and refined in her manner. Pacita had fine features, very light skin, high cheekbones, and a prominent nose; because of her appearance she could easily pass as an American or a Spanish lady. She kept a low profile by remaining in the house taking care of her aging mother, so the Japanese left her alone. Furthermore, her husband's last name, which sounded either Chinese or Spanish, provided her with additional protection. Had she publicly used her American maiden name, MacFarland, she would have been in trouble like all the rest of us who had white fathers because the Japanese rounded up the mestizos, forcing them into the concentration camps with their American and European fathers and Filipino mothers.

While sipping our coffee and speaking in low tones, I took a chance and confided in Pacita. After all, I thought, her father was a full-blooded American; surely she had some compassion for his own people who needed help. Besides, her husband was a doctor, so she must be accustomed to people in need. I quickly told her that there was a small group of Americans hiding in the jungles above Malaybalay who needed our help because they were ill and did not have enough medicine, warm blankets, and food. I asked her if she could help. Without pressing me for further details about who exactly needed help—because surely she knew—Pacita stood up and inquired what kind of medicines were needed. When I told her that the men suffered from malaria, she knew exactly what to do. She told me to wait there in her kitchen, that she would be back as quickly as she could. Pacita urged me to just keep on drinking my coffee so that my visit would appear natural. I knew what she meant because even her own maids could be sympathetic to the Japanese, so we could not take any chances. Twenty minutes later Pacita reappeared carrying a good-size bundle full of medicine and a blanket. She must have gone through her husband's medical supplies and gathered as much as she could. Just before we parted she whispered that she was giving me all that she had; she wished me well on my mission but begged me, please, not to come back for anymore of her help. Pacita did not want to jeopardize either one of our lives or those of our loved ones; she could do this much but no more.

I understood her concerns. So many people wanted to help the guerrillas but the likely retribution by the Japanese was horrifying. I knew I was taking a big risk: what if the courier was not who he said he was? What if that note was a clever forgery designed to deceive my dad's aging eyes? I thanked Pacita; we hugged each other before I left, and I kept my promise to her and never returned to her home. We never saw each other again. Many years after the war, I heard that Pacita had died of an illness. My only regret today is that I never got to tell her exactly what she did for the Americans and me: because of our combined efforts, many of their lives were spared.

That night the courier reappeared as planned under cover of darkness, and he was overjoyed when my dad gave him all the supplies I had gathered that morning. We even added some of our own provisions of rice, canned goods, and a blanket, even though our food supplies were getting very thin. My dad sternly told the courier that I had taken a great risk to gather these supplies so he had to take extra care that they did not fall into the hands of the Japanese because if they did, we would lose our heads. The man beamed with assurance as he replied that he would certainly guard these supplies with his own life and that his lips were sealed. He promised he would rather die than reveal our names for having helped Major McGee's men.

Before the courier left my dad gave him one last message for the Major, one I knew distressed him: he wanted his old friend Major McGee to know that we were alive and well but that we could not help him any longer because supplies were low and the Japanese watched us closely. The man nodded and then disappeared in the night. Much later we were relieved to learn that the courier was indeed Major McGee's right-hand man, that he successfully eluded Japanese soldiers to bring the provisions through the jungles. The medicine arrived in time to help many sick soldiers, so thanks to my friend Pacita they lived to see the end of the war.

I knew that the guerrillas suffered as did the soldiers still in concentration camps, and even conditions among the civilian population went from bad to worse. People became restless and frightened as they neared starvation. My parents and I resorted to rationing to make our food supplies last; still my dad began to show signs of deterioration due to his age and poor diet. Fresh meat for protein was scarce, and milk was unavailable except for what was available in cans. My mom was no better off because she ate small amounts of food so that my dad and I could have more. She had a heart of gold as she constantly put us ahead of her own needs. My mom was definitely a saint.

During the first week of December 1942, a year after Pearl Harbor and the invasion of the Philippines, my dad decided the time had come for him to step out of the house and see a barber in town. His thinning white hair reached down to his neck, his long beard fell way below his chin: he really needed a professional shave and a haircut as he was beginning to look like Father Time. My mom pleaded with him not to go because of the potential danger, crying and begging him not to take any chances. I believe she must have had another one of her premonitions, like the one she had the day the

Japanese soldiers almost raped me. But my dad proved stubborn as a mule that day, and he would not listen to her—he was tired of being cooped up in the house, and he wanted to look like his old self again. I believed it was my duty to accompany him because his legs were not as steady as they used to be, and he walked with the help of a cane.

The moment we stepped out of the house, everything went wrong. As we began ascending the slope heading to town, we spotted two vehicles carrying armed Japanese soldiers coming toward us on the opposite side of the road. They held their rifles with fixed bayonets while they rode on the running boards of the civilians' cars. As they came closer they stopped, ordering us to get into one of the cars. We felt like animals caught in a trap with no place to run or hide. For an instant I wondered if the courier might have been caught with the supplies that we gave him; then I thought of my visit with Pacita. Either action could have caused the Japanese to suddenly pick us up, but of course we did not know the real answer. We complied with their order, and my dad and I quietly sat side by side in the car; we did not dare speak for fear that the Japanese officer sitting next to the driver understood English. We had to stay calm even though we did not know where they were taking us or for what purpose. Halfway to our destination puzzling questions kept nagging me. Why, after over eight months of house arrest, were we being formally arrested? Did they finally have something on us that merited our being taken away? Who sold us out?

Immediately after the Japanese soldiers picked us up, a neighbor who saw it all from her window dashed over to tell my mom the bad news. My poor mom almost died of fright because we were all she had to live for. She told me later that her mind went crazy because she feared she would never see us again. Crying, walking back and forth in the living room she kept repeating to herself, speaking in her mind to my dad, "I told you so. I told you so. Why did you not listen instead of being bullheaded?" After she had a good cry she got on her knees and prayed to God for our safe return: she believed in a God who hears the prayers of a righteous woman, and she had great faith that her prayers would be answered.

The vehicle we occupied with our Japanese guards finally came to a stop in front of the old Bethany house, the same building my dad and I went to shortly after the surrender. At that time my dad and I tried to get a pass so that we could return to our farm in Kidapawan, but we were denied. Since then a new Japanese commander replaced the old one, and we both knew that each officer was unpredictable. The Japanese ordered us out of the car, and two of the guards stayed with us until we entered the building. Once inside a soldier took my dad to one room; I was taken to another. Our interrogations lasted an hour. My dad told me that he had to answer rapid questions about his nationality, his reasons for being in Malaybalay, and his sentiments about the Japanese Imperial Army.

My dad responded easily because he figured out what the Japanese were up to. He stuck to his guns, telling them through an interpreter that he was a Frenchman who owned a farm in Kidapawan, Cotabato, but because the Americans drove his family out we ended up in Malaybalay. He then tried to get a pass from the former commander here but he would not let us go home to our farm where we could grow our own food. When he came to the last question, my dad very carefully replied that the Japanese were good people, that he did not understand why the Americans were at war with them. He then claimed to be on the side of the Japanese! When I was a little girl my dad used to tell me that whenever he told a white lie, he crossed his fingers to ward off any evil spell that might follow. That day he not only crossed his fingers but his legs as well as he sat in front of the commander. Of course I understood the reason for his lies: we all had to tell white lies to temporarily appease our enemy, the Japanese. If we told the truth we would be in the firing line, and I would not be alive today.

Not knowing at the time what kind of interrogation my dad was going through, I had to rely on the good Lord, my keen ears, and my calculated responses. When the interpreter walked in, I was ready. First he asked me if I was that old man's wife, and I calmly told him, no, I was his daughter. Next he wanted to know what my nationality was, so I told him that since my father was French, I was also French. Knowing the laws in the Philippines, I understood that children born of a foreign father acquired their citizenship from the country of their father's birth, not from their mother's. Finally the interpreter asked why I had come to Malaybalay. I repeated the story that we had a farm in Kidapawan, that because of the war we were forced out of the way and evacuated to Malaybalay. Even though my dad and I did not have a chance to rehearse or exchange notes, the answers we gave were close enough to convince the Japanese that we were not spies. Of course I also believed that the fervent prayers of my mom, waiting and worrying over us at home, helped the situation. After it was all over we were sent home in a staff car, this time without the guards who surrounded us when we were picked up on the street.

As my dad and I rode home in a Japanese car, we remained silent for fear that the Japanese driver knew English but was playing dumb. Once we alighted from the car we hurriedly walked up the stairs, into my mom's embrace as she cried hysterically and laughed at the same time. After we all settled down, assured that none of us had been harmed by this frightening experience, my dad questioned me about my interrogation. When he discovered that the line of questioning was almost identical to his, we laughed, knowing that we had fooled the Japanese and kept ourselves together. The next time the subject of a haircut came up my dad acted much wiser; he had my mom cut his hair, and he trimmed his own mustache into a Van Dyke.

During the ensuing weeks, as time crept toward the Christmas holiday, the guerrilla forces gained more ground as they headed toward Malaybalay. Along the way the guerrillas released the Filipinos incarcerated in local jails; they and other able-bodied civilians joined in the fight to strengthen the guerrilla army. Although they had limited weapons and ammunition, their spirits were at an all-time high because they were on a mission to restore freedom throughout Mindanao. They had had enough of the tyranny, death, and destruction brought on by the Japanese, so they willingly fought to the death to get rid of the Japanese. The people remembered the history of the Filipinos' struggles in the past; they were tired of the oppression and the propaganda of a Co-Prosperity Sphere that the Japanese advocated after the invasion. This was why the courageous Filipinos came out of the hills determined to fight side by side with the guerrilla forces.

Even though the guerrillas had still not arrived in Malaybalay, Christmas remained a joyous holiday in our minds and hearts. Under normal circumstances both Catholics and Protestants enjoyed the happy occasion; however, the war brought on a new twist, so most civilians did not have quite the same unrestrained jubilation as before the occupation. The struggle for survival stayed uppermost in their minds, especially as food supplies became scarce. In our home I took the initiative to bring a little peace, joy, and happiness to my parents since I wanted to make this Christmas as normal as possible, despite the absence of my brothers. Exploring the wooded area in the back of our house, I quickly found a small tree and cut the top off of it, setting that piece on a cardboard box. Then I stripped all the leaves from each branch and covered it with the cassava flour and bright green paper I had bought from a store in town that sold favors and gift items including ribbons and colored paper. Because of the war nobody wanted or could afford these frivolous things anymore; the storeowners almost destroyed the items until I came along and retrieved them for nothing. The paper came in handy for decorating my tree: I put together strips of paper pasted on each end, made a fine chain link, and the completed work looked festive. For a finishing touch, I formed pieces of red paper into small balls, attaching them to the tips of each branch to make them look like berries.

This kind of improvising to make Christmas a real celebration in our home was better than having none at all; plus it was just about the best gift

I could think of for my parents, but I still wanted to do more: I had to have packages around the tree. For presents I managed to purchase a can of tobacco from one of the vendors for my dad and a secondhand dress for my mom. Without a doubt I made a good choice because they looked overjoyed when they opened their gifts from me. My mom and I baked a cake out of cassava flour for our dessert. Although we had no baking powder to make the cake rise, it tasted good enough. For our Christmas meal we ate corned beef, cooked rice, a spinach-like vegetable called tangcong, and we even had fried bananas with sugar from the moscovado, raw sugar extracted from the sugarcane in the area. It was not an elaborate meal, but we were thankful for that and for each other. I did not even mind that my parents had no material gift for me—the best gift they had given me was their abiding love that lasted a lifetime. Every moment we spent together in those trying times is etched in my memory.

One day in early January 1943, as I came home from my usual trip to town to see some vendors about trading some of our last supplies, I felt hot pains shoot through my body. Feeling feverish and shaky I dreaded the thought that I had malaria; my parents became alarmed because they had never seen me in such a condition before. There had been other times when I was sick—soaking with perspiration, feeling exhausted, drenched from a heavy rain—but my body would bounce back and I just kept going. Now, without a doubt, it had to be the wear and tear, the emotional tension and trauma from the war that finally brought my health down. My mom did her best to sponge me with cool water to lower my fever, but in spite of her efforts my temperature continued to rise. That night I became delirious from the fever, which scared my mom, who, while my dad watched helplessly, ran to the neighbor, hoping to get some medicine. The kindly woman next door had two aspirins to spare, very dear medicine at that point in the war, and she unselfishly gave them to my mom. She also told my mom that Doctor Cid had been released from Casisang Concentration Camp and that he returned to his wife and family in town, good news for me considering the urgency of my physical condition.

As soon as my mom returned she administered the aspirin then continued to sponge my body to reduce the fever. I soon drifted off to sleep and my fever dropped slightly. Early the next day, the same neighbor who gave us the medicine, concerned that my temperature had not yet gone back to normal, went in to town to summon the doctor. Doctor Cid grabbed his medical bag and immediately came to the house to diagnose my illness. On his arrival my mom quickly told him of my high temperature, aching joints, and splitting headaches, which the doctor recognized as symptoms of a bad case of influenza. Since his medicines for this particular disease had been used up at the camp on our soldiers he decided on a new treatment. He told my mom to ask the woman next door to find him a nursing mother who had just recovered from influenza and have her come to our house. When the neighbor found such a woman and brought her to our house, Doctor Cid explained to her that since she had been seriously ill with influenza but recovered well, she could help me, this girl on the bed, who suffered from the same sickness. Without her help, I would die before the night was over. The woman, thoroughly puzzled, asked what she could do to help, and the doctor replied that he needed some of the milk from her breast. Nodding her head, still puzzling over the request, she told Doctor Cid that, of course, she would be glad to give me some of her milk.

So the doctor called for a clean basin with boiled water, a cup, a tablespoon, a candle, and some matches with which to light the candle. Then he had the woman clean around her nipple with a piece of gauze that contained some antiseptic and she squeezed some of her breast milk in the clean cup. The doctor scooped up a tablespoon of milk from the cup, placed the spoon on the burning candle to sterilize the milk, and after the milk had cooled off he reached for his unused syringe, filling it with the sterilized milk. Then he plunged the needle into my buttocks and emptied the antibody milk in my body. Doctor Cid had never used this method before, but the emergency at hand prompted him to try the impossible—and it worked. Between the prayers of my mom and the practical insight of the doctor a miracle did happen on that evening. We thanked the woman for her unselfish act, and after she left we never saw her again. The doctor left soon as well and our paths never crossed again. Many years after the war, I heard that his beloved wife had died and that he remarried after his years of mourning. Although he may not have any recollection of what he did for me that night, I certainly have not forgotten his efforts: delirious as I was from the high fever brought on by the influenza, I never lost consciousness all together and remained fully aware of the doctor's endeavors to save my life. Even if the method had not been tested before and I served as a guinea pig for his experiment, it worked, and I am alive to tell about the innovative treatment. I was thankful that Doctor Cid applied his God-given common sense when he realized he no longer had the conventional medicine needed to effect my recovery from the flu. He dared to experiment on the immune system of a nursing mother through her milk that contained the antibody, and I lived.

The kindly doctor was like an angel sent from heaven, and I also found him nice looking: the Filipina ladies would refer to him as "poggie" (handsome). His hands were soft and gentle, and his face had the looks of a compassionate physician who cared about his patients. Although Doctor Cid was overworked after his concentration camp release, he did not hesitate to go where he was needed among the civilians. Because of his hasty departure I never had the chance to thank him personally for saving my life. Furthermore, I could not tell him about his wife Pacita, who helped me with supplies for the Americans, including our friend Major McGee, in hiding above Malaybalay. On the other hand, it may have been better that he did not find out about her generosity with his medicines and blanket—it may have upset him because of the risk she had taken. Today the good doctor must be in his late eighties, maybe even nineties, and some of the small details of his profession may have been forgotten. Thank you Doctor Cid wherever you are, for you were my angel unaware sent from God when my life hung in the balance. Strange how war brings all kinds of people into our lives. Some of them are like angels who touch us, and soon they are gone. In my case I discovered that even when I faced death, I thanked God that He sent the angels to minister to me.

7

Rescue at Midnight

After exhibiting their brutality during their invasion of the Philippines, it was only a matter of time before the Japanese met their match in the fearless Moros. Moro tribes occupied the provinces of Cotabato and Lanao even before the 1900s and were known as ruthless killers and enslavers of Christians. Even the Filipinos who lived near them feared them because of their unpredictability. I do not know whether the Moros from Lanao were fiercer than the ones from Cotabato; I only knew something about the Lanao Moros through my dad, who was stationed in that province when he fought with the Fifteenth Cavalry, C Company, of the United States Army. When I was a child he told stories of how the American soldiers were scared to death of the Moros, especially the horramentado, who ingested a hallucinogenic weed, went berserk with their weapons, and claimed that killing Christians and infidels gave them the right to go to heaven and their God, Allah. This was a fanatic of a different kind. Whenever a horramentado attacked a soldier, the American could pump many bullets into the man's body, yet he kept on going until he killed his victim with his native armament. In that era the American soldiers had an expression about the Moros: "The only good Moro is a dead Moro." And in World War II they used the same words about the Japanese: "The only good Jap is a dead Jap."

Hostilities with the Moros cooled off in time, especially when some of their children attended public schools funded by the Philippine govern-

100

ment. Moro children brought books home for their parents to see, and the adults loved to hear about the accomplishments of their children. Soon Moros went off to college and became good scholars in their field of interest. One such person was Salipada Pendatun, a full-blooded Moro from Cotabato. He was the son of a highly respected datu (chief), who was brilliant. Because of his parents' wealth and his eagerness to advance himself, Pendatun pursued his career by attending Harvard University in the United States. With his graduation from college he earned the distinction of being the first Moro to receive the highest degree from abroad. Upon his return to Mindanao from Harvard University, Pendatun was accepted in many circles of Filipino society. He spoke fluent English, was well versed in many Filipino dialects, and he improved the living conditions among his tribe and encouraged its members to pursue an education. To outsiders Pendatun looked like a man of steel, but insiders found him a wise, gentle person who cared about the oppressed and downtrodden. His people often came to him for his wisdom and counsel on matters pertaining to disputed lands or group rivalry that sometimes led to bloodshed. Pendatun was truly a born leader among his people, and his enemies envied him; therefore, he weathered character assassinations, petty jealousies, envy, and even threats on his life.

My entire family knew about Pendatun's friendship with my dad because their cordial relationship began even before the war, back when our family moved to Kidapawan in Cotabato to establish the Mindanao Oil Palm Corporation. This famous Moro leader took a liking to my dad because he was the only white man living in Kidapawan and because he had no left arm. Filipinos and Moros alike accepted my dad in spite of his handicap because he did not have the superior attitude sometimes found in white men who lived in the Philippines; he respected and loved everyone he met. Because of his outgoing personality the Moros called my dad the "pongkol Americano" (one-armed American), a distinction given to no other white man. The nickname did not bother my dad because he accepted it with a sense of humor. Besides, he found it unique! Each time his friends joked with him he simply laughed along with them, reciting the old joke, "You can call me anything you want. Just don't call old Dore late for supper!" The Filipinos and Pendatun surely knew my dad as hardworking and outgoing, qualities they appreciated and admired. When the Japanese invaded, the Moro leader found out about my dad's work at the war front in Digos, how he risked his life for the troops on the firing line. Pendatun also knew about my work at the field hospital in Kidapawan because he and Major Orbase served as officers in the Philippine Army attached to the USAFFE forces.

During the guerrilla offensive in Cotabato in 1943, Pendatun played

Original American and Filipino guerrilla freedom fighters from the Davao, Cotabato, and Bukidnon area in Mindanao. *Left to right:* Col. Thomas Cabili, Col. Robert V. Bowler, Gen. Salipada Pendatun, Lt. Comdr. Chick Parsons, Colonel Gutierrez, Mr. C. Fortich (plantation manager and possibly part owner), and Col. Edwin Andrews.

a major part in driving out the Japanese by rallying his people to rise up and overthrow the enemy garrison. With his military background, his birthright as the son of a chieftain, and his education at Harvard University, he proved more than qualified to lead his people in their revolt against the Japanese Imperial Army. His knowledge of the terrain and his proficient understanding of several languages gave him advantages lacking in other leaders. I observed the high emotions generated by the Moros in the midst of the guerrilla warfare even though I was only a girl of seventeen, and I thought them very commendable. Pendatun was definitely the man to lead his people, and his official rank as general suited him because he inspired and motivated them. They not only honored him, but they gave him the respect he deserved. Even if it meant giving up their lives for the sake of freedom, they willingly followed him all the way to victory.

General Pendatun, determined to serve the Allied cause, planned to rescue the American and Filipino prisoners of war at Casisang Concentration Camp in Malaybalay, Bukidnon. In order to do so quickly he needed military vehicles, including weapons carriers, ten-ton trucks, and several jeeps, to move a large body of men on the highway leading toward the camp. Unfortunately, the Japanese had captured most of these vehicles when the Americans surrendered in 1942, so the general's men had to cover the hundreds of miles between Cotabato and Bukidnon on foot, horseback, or in just a few motor vehicles. In spite of this tediously slow journey their morale remained high because their great leader inspired them. But the Moros arrived too late to rescue the prisoners in the camp: they found the place spooky and ghostly, and it gave them the shivers. Some of them shed tears because they felt guilty for not arriving in time to liberate their Filipino friends and relatives or the American prisoners in the camp.

Regardless of the disappointment they encountered at the prison camp, the guerrillas became more determined to eliminate the Japanese who stood in their way. Because a few of their men managed to infiltrate the enemy lines, they knew about the small Japanese garrison left in Malaybalay, and they discovered that the Japanese held Mr. Dore, the one-armed American, his wife, and daughter incommunicado and under house arrest in Malaybalay. When the report reached General Pendatun he was gravely concerned about our safety. Armed with bazookas, flame-throwers, hand grenades, machine guns, and rifles, the guerrillas followed the highway leading to the town of Malaybalay. As they exchanged fire with the Japanese, the battleground became dangerous for us even though the general had instructed the guerrillas to avoid firing at the building where we lived.

Being caught in the middle of a gun battle was an experience I shall never forget. Bullets zinged through our upstairs bedroom and other parts of the house; it was a wonder we did not get hit in the process. The guerrilla forces, meanwhile, could not have a clue that I was recovering from a serious bout with the flu or that my weakened condition had taken a toll on my body and that I had some difficulty with my legs. After the fighting subsided that day, when I began to walk a little more, my curiosity got the best of me, so with the help of my parents, I went to the large bay window overlooking the highway below. Dusk was approaching when we saw a gigantic carabao coming up the incline of the road heading toward the Japanese; on its back we could see beer bottles, cans, and other containers strapped to the beast. Recognizing the military implications of what was about to happen, we turned away quickly from the window and sought cover by lying flat on the floor. No sooner had we flattened ourselves than we heard a very loud explosion up the road. A couple of guerrilla sharpshooters had aimed and fired at the Molotov cocktails (beer bottles filled with gasoline and explosives) and dynamite harnessed on the animal. The explosion killed some of the Japanese and the poor carabao as well. Strange how the enemy soldiers did not recognize what was coming their way—they probably thought the beast of burden had gotten away from its master with beer and other supplies on its back. They may have even considered the possibility of slaughtering the animal for their hungry soldiers. Whatever the Japanese thought, the battle intensified after that incident, so my parents and I moved down to the first floor of the building and hid in a trench under the floorboards. We had hoped that the guerrilla forces would rescue us in time and move us away from the firing range. This did not happen. The Japanese, enraged at the deaths of their comrades, suddenly came down with all their fury. Through the crack in the walls of the building I saw flame-throwers pushing the enemy back during the night. However, the Japanese were better equipped and so had more firepower to battle with the guerrillas; therefore, our men had to retreat a few hundred yards away from our house. Then I heard a bull horn from somewhere up the hill. In plain English a Japanese soldier called out to my dad to come out from his hiding place and surrender, or they would burn down his house and kill all of us. We had only about five to ten minutes to show ourselves before the Japanese began to shoot and burn us out.

I felt like a rat caught in a trap with no way out. I knew we had to come out because the Japanese threats were real. My parents helped me to my feet, walking me along, with each one holding me up by the arm. From our darkened hideaway we finally came out to breathe fresh air once again; my lungs felt good after I inhaled the night air and I felt invigorated. We slowly ascended to the top of the hill where the Japanese with fixed bayonets waited. What a sad sight we must have been: an elderly one-armed man, his frail Filipino wife, and their sick daughter.

When we reached the top of the incline the Japanese officer questioned my parents as to why I was bundled up in a blanket, asking what was the matter with their child? My dad responded that I was very sick with influenza and was very weak. He thought we would get some help from the Japanese, but the officer offered none. He simply remarked that my dad was a wise father to surrender with a sick daughter. After a moment of silence the officer asked if we wanted to see what they had done to our house, and when we turned around toward the building we had come from we saw it engulfed in flames. I cried out that I had forgotten my pet Cheeta, that she was still on her leash and could not get away. I wanted to go back and save her. But by then the house had gone up in smoke; the structure was so dry and brittle it did not take much to burn it down. In spite of losing my beloved pet and still feeling the effects of the flu, I did not cry. I simply kept everything inside and kept quiet. I would not let the Japanese see me cry.

At first I thought we were the only prisoners that the Japanese had taken in. We discovered, though, that the Japanese rounded up government officials, their families, and Filipino civilians and marched them to a building (which turned out to be the municipal building) a few blocks away from the battle site. The Japanese intended to use all of us prisoners as a shield in the event the guerrilla forces broke through their lines and came into Malaybalay proper. Not satisfied with just taking us, some Japanese soldiers devised the idea of dressing up in women's clothing, thereby confusing the guerrillas, making them reluctant to shoot. But the word got out to our fighting men, and they were told that when taking aim at the enemy, they should look below the hemline of the women's dresses. If they saw bushy, hairy legs, it was a Jap soldier, so they should not hesitate; they should just shoot to kill.

The government-owned municipal building was a two-story building with the entrance facing the street, while the backside overlooked a panoramic view of the hillside with its edges sitting on a cliff. Large rocks and boulders sat at the bottom of this cliff so that anyone falling accidentally would meet with sudden death. Knowing the hazards behind the building, the Japanese decided to have their machine gun placed at the front entrance. Then they put a searchlight and some well-armed guards on the street side in case the guerrillas attempted to rescue the prisoners. They intended to slaughter every man, woman, and child in the event our men tried to release us.

Because of the overcrowding of men, women, and children inside the building, I felt like I was in a sardine can. People huddled together with their loved ones, not knowing when the end would come; children cried from hunger, while others feared the total darkness. The Japanese adamantly enforced a complete blackout, making it impossible for anyone to go to the latrine, which was out of order anyway. Some of the children defecated in their trousers and others used empty cans and newspapers to catch their mess. Either way, the stench became unbearable—it was suffocating and nauseating to those of us not accustomed to such conditions.

We dared not stir in the darkened building despite our growing discomfort. Fearing the trigger-happy Japanese soldiers who might randomly fire their guns at us, we remained still for about 24 hours. During the second night of our incarceration something happened. While seated between my parents on the bottom of the spiral stairway leading up to the second floor of that building, I noticed a bright light shining through the window above. The moon shone off and on then faded behind the dark clouds. I thanked God for that little bit of light in the midst of our desperate surroundings. Taking advantage of the light, we ate our cold rice and salted fish with our fingers; then we quenched our thirst with the water fetched from the faucet earlier that afternoon. At about ten o'clock at night I heard heavy footsteps coming into the building. Then flashlights illuminated certain spots, and I saw Japanese soldiers dragging young girls out of the building. The girls cried, kicked, and screamed in vain because the other unarmed prisoners could do nothing to help. The Japanese took the girls away from the building and raped them. My parents feared that I would be their next victim.

At midnight we had some mysterious visitors. At first I thought I was dreaming because I knew the building was impenetrable, but then I heard whispered voices asking repeatedly if the Dore family was here. Finally one of these seemingly bodiless voices reached the bottom of the stairway, and the actual body almost stumbled over us. Before he could say the words once more my dad spoke in low tones and replied that, yes, we were the Dore family whom he sought. But my dad wanted to know who was looking for us. Careful not to reveal his information to others, the man leaned over and whispered in my dad's ear that he was one of General Pendatun's men, and he was sent here along with some others to help us escape.

The thought of escaping to freedom exhilarated us. We roused ourselves quickly and made haste to depart from that hellish building. My parents and I made our way toward the back entrance of the municipal building, where five other men quietly greeted us with ropes. I understood immediately what was going to happen. My mom and I insisted that my dad go first because he had only one arm, and two of the men helped him down the precipice at the back of the building. When one of the men fastened a rope around my waist for the descent into freedom, adrenaline made my heart pump faster; I knew the danger involved. We might fall and kill ourselves on the rocks below us, or the Japanese might discover our escape and kill us without mercy. But we had no other choice than to make that precarious trip down the precipice. Luckily for us, the Japanese underestimated the ability of Filipinos to find a seemingly impossible way to rescue prisoners right under their noses. Like frolicking monkeys skilled at climbing trees, rocks, and ropes our young men learned to be much more skillful than those animals. Why? Because in their early youth some of them climbed coconut trees, mango trees, and any tree tall or short. Climbing up steep boulders meant nothing to them either because they knew how to use their bare feet, their toes, and fingers to dig into the crevice of the rocks. They also knew the importance of how to balance out their body weight so they would not experience any cramping or get exhausted while climbing. To me, those guerrilla soldiers became our guardian angels that night. God bless them. They risked their lives to rescue us away from our

"Devils Island"–type prison building. Now we all had to descend those well-secured ropes to escape the Japanese.

Just as the last of us reached the bottom of the cliff and we had all untied ourselves, someone in the building above us sounded the alarm. "Escape! Escape! The Americano and his family escaped!" I did not know at the time who informed on us, but I found out later. Only God knows what that person was thinking. With the warning sound the Japanese quickly turned their searchlight to scan the bottom of the ravine and the open field nearby. Then I heard the blasting sound of the machine guns, and we started to run like jackrabbits. Rat-ta-ta-ta! Rat-ta-ta-ta! Rat-ta-ta-ta! The bullets began to zing, zing, zing all around us. I heard my mom scream in the dark for me to run. Grateful for my physical education hundred-meter dash workout in the school grounds, I ran and ran without knowing exactly where I was going. The light from the moon helped me, but when it moved behind the clouds the sky went pitch dark. That was when I ran like h-e-l-l.

At last my parents and I arrived in the safety zone of the guerrilla army, whose territory covered a wide spread of land several miles away from Malaybalay. First we checked out one another to see if we had been clipped or winged by any flying bullets. Finding no blood oozing out of our bodies I hugged my parents and felt thankful we came out alive. The guerrillas then escorted the three of us to the nearest military tent, where we dropped from exhaustion, falling into a deep sleep, and I slept until ten o'clock the following day. The smell of good cooking over a hot stove woke me up, and my parents and I devoured a hearty meal.

Shortly thereafter a military jeep pulled up near our tent, and I heard a deep authoritative voice addressing my dad, asking him how he was feeling this morning, after last night's excitement. He wanted to know if his men had taken good care of us. The voice belonged to none other than General Salipada Pendatun himself, my dad's old friend. His immaculate khaki uniform, the gold stars on each side of his shoulders, the belt around his waist with a .45 automatic pistol dangling on the side, and his officer's hat made him appear like a knight in shining armor to me. This was how a seventeen-year-old girl characterized the man responsible for our harrowing rescue. Had it not been for his instructions to have his men make their own sacrifices to get us out, who knows what our fate would have been on remaining in the municipal building? Perhaps we would have been slaughtered, thus silencing my story forever.

Responding to the questions put forth by the general, my dad told him that we almost lost our lives from those damned Japs! He described how they were shooting the hell out of us right after our escape. But then he thanked the general and his men from the bottom of his heart because they worked hard to get us out from under the Japs' noses. He believed those men deserved a medal for their bravery. The general told my dad that the moment he heard the Japs held us prisoners in Malaybalay, he handpicked his men because he knew that they would not let him down—they were good boys and would be well rewarded. After further exchanges of greetings and thanks, the general told my dad that he had a big surprise waiting for us if the three of us would take a short ride with him in his personal jeep.

Dumbfounded, my dad tried to figure out what the surprise was but could come up with no answer. Turning to the three bodyguards, the general ordered them to ride in another jeep and follow us; my parents and I seated ourselves in the back seat of the general's jeep, and off we went. Riding in a general's jeep was like sitting in a king's coach, complete with pomp and circumstance. I never dreamed I would have this privilege, especially after the long incarceration we had under the Japanese. It felt simply wonderful. As the jeep made its way over the highway I acted like a child again, with the wind blowing against my face; inhaling and exhaling the fresh air had a different feeling since our arrival in friendly territory. I believe it was due to the freedom we deserved. Yes, freedom. How I know it so well! I learned that it comes with responsibility, maturity, accountability, and honor.

Two miles down the road to our right I saw tents and many of the general's men bivouacked next to some tall cogon grass. The jeep suddenly stopped in front of one of the tents, and we alighted from our vehicle, following the general. When our group entered the tent, the men stood to attention and saluted the general, who then called for Corporal Philip Dore to report to him at once. As my younger brother came toward us the general presented to my dad his youngest son, who had been serving under him with such honor and valor that he was proud to have him in his service. The 16-year-old handsome lad who moved forward had grown much taller, but otherwise appeared the same. I hugged him and we all cried. We stepped outside the tent, and my brother explained to us how the convoy had left him behind during the retreat in April 1942, that his curiosity about military life made him fall back with some of the soldiers. Before he realized what was happening the convoy vanished, and he could not catch up with us. To survive, he joined General Pendatun's Filipino-Moro guerrillas.

The reunion was overwhelming. It had been more than a year since I had seen Philip, and like me, he had lost his teenage growing up years because of the conditions brought on by the Japanese invasion. It robbed us of the better life that should have been ours, and instead we experienced many problems that we should not have had to cope with. Whether we deserved the challenge or not, that decision was out of our hands. Our only consolation was having our beloved parents with us; they were the bulwark and inspiration for our survival.

On seeing Philip my mom cried out with joy, for the lost son was finally found. I knew his absence especially tormented her because he was her youngest. Finding him alive and well, she pleaded with him to leave the guerrilla army and come with us, that he was just a young boy of sixteen and it took grown men to fight the Japanese. She told him he was too young to die. My mom's tears and her pleading touched my brother's heart, but he told her that despite his age he was a man now and that he could not go back to being a teenager anymore. Since he had become separated from us, he had learned a lot about growing up in the general's guerrilla army.

Pendatun, standing close to us, had a big smile on his face when he heard my brother, but he would not intervene with our family discussion. Just then my dad came to the rescue and spoke on my brother's behalf, telling my mom that their boy had grown up. Philip was, in fact, a chip off the old block, and my dad was proud that he was in the service of our freedom fighters. Not only that, he was under our friend General Pendatun, whom he trusted! My dad reminded my mom that he himself was not much older than Philip when he joined the United States Army back in 1901 and that he would do it again if he were as young as his son. He firmly believed that Philip was old enough to take care of himself.

Finally my mom reluctantly accepted the fact she could not talk Philip out of the service, and she let him go. After saying good-bye Philip returned to his duties, and the general brought us to his secluded headquarters for a conference, where Pendatun offered my dad a position with his guerrilla forces in the quartermaster department. Knowing that he had done this type of work for General Vashion, Pendatun believed this was the right place for my dad to work. On reaching their agreement the general turned to me and asked if I was interested in following up on what I had done at the Kidapawan Medical Dispensary. I could work back and forth between the guerrilla forces and the civilians, depending on who needed me. He offered to repay our services with a place to stay, food to eat, and a salary from the army. Realizing the position we were in and knowing Pendatun needed every able-bodied man and woman, my dad and I accepted the offer to join his organization. Now my dad, Philip, and I were members of the Pendatun guerrillas.

Because of the shortage of guns and ammunition, the guerrilla fighters did not always maintain the towns and barrios they liberated from the Japanese. They used the hit-and-run method in some of their skirmishes, which frustrated the enemy because, "First you see them, and then you don't."

Weapons used by the Moros or Muslims in the Philippines.

The Japanese should have realized that the Moros were well known for their jungle fighting. Their razor-sharp weapons were much better than guns because they crept up behind the enemy during their attack and the soldiers never knew what hit them—they just lay dead in their pool of blood. Because of the effectiveness of the Moros the Japanese called for reinforcements from Cagayan de Oro, and during August and September of 1943 additional enemy strength arrived. In the meantime the courageous Moros and Filipinos continued to fight side by side to eliminate the Japanese.

Prior to using the hit-and-run method, General Pendatun managed to hold on to the front lines between Linabo and Malaybalay. I remember seeing him with his prized Arabian horse that he captured from the Japanese; whenever he sat on horseback he appeared so distinguished in his full uniform. To me he was another hero like my dad because he believed in strategy, discipline, and honor in the military, and he was a no-nonsense type of man who served as an inspiration to his men. They were willing to follow him all the way to victory. Pendatun visited the front lines very often to inspire his soldiers. No white officer put himself in jeopardy by visiting the front lines so often—they stayed many miles away in the safety zone that the guerrillas established. Because General Pendatun fearlessly showed up where all the action took place, the Filipinos and Moros especially revered him for his courage.

General Pendatun, like everyone else, had a motive for living through the grueling war. His second wife, a lovely Filipina whom he married during the war, thoroughly supported him. She inspired this warrior by riding her own beautiful horse alongside him whenever he inspected the troops. This lady had an Arabian horse equal to the general's, and she routinely dressed in a khaki uniform; and because of her beauty, intelligence, and deep love for her husband, she became the envy of other women. But she also sparked some hostility because she embraced and kissed her husband in public, something not culturally acceptable. In those days kissing was a private matter done only in the privacy of one's home, so busybody women had a heyday gossiping and snickering behind the couple's back. This did not pose any problem for the Pendatuns because they were deeply in love. Like any young lovers who loved each other throughout a war, they knew that each moment must be lived because the next day they might be dead. Although the backbiting continued, the couple remained faithful to each other. They survived the war, had children, and lived happily ever after. I would not be so fortunate.

As General Pendatun and his guerrilla fighters recaptured some of the towns and barrios and held them for weeks and sometimes months at a time, his fame as a great warrior and leader spread throughout Mindanao. American soldiers hiding in the jungles for many months from the Japanese finally came out in the liberated areas and joined Pendatun, even though some of them were deathly ill from dysentery, malaria, and other tropical diseases. When they learned about the English-speaking Moro general who led guerrilla uprisings, they willingly joined his organization, and General Pendatun loved that they came aboard to fight alongside his men. His high regard for the Americans caused him to elevate many of them from noncommissioned officers to ranking officers, even putting them in charge of the Filipino men under his command. Pendatun initiated the officer's ranks among the Americans. Some of them had been attached to the Navy, Army, Marines, and Air Force but were all welcomed into Pendatun's guerrillas because the general trusted and respected them.

Good rapport developed between men of different racial backgrounds despite the fact that more Americans received officer's ranks and commanded Filipino and Moro soldiers. The general assigned some officers to the Ordnance Depot because of their knowledge of guns and ammunition; others he sent to the coastline because of their severe illnesses, and he assigned one, an American soldier who had a lot of savvy with engines and motor vehicles, to the motor pool. My parents and I met many of these Americans who stayed or passed through, men with names like Johnny, Tony, Sandy, Jack, Bob, Alex, Ken, Whiskey Bill, Tim, Lee, James, Taylor, Jack, and poor Chaote, who died of malaria. We reached out to help some of them when they first came out of the jungles deathly ill, and although they may have forgotten us, it does not matter. We extended our helping hands to them when they needed us, and I know our reward was much greater, as it came from a God who knows about all the things we have done for others.

My parents and I remained and worked under the general's protection and payroll for as long as he stayed in the area. However he managed to delay the advancing Japanese army, he helped pave the way for the return of General MacArthur and his mighty forces, although Pendatun never received enough credit for this. His guerrillas held the barrios of Linabo and Mailag the longest, and during this time Pendatun encouraged the civilians to set up a temporary government body to run the population. He felt this would build the morale of the people even in difficult times. As long as lawyers, judges, and other civil servants lived and worked in the areas, governments functioned and were acceptable in time of war because of the authentic credentials that these officials held. Even Catholic priests and Protestant ministers continued to practice and minister to their flocks. As a result young people caught in the turmoil of war found each other and were legally married by the priest, minister, or the justice of the peace. Sometimes these weddings involved big celebrations in which people dressed up in their finery, a pig was placed over a set of coals, and relatives and friends brought many edible foods. Groups of musicians with guitars, banjos, violins, and mandolins provided music, and everyone danced. It is well known that Filipinos love to dance as a mode of expression. They dance when they are happy or sad, when they are disappointed or exalted; they even dance to depict the dignity of labor, to express love of gaiety, and to show hope in the face of oppression. They dance for patron saints or for the birds in the rice field. Through their dances they preserve their identity as Filipinos; this is how they give clarity to their culture. In the absence of a wedding a fiesta was sometimes held in the community to keep the morale high among the people. Every now and then we took time to attend but not often because those attached to the guerrilla forces were constantly on the alert.

In one of the heavy skirmishes between the Japanese and the guerrillas during the early fall of 1943, the guerrillas captured some Filipino collaborators and spies. Because Moros have their own method of torture to extract information from traitors, the interrogating officer obtained some vital information from them, after which the general summoned my dad to his headquarters. When my dad arrived, the two men greeted each other like old friends do, with a warm handshake, and then the general asked my dad if he knew that right after our escape from Malaybalay we had become famous. The Japanese had put up a ten thousand pesos reward for each of our heads, dead or alive. The general expressed his anger at the collaborators and the spies who were out to get us, especially since those SOBs (as he referred to them) were our own people. He told my dad that from now on we must stay close to the troops and that as long as he was alive, he would make sure we were all protected.

Amazingly enough the news did not disturb my dad. Maybe the general's assurance made him feel confident or maybe because he had been through another war, threats from Filipino spies did not ruffle his feathers. My dad believed that when your number is up, it is up; simply put, when it is your time to die, you die. The Bible says this about dying: "Oh death where is thy sting, oh grave where is thy victory?" My dad had no fear of dying, and now neither have I because with all that I went through, I tasted victory in the end. I overcame the odds, and I survived; perfect peace is my companion.

Living and working among the few American officers, we felt a comradeship because we had good communications. We helped them in more ways than one because we understood the language and the culture. We had not forgotten what General Vashion had done by saving us from starvation, so we kept on doing things for the Americans as payback for the generosity of the USAFFE. In my mom's culture this is called "Utang nag loob," a debt that should always be repaid until death. Although the Bible says, "It is better to give than to receive," Filipino culture dictates, "When given a helping hand by someone, never forget it until you die. You must return the favor by giving back something of yourself."

I cannot give much of an accounting of what the guerrillas along the northern coast of Mindanao accomplished because the distance of several hundred miles kept me from knowing too much of what happened on that side of the island, although I knew they were brave, too. However, through the bamboo telegraph system, some names of the American officers filtered through: McLish, McClure, Childress, and others long forgotten. They were the heroes. I also heard about a mestizo American named Morgan, who single-handedly killed more Japanese than anyone else involved in the guerrilla war because he hated them so much. He had a woman companion just as tough as he was, and she too killed several Japs. Because of his popularity and his race, many people considered him a rogue rather than a hero; however, I give this man and his friend honor for their contribution to the war effort because they got rid of more enemy soldiers than anyone else. Unfortunately, as I heard the end of the story, the Japanese killed both of them.

These fighting men made such a great sacrifice that they deserve recognition from the Philippine and American government for their bravery. Some of them lived, and others died so that someone else like me might live. Since I survived the conflict, it is up to me to tell the world what really happened during the guerrilla war in Cotabato and Bukidnon in 1943. I believe that the Moros from Cotabato and their leader Salipada Pendatun should have their names etched in the history books of the Philippines, for without their effort many more would have died. Furthermore, the guerrilla organization in Bukidnon would have been a weak group of fighters if they fought by themselves. However with the original group of Moro guerrillas, the combined effort with the remainder of the USAFFE made them very strong. I could never understand why at the height of their victory a few American leaders managed to change the course of the leadership within the guerrilla movement. Was it a power struggle? Maybe not. Was it prejudice? Who knows? Perhaps it was an oversight? Not likely. Only God knows the answer to this.

In any case the Japanese could not long ignore the growing strength of the guerrillas on Mindanao during the fall of 1943. It was only a matter of time before they struck back with a vengeance, with a fury that destroyed my family.

The Guerrillas, the Horse, and the Family

Many books have been written about the guerrilla activities on Mindanao, but only those who actually experienced the war there can determine the accuracy of their contents. In piecing together some of the heroic accomplishments of the men who lived and died while serving the guerrilla units along the coastline of Mindanao, I cannot personally substantiate every incident of heroism because I was not everywhere. The hundreds, maybe thousands, of miles spanning the eight to ten provinces with high mountains and dense jungles made it impossible for any of us to know the truth about each other's responsibilities and activities. All I know is what I saw, heard, and became a part of while serving with the guerrillas in Malaybalay, Bukidnon, to deal with three types of enemies: the Japanese, the collaborators, and the unpredictable natives. We were not with the guerrillas for vainglory or future political recognition—we wanted our freedom back.

In the early 1960s, at a reunion in Denver, Colorado, my present husband, Jim, and I met several of the American guerrilla survivors who had been deployed along the coastline of Mindanao. The reunion, held at Colonel Wendell Fertig's home, marked the first time I learned that he served as overall commander of the guerrilla forces throughout Mindanao. General Douglas MacArthur had given the order when he finally received all reports from his envoys who came to Mindanao and held a secret meeting with Fertig. How extensive the intelligence gathering was of those three American officers, I have no idea; all I know is that they did not come to our location in Malaybalay. No matter how secret a mission might be, three people of this importance could not hide their presence from all of us in Malaybalay. Rather than probe into the background of what went on, I simply dropped the subject because we were guests at the reunion. Meanwhile, I listened to some of their stories and fumed at the injustices of those whose contributions were overlooked.

In mid–1943 General MacArthur sent two or three of his best men to scrutinize the guerrilla activities on the island of Mindanao in preparation for his return to the Philippines, as he had promised the Filipino people. The American officers left Australia by submarine and arrived at a secret rendezvous with Fertig. Their major task was to make sure that the radio communication system was adequate to inform each guerrilla unit scattered throughout Mindanao. The officers expressed amazement at the ingenuity of the salvaged radio parts that had been put together because some of the radios could send and receive messages from as far away as Australia and San Francisco. Likewise, MacArthur's men wanted a report indicating that the various guerrilla organizations were unified since there were a few disgruntled ones who preferred to be mavericks and wanted to do their own fighting. Satisfied in their findings and the reports they received from Fertig, they returned to Australia. Before long the Americans received full charge of operations in all guerrilla organizations, which received new names like 109th Military District, 110th Military District, and so on. I believe Fertig ultimately decided to give each American a rank according to what he learned about them.

General Douglas MacArthur was well known throughout the Philippine Islands even before the war. He spent his young life with his mother and military father in that country, and he understood the Asian mind—especially the Japanese—but most of all he loved the Filipino people for their warm friendship, hospitality, loyalty, and their eagerness to help themselves. His parents lived in Manila, in a home they called "Casa Blanca" or white house, and I believe they were within their rights to name their home as such because of the position the senior MacArthur held in the capital city of Manila. Another reason Filipinos revered the MacArthur name was because of his father's association with President Manuel L. Quezon, members of his cabinet, and the people at large. Casa Blanca served as a home where these Filipino leaders could come and meet with the MacArthurs for dinners and other special occasions. This was a warm, mutual relationship. Being a famous leader, however, General MacArthur had some powerful critics who could not see the depth of his ingenious military mind. In my opinion he never received full power of a command to follow his instincts of destroying the enemy; if he had been given that power, it is possible that all wars would have ended with World War II.

At that reunion in Denver I also learned that Fertig, authorized to command every guerrilla organization in Mindanao, had promoted himself to general and wanted to maintain that rank permanently. However, MacArthur refused to approve it, instead making Fertig a lieutenant colonel, which must have wounded Fertig. Whatever happened after that is beyond me. I only know that when the Americans received full authority to lead the Filipinos in the retaking of Mindanao, certain American officers and high-ranking Filipino leaders were demoted, and ultimately several names were removed from the final roster submitted for recognition and compensation. Two people I knew very well were affected by this: General Salipada Pendatun, who lost his command, and Captain John William Grant, reduced in rank to a lieutenant. As for my dad and I, we never received compensation for all our work, even though we continued our attachment to what was known as the 109th Infantry, 109th Division, 10th Military District, after MacArthur recognized the guerrilla movement in Malaybalay, Bukidnon. It does not matter much anymore, I suppose, because I have been blessed in other ways, but it still rankles that only certain people have been singled out for honors.

One of my lingering regrets over this whole situation is how General Pendatun, the man who began the guerrilla movement from Cotabato and brought his fighting Moros all the way to Malaybalay, never received full recognition of his rank or for retaking many towns and barrios, which cost significant losses on all sides. When MacArthur ordered Pendatun's replacement in the guerrilla movement, it almost caused a bloodbath in the town of Linabo because the Moros could not understand why their beloved general was not allowed to continue on with his leadership and his rank. During that electrifying hour the Moros prepared to slaughter all the American officers in the area because they were so furious about the way their leader was treated. I am not even sure if the Americans were aware of this, but I knew about it because I was there when it happened. Had the Moros been left to decide the fate of the Americans it would have been the bloodiest massacre of the war. Luckily the Japanese did not know what was happening because they could have had their moment of triumph by attacking that day due to the division and deep hurt among the guerrilla factions. Thank God Pendatun turned out to be the man of the hour: he subdued his people's anger and gathered them up to return to Cotabato.

My parents and I were caught in the middle of this conflict, but we simply stayed out of it because we believed we did not know enough facts to make a proper decision. Everyone worked harmoniously in the beginning of the war, therefore why not now? Why the sudden change when Pendatun was doing so well? The answer will have to be left up to God because my speculations might not sound very charitable. Anyway, when the general and his men left Bukidnon, he gave us the choice of coming along with them or of remaining behind, with his blessings. This made our decision to stay easier because although we felt indebted to him for what he had done for us since the beginning of the guerrilla actions, including providing us with food, work, and protection, we were tired of moving. The general even allowed my brother Philip to transfer to another unit so that he would be close to us. This decision to remain behind proved to be both the most joyous and most tragic of my life. I shall never forget Pendatun because he helped us get our freedom back. He and his Moro followers were our heroes.

The man that Pendatun assigned to run the motor pool and gave the rank of captain to would become my first husband, John William "Jack" Grant. Jack was dependable and responsible, and he worked well with the Filipino men under his command. Because of his expertise in putting together some of the abandoned military vehicles and making them serviceable again, he certainly deserved his rank, and his personal life, his decision to marry me, should not have prejudiced his performance and rank. He was, as the saying goes, free, white, and over 21; in fact, he was twenty-six years old when he made his decision, and no one put a gun to his head. Unfortunately, even in war certain actions get people blacklisted or shunned for no legitimate reason at all—only because of prejudice—but in spite of potential hostile criticism Jack and I took our chances. We were in love.

After he left Linabo, Mailag, and the whole of Bukidnon Province, Pendatun marched his Moro and Filipino guerrillas back to Cotabato in a massive exodus caravan that reminded me of the departure of the Israelites from Egypt. However awesome the caravan looked, those of us left behind felt sadness in our hearts for their unjust departure. We stayed behind because my dad believed this was our best chance for survival, and he hoped that after the war we could leave the country altogether and go to America to live.

Once the mighty Moro army left, my parents and I moved to Valencia, where we occupied a hut close to the highway so that in the event of a sudden attack we could remove ourselves quickly and hide. I continued my medical work there with the supply of medicines given to me by the guerrillas, and I helped soldiers and evacuees, anyone who needed me. One day, after hearing about a one-armed American who lived in Valencia, three American soldiers came out of the jungles because they were in bad shape: they were emaciated and haggard, and one of them had such a bad case of malaria that his teeth chattered loudly. The tall one, Tony, had a great sense of humor, which made him unforgettable—he always thought of something funny to make everyone laugh. Sandy, the other fellow, was short, but brother, could he cuss up a storm! The third man (whose name I do not remember), of Swedish or Polish heritage, hailed from Minnesota, and was more reserved. When the three of them got together, though, they made quite a team. Tony came to our place suffering from a terrible headache. After he introduced himself, he asked if I happened to have any aspirins because he had a splitting headache that wouldn't go away. He offered to trade me his horse for two aspirins. That was how valuable simple medicines had become by that point in the war—when someone would be willing to trade a useful animal so they could alleviate a common health problem like a throbbing headache.

But my ears perked up right away because I knew what a horse would mean, not only for my medical work but for my family as well. I thought the bargain was pretty good, if one-sided to my benefit, so I quickly fetched Tony a glass of water, gave him two aspirins from my medical kit, and asked him if he really meant what he said about the horse. He made the sign of the cross like the Catholics do in their church and replied, "Cross my heart and hope to die," an old saying that made me cringe at the time, given how many people were dying then. Tony swallowed the aspirins, and when I was about to claim my prize horse we heard a voice outside the house cussing and swearing about a horse giving birth to a colt. It was Sandy, naturally, doing the cussing he was famous for; but since my mom heard him, too, she forbade me to go outside, not because of the cussing but because of the birthing. She believed it improper for a young girl to watch an animal giving birth, so I remained inside the hut.

The poor mare delivered a stillborn colt, and after one of the soldiers hauled the dear little carcass away for burial in the woods nearby, I was finally allowed to go outside. To my utter disappointment, the mare turned out to be a bag of bones. No wonder Tony so eagerly traded her; he certainly had no use for a skeleton horse made up of a shadow of skin and bone—no wonder the two other Americans laughed so hard. The bargain was not as one-sided as I had originally thought, but regardless of the condition of that poor old nag, I felt glad to have something of my own. All I had to do was to remember the instructions my dad gave me about horses when I was a child. He had advised me to care for the animal by taking it to a river and getting its body in deep water so it would not be able to run away. Then I should scrub it down with a brush and rinse it off. After the horse was clean I had to dry it really well and take it to the nearest meadow where it could eat the rich green grass scattered in the field. Because I quickly followed my dad's teachings from many years before, I fattened that old nag until she began to really look like a horse. Tony never saw the improvements of his bag-of-bones horse because he could not stay around too long, but in remembrance of that day, of that trade with the American guerrilla, I called my horse Aspirin.

The three Americans spent the night under our hut with the stilts because we had no room for them, but I gave them native mats to lay on the ground and blankets to keep the chill out. Before retiring, the men got together with my dad and told him of the places they came from: Tony from Chicago, Sandy from South Carolina, and the third man from Minnesota. Because my dad had spent a few years in the United States in his early life, he enjoyed hearing about these places. I sold the soldiers some of the home-made cigarettes I made to bring in enough extra cash for us to buy fresh meats and vegetables. When the hour got late, the three men retired under the hut. Shortly after midnight I was awakened by a loud scream from somewhere, and I jumped out of bed quickly because I thought we were under attack by the Japanese army. When the sound of laughter followed the screams, I realized the commotion came from under the hut. Sandy was cussing up a storm because a centipede had crawled up his pant leg and bit him. As he struggled with his pants to get rid of the nightcrawler, he shook all over, and the other two men found the scenario so funny that they began laughing. One of them told Sandy not to feel too bad—at least it was not a snake. Sandy then shivered because he hated snakes even more than centipedes. Everything calmed down, I crawled back into my bed, and the men returned to their mats, where they slept the rest of the night. Between the horse and the centipede, how could I ever forget those incidents?

Shortly after the Mindanao guerrillas received recognition from the headquarters of General MacArthur in Australia, they asked us to leave Valencia. Pendatun had already left the area, and my dad was ordered to move my mom and me to Mailag. Without even being told why, I realized that MacArthur knew about the buildup of Japanese soldiers in Davao and the likelihood that they were headed toward Malaybalay. Valencia stood in the way of the Japanese convoy, so our lives were in jeopardy.

After we settled in Mailag my dad reported to Captain Jack Grant, who commanded the motor pool. Prior to Jack's arrival on Mindanao he survived the surprise attack at Clark Air Force Base in Pampanga, near Manila on the island of Luzon. In December 1941, as the men there celebrated the Christmas holiday, the Japanese attacked and destroyed most of the airplanes parked on the airfield, an attack that resembled Pearl Harbor. Jack and at least five other men managed to make their way to Mindanao, thousands of miles south of Luzon, where they first just wandered through the jungles, hiding from the Japanese. When they heard about Pendatun's anti–Japanese activities, they came out of the hills to join up with him, and they no longer had to suffer with hunger or go without clean uniforms and a bed to sleep in. But Pendatun soon noticed Jack's mechanical abilities and assigned him to the motor pool, where he was more than qualified to take charge because of his knowledge of vehicles. Pendatun always picked the right men for the right jobs.

After Pendatun left, however, the news went out to everyone who stayed behind that Colonel Robert Bowler would replace the general and take charge of the guerrilla units in Malaybalay. The colonel reportedly was a disciplined man with credentials from West Point, which I learned about firsthand when I briefly met with the colonel in person. Jack once sent me off as a courier on horseback to reach Bowler's hideout in the hills because he knew that I could be trusted with the message. Taking the top-secret message to the colonel was a duty I gladly accepted, so when I received my instructions from Jack, I willingly risked my life to go where I had not gone before. Jack gave me a map indicating Bowler's location and a message sealed in an envelope because of its secrecy. I easily located the hideout and found the colonel's hut, which sat on a hillside giving him a panoramic view of the area below. When I arrived on horseback, he and his companions were caught by surprise because they had not expected me. Two Americans and a Filipino bodyguard occupied the hideout; Colonel Bowler was one of the Americans, but the other kept his face from me so I never knew who he was. Because this happened so long ago and was but one small event during a tumultuous war, the colonel certainly may not recall meeting me. Delivering a message, no matter how important, is little cause for recognition, but I considered it part of my contribution for the cause of freedom. I did what I could for my God, my family, and my country.

The adventure of meeting a high-ranking officer hidden in the hills felt very exciting to me. I neither asked foolish questions about his command, nor did I give him information about myself, although I immodestly assumed he knew who I was because of my dad's reputation. When I arrived at the hideout, the armed Filipino guard became annoyed because he was very protective of the colonel and the other American. After telling him very briefly who I was and why I was there, I gave him the brown envelope, and he handed it to the colonel. As soon as the colonel read the message, I asked if there was a reply; he said no, and I left in a hurry because I wanted to be back in my safety zone. That was the first and last time I saw Colonel Bowler in person. The Filipino people, however, whispered his name as one they highly respected, revered, and obeyed. Like many of us he was caught in a dangerous situation, and he just wanted to end the war and reestablish our freedom.

With my dad's assignment to the motor pool in Mailag, my family was also entitled to live in the same hut with Jack Grant and his men. My dad's duty was to help Jack locate motor vehicle parts because the guerrillas knew my dad had a good rapport with the civilians in the area and could get important information and supplies out of them. Reflecting back fifty years, I believe we were moved back to the motor pool because of Colonel Frank McGee's influence with the American guerrilla leaders who had taken control. He knew how valuable my dad had become and about the medical work I did. But in addition to this work, I went on secret missions that few people knew about. As long as my dad and I worked for the USAFFE, it provided us with a place to live, food, and a salary. Colonel McGee made frequent visits to the motor pool when he passed from one military mission to another. He had not forgotten that my family helped save his life and those of his men with quinine medicines, blankets, and food while they were in the hills of Malaybalay; neither did he forget his long friendship with my dad. We would have been related had my cousin Betty from England accepted his marriage proposal. McGee showed his friendship by securing good positions for us with the guerrillas.

The American officer in charge of the motor pool was a very private person, who enjoyed his work. John William Grant was born on June 18, 1919, to Charles and Kathryn C. Grant of Cuyahoga Falls, Ohio; he was an only child. After Charles died at an early age, Kathryn raised their son on her own. During the 1920s and 1930s Jack helped his widowed mother in the store she owned while he went to school, eventually graduating from the Falls high school in 1938. Like some mothers with an only child, Kathryn wanted her son to grow up and marry the girl she had chosen for him, a girl who lived across the street from the Grant home in Cuyahoga Falls. Even though he tried to be an obedient son, Jack was irritated that his mother nagged him about whom she wanted him to marry, so rather than comply with his mother's wishes, Jack joined the Air Force to get away from home. At first he was stationed at Hickam Field in Hawaii, assigned to the 11th Air Force Bomb Group, where the men received tough, extensive training.

Jack's former sergeant, now a retired major living in California, filled me in on his Hawaii military training because Jack himself never spoke of it to me in our short time together. Major Bernheim and his wife visited my present husband, Jim, and me in the summer of 1989 after he discovered I was Jack's widow. The major encouraged us to accept the invitation and hospitality of the people of Cuyahoga Falls to visit Jack's hometown on September 25, 1989, and we followed the major's advice, providing us a most unforgettable experience. Jack's only daughter, the one I gave him, Jean Louise, and her husband, Arthur, traveled with us. The mayor of that city honored us, and the "lunch bunch" ladies entertained us along with their spouses. The ladies, all high school graduates from the 1930s, classmates and friends of Jack's, were simply wonderful. We had the opportunity to see the home where Jack grew up, and these kind people of the Falls high school asked me to share some of my wartime experiences with the student body. The young boys and girls seemed engrossed as I related the story of how one of their own hometown boys traveled so far, ending his journey in a foreign land during a brutal war. The man who made the trip to Cuyahoga Falls possible was Craig Wilson, a newspaper editor from the *Beacon Journal*, who covered these events for that paper, which sold a quarter of a million copies when my story appeared on May 28, 1989. I am indeed grateful to this man for helping preserve Jack's memory in his hometown in Ohio.

By American standards Jack Grant was short in stature, and because a controlling mother raised him, he tended to be shy and reserved with the girls. He preferred to wait for the right girl to come along in his life rather than to allow his mother to dictate whom he must marry. No doubt he had a good upbringing by his mother, though, because he acted neither vulgar nor rowdy; instead, he was kind and considerate, with a pleasing personality. His hometown friends indicated that Jack loved to tinker with automobiles in his high school days, a passion that kept him busy when he was not studying. Since Jack proved very good at putting motor parts together, he earned the right to be in charge of the motor pool in Mailag during the guerrilla days of 1943. By all accounts he deserved to retain his rank as captain and even achieve major because he was so conscientious, but MacArthur's decisions about guerrilla organization changed, and the leadership was put in the hands of the American colonel on Mindanao. Jack had no time for triviality, and in his leisure time he remained a loner, which his army friends never understood; but in time, I did. I admired him, and eventually I married him.

I first met Jack when General Pendatun introduced my dad and me to him shortly after we made our escape from the Japanese in Malaybalay. The meeting was very formal and polite, and neither Jack nor anyone else paid much attention to me because I was an unsophisticated young girl, overshadowed by older military men. Wearing khaki pants and long baggy-sleeved shirts, I probably looked more like a boy than a girl, but my appearance did not concern me either because I was too busy with my work. As long as the soldiers respected me as one of their peers, I was satisfied. Anyone who dared try to mistreat me, though, had my dad to answer to.

One night after our arrival in Mailag the townspeople put on a dance, and since the women had to wear dresses for the occasion, I had to find one to wear. When I shed my uniform shirt and pants my young womanly figure came to light: my chest had developed and my tiny yet curved figure fit in to a size seven dress, a cast-off of my mom's. Once I was in that dress, the men began to notice me. Feeling a little out of place and self-conscious about being out of uniform, I insisted my mom and dad escort me to the dance, as was proper anyway. As we entered the town plaza I suddenly heard some wolf whistles. I felt flattered. My dad observed that I was certainly growing up if the fellows out there were now noticing me. He asked if I heard their whistle calls. Pleased but still uncomfortable, I told him that they were just kidding, that nobody was serious about anything these days except their work.

At that moment both men and marriage were the furthest things from my mind. I had been raised to believe in the sanctity of marriage, and I wanted to wait for the right man to come along before giving myself to him alone, so I had no time for fooling around. That evening I danced with a few fellows then returned with my parents to our living quarters in the motor pool; the next day I donned my khaki pants and my baggy shirt, going to work as usual. I was no wartime Cinderella.

A middle-class family must have owned the building used for the motor pool in Mailag because it was spacious. Several tall stilts boosted the main floor high above the ground, making it easy and convenient for the mechanics to work on the military vehicles. Inside, the home contained two bedrooms, a large living room, a kitchen, and a bathroom. The room my parents and I occupied accommodated two rattan beds, one for my parents and the other for me. My mom took charge of the kitchen meals, and I helped her once in a while by buying supplies at the marketplace. During the months we lived in that motor pool we had no friction or disagreements with Jack Grant; everyone just worked together on the assignments given to us. Jack and I hardly noticed each other because our responsibilities remained uppermost in our minds.

While working together in the motor pool, Jack and my dad developed a father-son relationship, my dad serving as a substitute for the father Jack never knew. They got along so well that I do not recall any argument between the two of them. Moreover, we became his substitute family as well, so our survival as a family unit became very important to all of us in that motor pool. Jack managed the motor pool in a professional manner while my dad ventured out to procure vehicle parts from the locals. Even when the motor pool needed gasoline to run and test the motors, my dad somehow managed to find this very scarce commodity for the guerrilla army. I continued my medical work in a low-key fashion. Our family was still on the wanted list of the Japanese army; the less they knew of our activities, the better for us.

In an attempt to keep up the morale of the soldiers and civilians while everyone was still on constant alert (we did not know when the Japanese would make their big drive to attack our garrison), coffee shops and restaurants opened in Mailag. Filipino families operated these eating places, and a few were located across the street from the motor pool. My mom's cooking usually sufficed for my dad and me, and we simply had no need to eat out; however, some of the native desserts served at the restaurants were so delicious they lured us away from her kitchen. As weeks went by, Jack and I took time out to meet in one of those restaurants for coffee and conversation. Since my parents considered him part of our family, they let me go with Jack, no questions asked, because they trusted him completely. So did I.

Jack Grant was six years my senior. In the beginning our relationship resembled a familial one; we had great respect for each other, and somehow I always felt safe when he was around. He acted maturely, and he treated me like the sister he never had; I also missed my own brothers, who had been so close to me, initially adopting Jack as a good stand-in. Best of all, Jack was not the aggressive type, so I had nothing to fear when I was alone with him. After several of these coffee breaks Jack shared a few things about his mother and his life at home. One day he asked me if I knew why he joined the Air Force, and before I could even respond he told me that it was because he wanted to get away from his mother. He explained how his mother was determined to marry him off to the neighbor girl across the street, but he rejected the idea that just because they grew up on the same street, they had to get married. When it was my turn to speak, I asked Jack if he was sure he was really not running away from the neighbor girl, that he might be in love with her and did not know it. Without hesitating Jack replied with one of his favorite American phrases, "Heck no!" He said he never gave the girl a second thought, so how could he be in love with her? It was all his mother's idea. Then he told me of his hometown in Cuyahoga Falls, a name difficult for me to remember because of its pronunciation.

Our coffee breaks never lasted too long, but we began meeting a little more often at the same place. The informal talks took on a more personal tone, although in my naiveté I never sensed what Jack was leading up to because my only experience of camaraderie with men had been within my own family—my dad and my three brothers. Jack did much of the talking, and I listened, which at the time seemed proper to me; consequently, he never had a chance to know the kind of home or education that I had. He did not even realize that I led a very sheltered life or that I attended a private Christian school, where girls certainly were not promiscuous at any age. He did not know of the Filipino belief in premarital chastity. Whenever Jack talked of his desire to be with a woman, I felt uncomfortable but told him that the kind he was looking for were available—all he had to do was inquire from the men working for him at the motor pool. A red-blooded American like him should not have any trouble finding a girl.

Jack's need to have a woman in his life did not bother me because I had heard whisperings about men's urges and knew that there were "good" women and "bad" women. I thought as long as he was not referring to me, why should I care? After all, I was not his mother. But when I told him about the prostitutes available for the men, he became so embarrassed his face got red as a beet, and he dropped the subject right away, never to speak of it again. In the meantime our friendship continued to deepen, yet he never attempted to kiss me, which would have damaged our relationship. He was patiently biding his time, and for this I developed a strong liking for Jack.

Before Jack had the opportunity to reveal his feelings for me, someone else noticed me. One night this young man came calling at the motor pool, and since my parents knew him they allowed us to sit on the porch and talk. I do not even remember what we talked about, and I would just as soon forget what happened that night. I had known this handsome fellow since we were rescued from Malaybalay, and I did like him a lot, but in the course of our sitting in the dark talking about many things, he suddenly wrapped his arms around me and kissed me. He had powerful arms and his kisses gave both of us a good feeling. This was a first for me in a long time, and the pleasure was ecstatic and surprising; but we were careful not to go beyond that point. He remained a gentleman, something I always remembered him fondly for. Remaining in the dark did not help the situation because we just wanted to go on kissing. Suddenly my dad stood in the living room and began scolding me, demanding to know what in the hell was going on. The old man's desire to protect his young daughter fueled his rage so that the embarrassed visitor left in a hurry. The incident left me feeling so guilty and ashamed that I wanted to die.

I felt doubly humiliated when I realized that Jack Grant remained quietly wide awake in his room during this entire episode, where he heard everything but said nothing. This was a family matter he did not want to get himself into. My mom kept very still because she did not want to interfere with my dad's anger, and he finally ordered me to go to my room, announcing that we would talk about this in the morning. And like a whipped puppy I made my way inside, feeling full of guilt, confusion, and despair; my chin dropped to my chest, and I dared not look at my dad. It took me a long time to get over that terrible embarrassment of being caught by my dad kissing a man that I was attracted to. Fortunately I no longer feel any shame for what happened that night because I realize that it was a normal part of growing up.

Sleeping that night proved impossible as terrible thoughts built up in my mind. I thought that I must get away from there, that I would never be the same again because I felt so cheap after being caught kissing a man. I believed my dad would never forgive me. I quietly waited for the right moment to make my move, and when I heard my dad's loud snoring I knew the time had come. I gathered a few of my things, rolled them in a bundle, and tiptoed out of the room and down the stairs. It was pitch dark, and nothing stirred outside as I retrieved Aspirin's saddle and bridle and started to prepare the animal for my getaway. After mounting the horse I headed in the direction of Linabo, and beyond it was the front lines. Having traveled on that road many times, I had no difficulty following the highway even in the blackness of night. I allowed Aspirin to walk at a slow pace, my fragile emotions shattered by my dad's anger. This was the first time in all my life that he really got angry with me, and I just wanted to run away and die because I believed I had committed an unforgivable sin.

Looking up at the sky I saw a few weak stars trying to light up my way. If they could have talked they probably would have said, "Don't despair, my child, for you have not done something that cannot be forgiven and forgotten." But I thought I knew better, and I kept on going. Then from out of the darkness I heard a real voice shouting for me to wait up, asking where I thought I was going. That voice was so familiar to me, yet I could not believe it was real. The hoofbeats of another horse approached, and sure enough the voice belonged to Jack Grant. When our horses stood side by side, without shame I threw my arms around Jack's neck and sobbed in his arms, asking him if he had heard everything that had gone on back at the house.

He told me that he had because he was awake the whole time. I told him that I felt so hurt and so ashamed, that I didn't know why I let myself go the way I did. I explained that I had tried to keep from any temptation, yet my dad caught me kissing that young man. I asked Jack if that made me a bad person. Jack reassured me, calling me "honey," telling me that certainly I was not bad. He told me that it was all over now, so we had to get back to

John William "Jack" Grant stationed at Clark Air Force Base in Angeles, Pampanga, in the Philippines at the beginning of the war.

the motor pool. But I was still afraid, and I confessed that I thought that my dad would kill me if he found out that I tried to run away.

Before I knew what was happening, Jack held me tight in his arms and kissed me passionately. He assured me that everything was going to be all right; then we turned our horses around and returned to Mailag. The cool evening breeze brushed up against my cheek, renewing my spirit. When we arrived at the motor pool and alighted from our horses, Jack suddenly asked if I would marry him. He explained that he had bought a gold wedding ring from one of his men so we could get married right then. He begged me to say yes. The proposal caught me by surprise, but in a way I realized that Jack's affection for me was not surprising. As soon as I agreed to marry him, I knew our fate was sealed, for good or for ill.

Jack made his way up the stairs with me following behind, holding his hand. He went to the door of my parents' room and called out for my dad to wake up, that he was going to marry his daughter right now and wanted his consent. My dad came out of the room half asleep but smiling like a Cheshire cat, and he gave his approval without asking any questions; his anger toward me had suddenly vanished. Jack's Filipino sergeant went off to get the justice of the peace, and in front of friends and witnesses, Jack slipped the gold ring on my left hand, fourth finger, and we were married. Our marriage took place on October 31, 1943, and a small celebration followed.

Despite the swiftness of getting married in those wee hours, everything was legal, from the justice of the peace to the witnesses. Jack Grant was twenty-four years old and I was eighteen. The only thing that troubled me was that we were not married in the church. Due to the influence of the large Catholic population, many Filipinos emphasized the idea that only marriages in the church were legal or real. Part of me believed this as well, and it took me some time to come to the conclusion that my marriage to Jack was just as legal and as binding, even though it did not take place in a church.

The truth about my dad's anger toward the young man who kissed me that night finally surfaced after I married Jack. My dad thought so highly of Captain Grant that he hoped the man would ultimately become his son-in-law; no other officer, American or Filipino, was good enough for me, his only daughter. He and Jack had developed such a strong friendship that my dad did not want anyone to come between them. As much as my dad supported the marriage, my mom was very much against the idea because she did not feel I was old enough; plus she did not believe that the time was right because of the war. She wanted me to wait until the war ended, finish high school, and go on to college. My mom tried to plan my life like other mothers; however, her plans were not meant to be. Jack and I did not wait for the war to end because in our hearts we knew we had to live every moment of our lives to the fullest and accept the consequences. Our destiny and our fate had already been sealed when we first laid eyes on each other.

Everyone in the Philippines during World War II lived on borrowed time, whether they were young, middle-aged, or elderly. To marry or wait, have children or not, to sacrifice one's life so that others might live—these represented just some of the day-to-day crossroads we all faced. As for Jack and me, I believe destiny brought us together. For him to leave Cuyahoga Falls in Ohio because of his mother's domineering ways and to find himself over ten thousand miles away on an island in the Philippines, who could have planned that? As for myself, even though I had a white father and a Filipino-Spanish mother, I never dreamed I would end up marrying an American soldier at the age of eighteen. Only God could have laid such a plan; only He could have given me the strength to see it through because He gives us only what we can endure.

9

The Trail to Murder and Death

Reliving this chapter of my life is not an easy thing to do because of the trauma and the excruciating pain it caused me for many years. Yet I know it must be told, not because I am looking for sympathy or pity but because my experiences during World War II in the Philippines are not complete without this episode. For me to exclude this portion of my story would be to deprive my own family and friends of knowing how I really survived and what that survival cost. It might lead people to think that the war was nothing more than a strenuous adventure. It was not adventure but horror. There was suffering, the loss of loved ones, the loss of prized possessions, yet there was also the courage to take responsibility for jobs without experience and the fortitude of finding my way out of a jungle I knew nothing about. Above all, there was the courage to live in spite of the many obstacles constantly before me. This was how I spent my teenage years, growing from and suffering with loss.

I took a big step toward adulthood by marrying a handsome American officer six years my senior. Timing was a factor in both our lives because of the high stakes involved in war. Despite the old adage "All is fair in love and war," Jack and I were not sure what was fair about a war with the Japanese that kept us on the run and threatened our happiness and our very lives. As providence dictated, we went ahead with the marriage so that we might laugh together, work together, then live and love together for our allotted time. Our decision may not have pleased everyone, but we did not have to answer to anyone else. Our accountability was to ourselves and to God, who judges all.

Celebrating our marriage with the traditional feast was not easy because the area was on a constant alert; however, Jack and I made the most of it. The jubilation in the motor pool continued until morning, with friends and strangers from the surrounding area bringing in food and drinks, but just as daylight finally arrived to brighten our day, the general alarm sounded. At last the Japanese launched a three-pronged attack on the guerrilla forces, planning on outflanking the organized guerrillas and scattering them in three different directions, with Japanese soldiers assailing from the left flank, the right, and the center. I found out later that they had to make this push to clear the highway from Malaybalay to Davao because the guerrillas had occupied some parts of the highway for months, and the Japanese needed to secure it if they were to hold the island. This desperate move by the Japanese was prompted by the news they heard: that General MacArthur was on his way back to the Philippines with his mighty force to first retake Mindanao and make it his main base in reconquering the rest of the islands. The general's promise of "I shall return" to the Filipino people kept the Japanese nervous since their spies and collaborators were not sure how the general intended to carry out his operations. For this very reason the Japanese shifted their position, bringing in many more troops to fortify the island of Mindanao. Their top priority was to clear the highway that the guerrillas held, to link their military forces from the north to the south of the big island. Troop reinforcements landed in Cagayan de Oro and moved toward Malaybalay to make their big assault on the guerrillas.

The Japanese held the element of surprise because the guerrillas never expected the magnitude of the three-prong attack. Even though our soldiers fought valiantly and tried to hold their lines, the volume of well-armed Japanese soldiers proved overwhelming to the guerrilla fighters. As a result guerrilla officers issued orders for the immediate burning of all documents and the concealment of any usable vehicles in the nearby jungles. When the unexpected orders came to the motor pool, the first thing we all had to do was to abandon our jubilation over the marriage event and get ready for the mass evacuation from Mailag. We only had a day, at the most two, to withdraw from the area and flee across the Pulangi River to seek the sanctuary of the dense forest. While Jack occupied himself with helping my dad and me destroy all motor pool documents, he also worried about our safety. He ordered my parents and me to pack a few food supplies, medicines, blankets, and clothing so that we could abandon the premises in time to get across that river. Jack was my husband now, as well as my commanding officer, so I was doubly bound to obey him, but my heart sank at the thought of being separated from him so soon.

A few days before, a tropical storm had hit the area, causing the Pulangi River's waterline to rise above its normal height. The resulting turbulent flow of the water produced mud and floating debris, which made crossing the river hazardous. By the time my family reached the edge of the river the morning after Jack and I got married, many of the frightened civilians had already congregated there, contemplating how to make the crossing. Some who could not wait plunged themselves in the river hoping to get a head start from the rest of the people, and the mighty current quickly swept their fragile bodies away to their deaths. That wild river claimed many old men, women, and children as its victims; we could only watch helplessly on the bank. Understanding the consequence of any more reckless plans to cross to the other side, my dad took charge of the situation. He instructed two of our soldiers to tie a rope around their waists, get into the water, and allow the river to sweep them at an angle until they reached the opposite side. Each soldier had to support the other to avoid drowning; still the first attempt to cross was almost a disaster because both men got dragged under water by the swift current. My dad and others, holding on to one end of the rope on shore, had to pull the soldiers back to safety, but because of the urgent need to get everyone to the safe side we risked a second attempt, which succeeded. Cheers and clapping erupted when the two men finally emerged from the river and tied the rope to the biggest tree trunk on their side. Then began the exodus of civilians, with women and children being helped across by strong men, both military and civilian. When it came to our turn, my mom and I made sure my dad went first with two soldiers flanking and protecting him because of his single arm. While holding on tightly to the rope my dad slowly moved his body on that treacherous current with my mom, another soldier, and me following behind. At one point we thought we lost my dad because he sank under the water with only his campaign hat showing, but the alert soldier pulled him up quickly and we continued on. My fragile mom had great difficulty but luckily a third soldier kept track of her, and all of us made it safely across.

Now that my parents and I were safe I had more time to worry about Jack. Since we left the motor pool I had not seen or heard from him, and I feared for his life because I knew how much the Japanese hated the Americans. If they caught him they would not hesitate to torture and kill him. Just before sundown I waited at the edge of the river, and I felt relieved when he finally appeared with the rest of his men, tired but still looking handsome. I called to him from across the way that there was a rope tied on both sides of the river so they could all cross like we did, and I urged him to hurry while it was still light so that he would not have trouble making the crossing. When Jack heard my voice, he smiled, obviously pleased that we were temporarily safely beyond the reach of the oncoming Japanese army. He and his soldiers made their way to our side of the river; then Jack released the rope, allowing it to float away with the current. As soon as he came out of the water we embraced and kissed each other passionately; neither of us cared if anyone watched. Our honeymoon had not even begun because of the unexpected full-blown attack by the Japanese, but as long as we were together we knew heaven could wait for that moment. We reluctantly broke our brief embrace, though, and turned to more immediate matters.

My parents and I had found a large hut underneath a thick clump of trees to serve as a resting place for all of us. We believed that once we crossed the Pulangi River and now that darkness had finally come, we were temporarily safe because the Japanese knew better than to travel in the dark for fear of a guerrilla ambush. I led Jack and his men to the hut because I knew they were hungry and exhausted from all the rushing about in Mailag, where they had helped bury and burn items of importance to the guerrillas that they did not want to fall into the hands of the Japanese. Those articles of less importance they either discarded in the bushes along the trail or left behind.

As soon as we arrived at the hut we all sat down over a hot meal that my mom had prepared, and my parents informed us that my cousin Beth had turned up during the evacuation. She was one of my Aunt Mary's children who lived at our home years before the war, one of the cousins my dad and mom helped to get an education, but we had not heard from her again after she returned to her parents' home in Kling, Cotabato. Now that we were all reunited in that evacuation hut, Beth told us she married a soldier assigned to Pendatun's guerrillas. When a group of Moro soldiers returned to Cotabato, they decided to stay behind and join the Filipino guerrillas in our area, those connected with the 109th Military District. As the Japanese executed their massive drive to wipe out the guerrillas, Beth and her husband escaped by following the trail that led toward the Pulangi River, but he drowned in his attempt to cross the river. Beth was too distraught to tell us how she made it to safety. I felt dreadful: our situations seemed so similar, and I knew that I would react the same way if I lost Jack. Since Beth was alone and incapable of looking after herself, we naturally took her in, and she became a part of our family again.

Exhaustion quickly overcame everyone who joined us that day, and they retired early to sleeping places they had staked out in and around the hut. Jack took hold of my hand, and we walked out the front door—we were two young lovers heading off together in the dark. I heard a multitude of birds singing in the night, and the sheer beauty of the evening caused us to clasp hands even tighter. From somewhere in a tree I heard the wise owl hoot, causing me to wonder for a moment if it was really an owl or a signal by the Japanese. I tried to push thoughts of the war out of my head because this was a time for Jack and me, loving newlyweds, not guerrillas, at least for one night. Jack soon spotted a small clearing laden with moss and we sat down together. He had patiently waited so long for this moment to be with me, and it had finally arrived; he kept his embrace gentle yet his kisses were exciting. Then I gave up my virginity and discovered the meaning of heavenly sex in marriage between two people in love. The tender emotion, the sweetness of the hour, and the lovemaking were things I had never experienced before that night. My young body gave in to my husband's need to be loved, and I enjoyed being consumed by his passion. The sweet aroma of wild orchids and Ilang-Ilang blossoms added to the atmosphere of ecstasy, and we made love until we were exhausted. Jack was all man, and I loved him for his gentleness. I have no regrets in saying that we strolled into the forest many more times after that, happy to be in a world of our own. Little did we know that our world, our dreams, our love, and our marriage hung on a thread that was going to be severed then destroyed. Our destiny was not our own—we were both in God's hands.

Jack and I knew that we could not remain in the forest all night and we reluctantly made our way back to the hut, where the others (except for the guard posted outside) still slept. The guard smiled when he saw us returning. Early the next morning we were all awakened by the crowing of an old rooster somewhere in the distance, and even though it was still dark, we had to get a head start before the Japanese arrived on the other side of the river and attempted their crossing. As we ate our breakfast, everyone agreed to stay together as a group, and we quickly left the hut, all of us carrying our own load on our backs or underneath our arms. Rather than staying on an established pathway that might bring us into contact with the Japanese, we moved further inland and made our own trail toward the mountains. It made for tough going because none of us were accustomed to the conditions in the dense jungle. We walked all day and only stopped for short intervals so that we could rest our tired bodies and drink the water we carried in our canteens. Finally we reached the bend of the river, the end of the line, where our only options were to go up or to go down and cross the river without knowing what was on the other side. We all voted to make the climb upward. The treacherous cliff was made more difficult because of the things we carried: back packs, bedrolls, food rations, and cooking utensils. Jack sent one soldier ahead of the group so that he could dig holes in the cliff, which would allow the rest of us to nestle our shoes in the holes to make the climb easier. We all felt drained by the maneuver—my parents suffered the most because of their age—but we were all relieved when we reached the top of the cliff.

Our group had experienced no casualties, but the hot sun, treacherous climb, and general uncertainty about what we would encounter sapped our energy. My clothes, saturated with perspiration, stuck to my body, and the humidity continued to rise. Jack allowed us to rest but not for very long because the people we occasionally ran into on our trek told us that the Japanese continued to follow everyone's trail, led by Filipino spies and native guides who knew the area well. Once we heard this we knew we had to keep moving; however, the further we went into the jungle the more we discovered we had other problems to face.

Underneath the damp and darkened forest lurked blood-sucking leeches. Tropical rains allow the creatures to survive in large numbers because they live on muddy soil or the wet surfaces of tree leaves. Whenever leeches attached their worm-like bodies to human flesh, they sucked up blood to fatten themselves, and the only way to release their hold was to burn them with a lighted cigarette or apply some chewed up tobacco spit. The leeches were like little vampires living on human blood. I still squirm when I think of the time when one attached itself to the tip of my tongue, my anxiety relieved only after I removed the terrible creature. After that everyone teased me for talking too much when I should keep my mouth shut. In addition to the bloody leeches, we dealt with poisonous snakes that hid under rocks or slithered across our path, and since we had no antidote for snakebites we had to be especially careful of them. We also had to face malaria mosquitoes that lived in swamps or in dampened areas underneath the trees; they became not only a nuisance but also a threat to our health since we did not have any quinine. In the course of our evacuation, as we moved in and out of native huts, we did not immediately realize that we had picked up some creepy crawlers from the dirty walls and floors of the shacks we occupied: we all had an infestation of body lice. The disgusting insects had laid their eggs in the seams of our clothing and in our hair, and even though we tried to boil our clothes some eggs remained and the lice multiplied all over again. Like the vampire leeches, the body lice lived on human blood, and only real delousing and new clothing could eliminate them.

The strenuous trek through the jungle and the high mountains took the wind out of my mom. She had difficulty keeping up with the rest of us; the weakened condition of her tiny frame was evident to everyone in the group. We made special stops just so she could rest but I knew that she had reached the peak of her strength and was ready to give up the struggle. Before the setting of the sun on that long, difficult day, Jack located an abandoned nipa hut in a small burnt-out clearing the natives called a "kaing-in." I knew that the former occupants were nomads, people who moved from place to place, clearing a small piece of land, planting their seedlings, and returning when they thought the vegetables or corn had grown enough to be harvested. After each harvest they started the same process all over again somewhere else. Most of the natives in the jungles of Malaybalay preferred to live this way; however, a few of them became Christianized by missionaries who taught them how to read, write, and embrace a Christian God. Even after becoming Christians they continued to live in the same way with their customs and culture, maintaining their chief, a man they called "Datu," who was allowed to have many wives. While the wives did all the work, the datu simply sat around, ate, or went fishing to pass the time away. This was certainly not what the missionaries had expected of them.

At the time I did not know much about the people who lived in the jungles but discovered later that, as with any group of people, they were made up of two kinds: the good guys and the bad guys. The bad ones appeared friendly but had evil intentions—not at all motivated by the war. I learned that a Chinese merchant happened to evacuate in their part of the forest, and the bad natives decapitated him and stripped him of all his belongings. His Filipino servant was more fortunate because he managed to escape and report the murder. Even though we knew about this, we had no other place to hide out except in the vast jungle itself; it was our only possible salvation. As it turned out, the big problem with the path we chose was that we now had three enemies pursuing us: the Japanese in front of us, the unfriendly natives in back of us, and the spies or informers between.

The soldiers in our group investigated the abandoned hut, assured us that the natives had gone, and by nightfall Beth and the soldiers had prepared a hot meal for us. Because of the long journey almost everyone in the group dropped off to sleep immediately after eating, but again Jack had other plans for the two of us. He winked at me, motioned for me to follow him, and we headed out for a stroll into the woods nearby, the brilliant stars lighting our path. When we were far enough away from the hut we spread out a blanket and lay on the ground, Jack's fatigue quickly vanishing as soon as we were in each other's arms again. Our youthful and vigorous passion for one another could not be contained. Although Jack continued to be gentle with me, I understood that he had been deprived of sex for a long time and that he wanted to make up for it, so we did not stop until we were completely exhausted; then we fell asleep in each other's arms. Our jungle honeymoon did not disappoint either of us: we learned we were compatible in every way.

The sound of approaching voices awakened us the following morning, and Jack and I tidied up a bit and returned to the hut. We were puzzled to find everyone still asleep when we got there, so we woke them up, telling them we had heard people approaching. Soon those people came closer and we waited in quiet trepidation to see who they were. They said they were civilians trying to run away from the Japanese, but we were suspicious because they were in fact heading right into the arms of the enemy. We tried to convince them to go another way, but they would not listen, and they left. After breakfast our group gathered up all of its equipment to continue on with our journey to safety, but that particular trail turned into a dead end, so the soldiers had to use their bolos to cut our way out of the heavy vegetation. Having no native guides to lead us, we soon discovered we were lost.

After another long and tiresome day we fortunately emerged in an area occupied by American officers from the ordnance depot in Linabo. Jack was glad to see them again because none of us knew whether they had gotten away during the Japanese attack. Once the alert had sounded that confusing day, the general policy was "Every man for himself" until the guerrilla forces could regroup to assess their position. After they found each other in the jungles that day, the Americans made new plans, ones detrimental to my family: they no longer wanted an old man and three women traveling with them because they believed we would slow them down. This put Jack in a horrible position because he was torn between his desire to join these men or to stay with his wife and her family. Sensing Jack's concern, one of them suggested that he remain with us, and help us continue on with our journey so that we could locate a well-known friendly datu who would protect us. This native chief was Frederick Walter Taylor, a datu known among the missionaries for his belief in God. His Christian faith changed him from a rebel outlaw to a man who cared about others, especially the Americans, and he allegedly had taken in other Americans in the past, willingly sheltering them in his hideout. Once we were settled in a safe location, Jack would send a soldier back to guide the other Americans to our hideout, but this was not destined to happen.

Datu Taylor, four feet eight inches tall, wore a turban wrapped around his head, a cloth that signified his status among his tribesmen. He had jet-black teeth, caused by chewing betel nut. In place of tobacco these natives took a green leaf called "bouyo," spread it with lime powder, made it into a paste, then folded it into a ball, and chewed for hours. Whenever I saw a group of men sitting around all chewing at the same time, they reminded me of a bunch of cows in a barn. The only difference was the red saliva that built up in the men's mouths, which they spit out, leaving a crimson-black color on the floor. Unsanitary to some people, but they did not think so. Even their women chewed this same betel nut because they believed that black teeth made them beautiful, and though I thought they looked ugly, "Beauty is in the eyes of the beholder," and I had to respect their culture for what it was.

The datu took his name, Frederick Walter Taylor, long before World War II. Missionaries came to visit him in the early part of the century and introduced him to the teaching of Jesus Christ in the Bible. Before his conversion he and his men lived as nomads, following a life of crime by killing Filipinos and Christians: stalking, kidnapping, decapitating, and killing their victims meant nothing to them. Only after the datu converted to Christianity did he and his people change their evil ways; they became a peaceful tribe and learned to associate with the outside world. They kept their primitive weapons because these represented their means of hunting wild pigs, deer, monkeys, birds, and snakes and of protecting themselves from rival tribes. The missionaries introduced simple books to the datu's children, who eventually attended the rural schools nearby, and when the children brought the books home, the chief was elated because he wanted to learn the English language himself. In time he adopted an American name to impress his people and the missionaries who became his inspiration. Although the man no longer lives, no doubt many who experienced the war on Mindanao remember him for his unique name and his kind reputation.

When our group finally decided to go find Datu Taylor, Jack left one of his soldiers at the hideout of the American soldiers from the ordnance depot to await his instructions as to how to reach the datu's hiding place. Jack then led our group away from the soldiers and on our way to the datu. Even though a promise had been made on both sides to help each other, it did not end that way: the American officers did not wait around; instead, they made their way to the coastline and joined up with the guerrilla forces in the northern part of Mindanao. Jack never learned that his American friends left us behind, but I did—years after the war was over when I met up with two of them.

My mom soon found it impossible to keep up with the rest of us, and she finally gave up, asking that she be left behind with one of the soldiers. Her weakened body simply could no longer stand the strain of hiding from the Japanese; she wanted to rest for a while and promised that she and the soldier would soon catch up with us. My mom quietly explained that she could no longer keep up with the grueling course we were following, that her feet were full of blisters, her legs had sores, and she was just exhausted. No matter how much I begged her to keep going, no matter how strenuously my dad pleaded and threatened not to go on himself, she refused to budge a step further. She insisted that because she was an old woman, that if the Japanese captured her they certainly would not harm an old lady like her as she was merely a civilian. My mom was only forty-six years old at this time, and I was astonished that she considered herself an old lady. To me, my mom, despite the hardships of war, was bright, vivacious, and funny, not an old lady. She turned to my dad and told him that it was the three of us (he, Jack, and myself) that the Japanese were looking for because we were white and we worked for the guerrillas. She reminded him how much the Japanese hated the whites and encouraged us to go quickly, reminding us that God would be with us until we saw each other again. My dad and I, heartbroken, nevertheless knew she was right, so we reluctantly left her behind with some supplies and a Filipino soldier to look after her.

I struggled with my inner self because I was torn between my love for my mom and my love for Jack. I had a duty to both of them but had to choose one; in the end my mom helped me make the decision to go on with her insistence that my place was with my husband, that I was in more danger than she was because of my American heritage. We hugged each other amid tears and reassurances that we would be together again soon; then we waved good-bye and the soldiers and my family trekked into the forest. That was the last time I saw my mom alive. Our parting words haunted me for more than ten years after the war. I was troubled in my soul with questions: Where should my loyalty have been—to my mom or to my husband? According to my mom's Filipino culture, since children come from their mother's womb and are nurtured by her and blessed by her, they should never abandon her when she needs them. I felt I turned my back on her when I decided to remain with Jack and my dad. I tried to justify my actions with religious teachings, as the Bible teaches that when a man takes a wife, she will leave her mother and father and cleave unto her husband. The conflict between the two beliefs played havoc in my heart and mind for many years after her death. I felt so guilty for having left her.

At the end of the day Jack spotted a large house nestled deep in the forest, crammed with many fleeing civilians trying to recover from their own hardships that day. We were all just trying to get away from the Japanese, to be safe. While some refugees rested their weary bodies upstairs, a few remained under the house, tending fires to cook their meals. As we cautiously approached the house we watched out for spies and collaborators who continued to hound us with their treachery; they could not be identified easily because they dressed like everyone else, mingling with people who claimed they were relatives. Since Jack and my dad felt uneasy about the actual loyalties of some that were in the group, they decided we should distance ourselves and instead choose a place close to the stream that was further ahead. We planned to stay overnight, hoping my mom and the soldier would arrive the next day and we could be together again to continue our journey. Once again when it became dark, Jack and I snuck away, found a quiet place of our own, and made love in the midst of sweet-smelling forest flowers, momentarily losing ourselves in our own world of peace and happiness. We lived on borrowed time because we never knew what would happen from one day to the next.

Some evacuees remained awake all night, fearful of a Japanese attack, so guerrilla soldiers guarded strategic areas to warn them in case the Japanese came while they slept. Children fidgeted in the night because of crowded conditions, while others experienced nightmares because of the trauma they had been through. Jack and I slept after our lovemaking to shore up every bit of our strength for the next day. At about four thirty in the morning an old rooster began crowing, waking us all up, and the four of us decided to move out before the other civilians noticed. Rather than wait for my mom right there, we thought of moving upward in the forest and out of sight, but not too far away from that house, which she and the soldier were certain to find.

The stream on whose bank we spent the next night flowed about a hundred yards from the house; its crystal-clear water came down from the mountains and tasted sweet. Thick bushes covered much of the area so that in certain parts the building was not that visible. Just before we left the area, one of the guerrilla soldiers who had come along with us had a brilliant idea: he told us to walk in the stream as we headed toward the forest so that our footprints would not show on the ground. Since we were all concerned about native trackers, experts in searching for any shoe imprint on the soil, we eagerly followed his suggestion. Giant trees had fallen down across parts of the trail but we continued on, ducking our heads to go under the trees or balancing ourselves while walking on the large trunks of the fallen trees. Even though we left some tracks on dry parts of the huge trees, the wet prints of our shoes dried up in a hurry because of the blazing sun that day.

Tired and hungry from having skipped breakfast we stopped on a hillside clearing to rest, and Beth opened a can of beans that we ate with cold rice. We did not dare build a fire because the Japanese could spot the smoke coming from the trees and could then sneak up and ambush us as we cooked our meal. Satisfied with what food we had to feed our hungry stomachs, everyone stretched out on the grass for a breather since we planned to continue to wait there for my mom's arrival. Suddenly I felt very restless from within, yet I could not understand why; I had an urgent need to backtrack and return to the house we had left earlier. Without telling anyone for fear they would stop me, I simply told Jack that I was going for a walk nearby. He advised me not to go too far away because we were not familiar with these woods. I left the group, walked on the stream, and climbed over the dead logs, making sure all the while that this was the same pathway we followed when we first ascended earlier that morning.

I found my way easily. As long as I did not stray from walking on the same water, I had no problem. I took my time with my walk across the last big tree lying parallel to the stream, being careful not to slip, when suddenly I heard a volley of rifle shots and machine gun fire in the direction of where the house stood. My sixth sense told me those were Japanese weapons because of the amount of shots being fired. I was right, although I did not know this until much later. When I heard the shots I turned around and ran back to my group. Jack spotted me first, came and wrapped his arms around me, and said that I must have heard all those shots because they did too. He feared that the Japanese had run into me and caught me. Some of his concern vanished since I was back, but realizing that the shots were too close for comfort we decided to retreat to a higher place away from the Japanese.

Once again we packed up in a hurry and left while some light remained in the forest; since we did not know our exact location, we made sure not to travel in the dark. By late afternoon the one soldier faithful to Jack who stayed with us spotted a large tree that had a platform built fifteen feet or more above the ground, and a smaller tree leaned on the big one with notches cut out to fit a person's foot. He and Jack decided we should spend the night under that tree. While everyone slept, Jack and I searched for our own private domain, and rather than waste our time in conversation, we simply fell into each other's loving embrace, temporarily forgetting the world around us. We acted as if that was our last evening on earth to be together, so consumed were we with each other's affection. With every precious moment we shared, we realized that our marriage was not a mistake after all. We loved, we laughed, we shared one another's hardships in our struggle to survive, and we lived.

The next day we all sat around in a circle to discuss our plans, and just as we started our cold breakfast, two half-naked men suddenly appeared from nowhere. They both carried spears, and daggers in crudely made sheaths hung on one side of their waists. They wore only a G-string, a narrow cloth strip tied around their waist with a wider piece of cloth about three to four inches in diameter hanging from it and barely covering their crotch.

They had no shirts and wore no shoes. One of them spoke in fluent Visayan, a dialect Beth and I understood perfectly. He wanted to know why we were in their jungle and where we were planning to go. Beth and I, impressed by the fluency of his language, decided to trust him. I do not know why I ever equated language fluency with civility; my instincts had never betrayed me before. I responded that we were looking for the hideout of Datu Taylor, who was a friend of the Americans, and asked if they were members of his tribe. The fellow replied that they knew who the datu was and that they were willing to lead us to him, but we had to leave right away because we had to travel very far to reach the datu's place deep in the jungle.

After I translated to Jack, who was extremely anxious to know what was going on, he agreed with me that this was our only way out; however, we thought it best to have my dad stay behind with the armed soldier in case my mom showed up. Jack and the soldier helped my dad climb up to the tree platform where he looked just fine as he settled in, enjoying the scenery overlooking the forest below, on the alert for his beloved wife. Then Jack instructed my dad to remain with the soldier until we reached our destination and sent someone back for them. Beth, Jack, and I picked up our backpacks and followed the two natives through cogon grass and on into the forest. The two guides led the way, and we trustingly followed. After traveling for two hours in silence, our native guide spoke up, saying that he had relatives waiting in a hut beyond the trees, members of his chief's tribe, but he did not mention the name of the chief. He asked if it was all right for them to come with us.

Without even seeing the ones he spoke of, I agreed that they could join us because I believed that the more natives that were escorting us, the better protection we would have from a Japanese attack. The two men led us to a lean-to hut that had no walls but had wide palm leaves for a roof. We saw several people from a distance; when we approached we found three men dressed in G-strings like our guides and four bare-breasted women wearing short, tight skirts. All of the women had small baskets containing betel nut, lime, and other chewing ingredients dangling from the back of their heads with a braided string that hung behind their backs. One of the men had just finished cooking rice over a small fire, and they motioned for us to eat, as it was noontime. The rice had to be dished out on banana leaves that served as plates, and chips of rock salt sat close by for anyone who needed it to flavor the rice. During their preparations we noticed that they acted friendly, yet they often talked among themselves in whispered tones; but none of us understood that particular dialect. As soon as everyone sat on the floor, we began eating the rice with our fingers because there were no utensils around. I suddenly noticed that when we put our food in our mouths and swallowed, they allowed their rice to drop right back on the banana leaves uneaten. I later learned that with this tribe, not eating with guests was a telltale part of preparing them for death, but as I was unfamiliar with this tribe at that time I did not recognize the sign.

Before we had even finished our meal, the guides hurriedly motioned for us to leave with them, claiming we still had a long way to go. As soon as we hit the trail I realized there were a total of five men and four women, giving us nine guides including the original two, and these natives outnumbered us as they took us deeper into the jungle. While the men led the way, they held their poison-tip spears in their right hands, with their bolos hanging on the right side of their waist. The trail seemed endless because we were worn out from all the hiking that day, and although I looked anxiously with every step, I saw no villages along the way or any signs of the datu and his community of tribesmen. Then I observed other strange behavior by our native guides. When the trail came to a dead end, they cut out their own passageway but only laid wide leaves on our path for us to walk over. Again I did not know that this marked the final signal that death was just around the corner for the three of us: we were sheep being led to the slaughter, and we did not even know it.

I entered a grove after the others and stumbled over a very large tree that had fallen down on an embankment close to a stream about fifty feet below. I felt a terrible pain in my stomach unlike any I had had before, and I began to suspect the natives had put poison in our rice or our water. Whatever the source, the pain simply would not go away. When I finally buckled over, I called out to Jack to stop and help me, that I had an excruciating pain in my stomach and I needed to rest a while. As soon as Jack saw me wrenching in agony, he became deeply concerned, telling me in a kind voice that I had the right idea, that we did need a rest after all the walking we had done. He approached me as he talked, put his arms around my waist, kissed me, then suggested that I stretch my body out along the giant blown-down tree. Beth, in the meantime, decided to cook some rice in an empty pineapple can in preparation for our evening meal, and she thought I should eat a bit of the rice in case my pain stemmed from hunger. She located a level spot near the water's edge, gathered three large rocks from the bank of the stream, placed the rocks in a semicircle, gathered some twigs and dry pieces of wood, and ignited the twigs to start a small fire. While that was going, Beth added the correct proportion of water to the rice and set the can on top of the large rocks with the burning wood underneath. The three of us never ate that meal.

Jack looked astonished at the way Beth managed to put things together to cook the rice; he had never seen such ingenuity before. After the fire got going Jack decided to smoke a cigarette for relaxation. He felt so happy and secure that before leaving my side he unbuckled his gun belt and laid it at my feet. His belt held a .45 automatic pistol, extra ammunition, a mess kit, canteen, and a sheath with a large dagger in it. As far as I can remember Jack always kept that gun belt around his waist, yet for some mysterious reason that day he removed it and left it with me, showing more concern for my own safety than for his. As he headed off to smoke his cigarette, Jack comforted me once by saying that we had traveled a long way but that it would not be long now before we reached the safety of the datu's community. He hugged and squeezed me tight and gave me the longest kiss—our last.

While Jack made his way to the fire below the embankment, I laid my head backward on the old tree, and for a split second I allowed my mind to wander into space, my eyes gazing toward the sky to enjoy its beauty. All at once a soft mysterious breeze blew gently through the trees and surrounded my whole body, just like a mother would caress her child in her arms, and somehow the peace and tranquillity eased the pain in my stomach. The aura of that moment suddenly shattered into a terrible warning scream as I heard Jack's desperate call for me to fire the gun. I quickly rose to my feet and looked on in horror as nine native guides, now turned into assassins, surrounded Jack and Beth. The moment Jack had reached the bottom of the embankment and came close to the fire, the natives positioned themselves so that their innocent victims did not know they were being surrounded. Five men led the vicious attack with their spears and bolos while the women encouraged them to kill their victims. As Jack turned to bend over and ignite his cigarette with a lighted twig, the first native launched his spear with great accuracy and hit him in the back. Jack, surprised and in pain, turned around to give me the warning cry, while the second native, using his bolo, struck a four-inch diagonal deep cut across his forehead. The third man thrust his spear into Jack's heart, causing him to fall backward. I knew he was dead. I had stood petrified for the seconds it took the natives to murder Jack, but still hearing Jack's cry in my head, I finally jolted myself back to reality and reached out to remove his gun from the holster. I pulled the trigger, but the gun would not fire; nervously, I pulled it again and the gun still did not fire. In an instant I realized the safety latch was on, so I released that, aimed with my shaking hand, and fired a third time. That time the gun caused a loud explosion, causing the natives to disappear into the forest; they knew that none of their weapons were any match for a gun. But it was too late to save Jack—he was gone, out of my life forever.

Now holding the pistol in my right hand with more confidence but moving with dread, I walked down the embankment toward Jack and Beth. This time I kept the safety latch off because I wanted to be prepared in case the natives returned to finish me off. I believed they intended to kill us all so that no one would be alive to tell what happened on that dark and dreary day in the jungles of Malaybalay. Had they made a second attempt to attack, I was ready to meet the challenge: it was my life or theirs. Thank God they stayed away, and thank God that He allowed me to survive without a scratch, to tell the world we were attacked by our second enemies, the evil Magahats who lived in the Philippine jungles during World War II.

Even before I reached Jack's still body, I knew he was dead because I had watched as the Magahats inflicted those awful, fatal wounds on him. Then I heard a moaning sound from the opposite side of the place where Beth had tried to cook her rice and saw that she still lived; she lay in a fetal position, rocking back and forth, mumbling words I could not understand. When I called to her she would not answer me, and she was so traumatized from the attack that I had to get close and shake her out of her trance. Only then would she allow me to find out if she was hurt. As I examined her, I had to tighten my stomach so that I would not vomit; despite my wartime medical training, I found it difficult to look at such horrendous wounds on a family member. Two of the natives managed to use their bolos on Beth: while one native almost sliced the thumb off of her left hand, the other cut her in the back of the head deeply, parting her dark hair and leaving a three-inch horizontal wound. He struck a second time with his bolo, cutting her on the right side of her buttocks, resulting in a four-inch vertical wound. The trauma was almost as overwhelming for me, even though I had not been attacked, and I had to keep my wits about me, knowing that the natives still lurked somewhere. We simply had to get out of there as fast as we could.

With this in mind I urged Beth to get up from her sitting position and to help me carry some of the backpacks. I strapped Jack's gun belt around my slender waist and picked up his knapsack and slipped it over my back. Then I walked over to his cold, prostrate body and covered his face with his officer's hat, but I could not even shed tears for the man I loved and married. Even though he saved my life by screaming out for me to fire the gun, I felt no happiness about my lucky survival. I felt nothing. Was I in total shock from witnessing the murder? Perhaps, but I really don't know. My strongest feeling at that point was the urge to scramble out of there. As I placed his hat on his face I whispered, "Good-bye Jack. You will always be in my memory. I love you." Then I went over to where Beth sat, still barely aware of her surroundings, and told her that we had to get out of there, that those natives would return soon to kill both of us. I urged her to hurry.

Beth responded wearily that she wanted to be left alone. With the extent of her injuries she believed that she was finished anyway, so she told me to leave her to die. As she talked, I realized that she was still traumatized, but I still felt agitated because I was trying so hard to save both our lives. I desperately tried to convince her that although her wounds were serious, she was not dead yet, but if I left her there, the natives would return and finish her off. Evidently my words finally penetrated her shock, and with my help she put on her knapsack. I would have carried her backpack, but I already had Jack's and my own plus the military belt wrapped around my waist; although I had a good, strong athletic body I could not haul everything.

Beth and I left the area, slowly making our way above the stream, intending to follow the source of the water to find some evacuees to help us. Picture two teenage girls, one sixteen and horribly wounded, the other eighteen and freshly widowed, alone in that unfamiliar jungle. Our longing to find and connect with some Filipino civilians kept us on the move; even though the two knapsacks and the gun belt weighed me down, I felt my strength stimulated by the desire to get out of this situation alive. I noticed that in addition to my super energy, all my senses had gotten clearer and sharper: smell, sound, touch, taste, and thought had come alive! As Beth and I continued on with our trek, listening carefully for footsteps, I kept Jack's loaded gun in my hand in case of an ambush. Whenever I heard twigs snap I tried to figure out whether the sound came from an animal or the natives, which would pose the biggest danger to us. After half an hour, we came on a clearing leading down toward a stream, and to my horror we found ourselves back in the same place where the natives ambushed us. I saw that Jack's body had been pushed into the stream, his face down in the water, so Beth and I pulled his lifeless body back to the side, faceup, and again I covered his face with his hat. Without a doubt I knew those natives still prowled around trying to find Beth and me because only they could have shoved Jack's body into the running water. More than ever I felt we had to get away from that place, and this time I decided to follow the running stream downward in the hope that that direction would lead us to safety. The light in the forest faded away quickly, indicating that we needed to find somewhere to spend the night. After following that stream for three quarters of an hour we came on a marshy pond, and because of the high embankment on our side, Beth and I had to walk into the marsh clinging to vines and dead trees growing from above the high bank. We started out fine until we reached the middle where we began to sink deeper in the mud—or was it quicksand that we were in? I did not wait to find out. As soon as the chance presented itself I told Beth to grab for the largest vine, and as she tried to pull herself up, I pushed her from below with all the strength I could muster. She had become heavier because she had lost her own strength from the three serious wounds on her body.

As the barest of light came through the trees, I at last managed to get Beth to the top of the embankment, and I followed. Moving a hundred feet away from the side of the marshy pond, I found a level place where we could spend the night; then I cut some wide branches from nearby trees, laid those on the ground, and spread our blanket over them. I also had to set up our mosquito net or else we would have been eaten up by millions of mosquitoes and would have likely contracted malaria, something I did not want to have to deal with at this point in our journey. By the time I finished with getting our bedding together, the rain started—just enough to soak us—and despite having a spare army blanket to cover ourselves, our wet clothing made us miserable. Beth and I were cold and hungry as we tried to get some sleep, Beth moaning in her sleep because her wounds were starting to get infected. I tried to keep at least half awake in case of attack. Falling asleep proved a real struggle for me, anyway: my eyelids felt as if they were screaming for me to let go, but my brain kept fighting to stay awake. Whenever I heard the slightest noise, I reached for Jack's pistol so that I could shoot first and ask questions after. I listened carefully to the sounds coming from the swamp Beth and I pulled ourselves out of, wondering if they were made by crocodiles or iguanas frolicking in the muddy water. Dangers were still all around us.

I knew that I had to rejuvenate my body if we were going to survive the next day, and I desperately tried to cover up with the extra army blanket and get some sleep. The blanket did not help much, so I hit on the idea of sleeping back-to-back with Beth so that our combined body heat would supply us with natural warmth. This worked better than the blanket for a while, but with the continuing rain, I shivered incessantly; so I allowed my mind to wander back to the security of my childhood, where I had my saintly mother by my side. She never failed to come to my bedside every night, where she had me repeat the prayers she learned to ward off any of her fear or anxiety. At that moment in the jungle I longed to be back in my sheltered home with my dad, mom, and three brothers. We had laughter, fun, tears, and conflicts just like any other family, yet we had plenty of love and hugs in our family to make up for all the hurts, misunderstandings, and occasional lack of communication. I believed we were a normal group of individuals who learned from each other about how to get along and live together in peace and harmony. My family, as I remembered that night in the forest, will always be cherished in my memory as the best, because we knew how to live and how to love.

The pleasant flashback to my childhood, my home, and my parents soon had to be set aside because I had to think about the frightening situation Beth and I were in. Beth's condition was uppermost in my mind: I not only worried that she might die but that then I would be left alone to find my way out of the jungle. However, I refused to allow negative thoughts to over-power my sense of hope for our survival. Since everything rested on me, I had to remain strong in body, mind, and spirit. Yes, I now needed to tap into my spirituality; the answer was there all the time in the prayers that my mom taught me as a little girl, especially the Twenty-Third Psalm and the Lord's Prayer. I began to say the words, taking extra comfort in the phrase: "Yea, though I walk through the valley of the shadow of death, I will fear no evil: for thou art with me; thy rod and thy staff they comfort me." When I finished the Psalm, I followed by saying the Lord's Prayer, remembering that as a child kneeling next to my bedside, I repeated this prayer word for word in the presence of my mom, who smiled as she laid her right hand on my little head. As I finished up with this prayer and had spoken the last word of "Amen," I finally fell fast asleep. I am convinced that the power of prayer can truly bring peace, comfort, and assurance that God watches over all of us, even in the midst of a storm that shatters our lives. And my storm continued.

10

A Gift
Worth Living For

A beautiful ray of sunshine broke through the opening in the trees, waking me up the following day. This day had to be better than the day before; I could not think how it could be worse. Beth continued to moan in her sleep, so I left her alone for another half hour to rest, but after thirty minutes I felt nervous and knew it was time for her to rise, help me pack our things, and get out of that place. Before we left, however, I had to check out her grave wounds, and to my horror I saw they were all inflamed and red, sure signs of infection. Reaching into my knapsack I brought out some sulfanilamide tablets; then I knelt on the ground and began chopping away with my little scissors, grinding the tablets to a powder while Beth sat up and said nothing. I had to cut away portions of Beth's hair from the laceration on the back of her head before I could apply the medicine; her passivity made it easier for me to sprinkle the medication on her wound. The rest of the powdered medicine went on her injured hand and her buttocks. After completing my nursing duties, I opened a can of peaches with Jack's dagger, and Beth and I ate everything up—juice and all to quell our starving condition. With Beth still in shock I had to take full charge of the situation: we had to come out of there alive!

The only weapon we had, Jack's gun, was soaking wet, so I decided it was worth the time to clean out the barrel and make sure it would fire again. I turned the barrel away from me to move the topside back and forth to release any bullets lodged in the barrel, then I pulled the trigger. The gun was now safe for me to dismantle so I pressed below the tip of the barrel, releasing the spring, and the gun came apart. Knowing that the firing pin was the key to the whole weapon, I was careful not to lose it. I cleaned out the inner chamber with a dry piece of cloth and put each part back together again, simply reversing the procedure I used when I had taken it apart. Then I tested it by aiming the gun away from Beth and me and pulling the trigger; the firing pin went off—success! I felt triumphant because I had never taken an automatic pistol apart at any time in my life. The only knowledge I had I acquired by watching the men from the ordnance depot working on rifles and guns, so I paused to wonder if my quick memory was hereditary or a gift from God.

Even with Jack's gun, Beth and I were still vulnerable to the native murderers, the Magahats of Tigwa. In daylight the Magahats would surely find us because the forest belonged to them—they were the marauders of the jungle. I later learned that this tribe in the upper Bukidnon and Agusan Provinces was regarded as a real terror; even other natives feared it. Because Beth and I had become their victims but survived, they would not want us to escape and report their heinous crime. I am convinced that the only way we managed to elude them was that the good Lord surrounded us with His invisible, protective shield, preventing us from being seen and then murdered. The natives' vision seemed thwarted as long as Beth and I remained in the dense jungle, and we were thankful in our hearts; but I could not remain passive and rely solely on God's help. I needed to take action.

Never having lived inside a jungle and deprived of any expert assistance, I thought hard about our dilemma. I recalled what my dad used to tell me as a child about using common sense; somehow I knew there would be an answer. My nerve cells jittered as I searched for answers to this puzzle, and all of a sudden my wired brain stopped at the right place. My history teacher in grade school once told my class that usually the origin of rivers and streams comes from the high mountains, that if you follow along the bank, you will eventually end up in civilization again. I realized how much that made sense, the same common sense that my dad drummed into me.

With this in mind Beth and I set out in search of the Pulangi River; all I had to do was listen for a certain sound. I completed the packing because Beth still sat motionless and useless, but soon we were off on our mission to find the river. I kept Beth ahead of me in case she stumbled or fainted from the pain of her wounds. After an hour of walking through the jungle my ears perked up when the sound of flowing water became clear, and it did not take us long to arrive at the bank of the Pulangi River. God smiled on us again because the river water rested at its lowest point, allowing us to make the crossing without any problem. The only deep spot Beth and I had to go through was in the middle of the river, where the water came up to our waists, but even though the depth frightened us there was no turning back now. I was even more determined to distance us from our murdering guides. Just as we emerged from the water I heard loud voices coming toward us, and I could tell they belonged to natives because the voices used a dialect I was not familiar with. Quickly hiding behind some big boulders, we watched as they came through the trees. I summoned all my courage, peeked to find out who they were, and sure enough I saw four half-naked men talking to one another as they approached the bank of the river only fifty yards from where Beth and I hid. Raising my finger to my lips I motioned my cousin to keep silent at any cost, my right hand tightly gripping Jack's gun, making ready to shoot if we were discovered. Luckily the natives did not see us; they crossed the river and disappeared in the dense forest. Only then did Beth and I come out from behind the rocks and continue to follow the water downstream. We were still lost, but at least we were on the safe side of that river—that made me breathe a little easier.

The cogon grass had grown thick along the riverbank of the Pulangi, and because there were no paths for us to follow, we made our own. Shortly after going through the cogon, Beth and I found ourselves back in the forest again. I made sure we stayed close to the sound of running water to better our chances of survival, but this all proved exhausting for poor Beth. She cried out from the pain of her wounds, yet I could not allow us to stop; so we walked until I became hungry, and then we finally rested. After finding a spot where I could leave Beth within the safety of some bushes, I told her to lie down while I went in search of some berries we could eat. She hesitated at first because she did not want to be left alone, but when I assured her that I would not be too far away, she allowed me to go. I found an abundance of wild berries a short distance away, gathered as many as I could, and brought them back so we could feast on fresh fruit. The food did not revive Beth; instead, she complained again about the pain from her wounds. I pulled her panties down because the buttock wound seemed to bother her the most and I was horrified by what I saw: several fat maggots were feasting on the wide-open wound there. The white pudgy things squirmed about in the four-inch vertical wound. I told Beth to stretch out on her stomach and I went to work picking out each maggot with my tweezers, the best I could do since I was completely out of the sulfa drugs. I could only hope that those little pests would not return because I did not know how long we would remain in the jungle without any medical treatment for Beth.

With Beth still in pain and me grimly determined to secure our survival, we continued our journey through the forest. I worried about Beth's infected wounds, and I knew her thumb could easily fall off her hand if she did not get help in time. The humidity rose with the heat of the day, soaking our clothing with perspiration, yet I was happy to know that every step took us further away from the murderous crime scene. By late afternoon I spotted a hut on the hillside and we got excited; surely whoever lived there could help us. As we got closer, though, I realized it was uninhabited, empty and silent except for the sound of the wind whistling through the hillside. While Beth rested, I scouted around for food. I spotted a camote (sweet potato) patch and some corn growing close by, and I plucked a few ears of corn, removed the husk from one of them, and immediately devoured it. A few papaya trees grew there as well, and I helped myself to some of that fruit. Then I returned to Beth with some of everything that I had found, and we ate the green stuff without taking time to cook them. Once our famished and tired bodies had been satisfied I heard the sound of the crickets all around us; their audible noise told me that darkness was about to close in on us. To avoid the possibility of another ambush we removed ourselves from that hut, crawling under some bushes a long way from where we ate, spreading our blankets out just before we fell asleep. This day had been only marginally better than the day before.

A bunch of noisy birds called *kalaw* (toucans) woke me the next day. These fairly large birds, longtime inhabitants of the forests in the Philippines, have brightly colored yellow and brown feathers with bright red beaks. I allowed Beth to sleep while I returned to the sweet-potato patch to gather some of the vitamin-rich leaves, and the tubers themselves tasted good after cooking. I stopped to pluck a few more ears of corn for our meal, making sure that the corn silk, which I used for my cigarettes that drove away the pesky mosquitoes, remained intact. I thought Beth would be thrilled with the food; instead, she only shook her head, wordlessly. Her reaction troubled me but there was nothing I could do. The day passed quickly and quietly, and we spent another night in the bushes to build up our strength for the next phase of our journey. But then on the third day, as I began to cook our meal, two half-naked natives, one carrying a spear and the other sporting a bolo, appeared at the entrance of our hiding place. I had not heard any footsteps coming toward us or any conversation between them; they seemed to have dropped in from nowhere. The moment I saw them, the hairs on the back of my head stood out in fright, and as I reached for the gun, one of the natives spoke in Visayan, asking who we were and what we were doing in the bushes.

Understandably, I did not trust them, so I responded that Beth and I were evacuees who had become separated from a larger group and had become lost. After the ambush Beth and I had been through, perpetrated by natives dressed just like these two, I had to be careful about the information I gave them. The observant young man noticed Beth's swollen hand and spoke again, wanting to know how she had come to be so badly wounded. I told him that Beth had fallen into some sharp bamboo stakes, which resulted in a severe cut, then I asked which tribe they were from and how they found us.

The response came quickly from the second native who claimed that he was the son of Datu Frederick Walter Taylor, that they saw our smoke from above the bushes so they came to investigate. Then he offered to take Beth and me to his father, assuring me that he had two Filipino men staying in their camp across the river. Concerned with Beth's infected wounds and the fat maggots that kept coming back, I decided to take a chance and go with them—after everything that had happened, I had to take something on faith. As Beth and I put our things together the natives watched us closely, and when we were ready to leave, they suggested that we walk ahead of them, but I refused. I had learned that much from the last time, and I wanted to keep an eye on them from behind; should they make a false move, Jack's gun would protect Beth and me. The two natives led us downstream, much to my relief, and then we crossed the river once more, with the low waterline in our favor. Returning to the dense jungle did not bother me because I was preoccupied with watching those natives, and I could not wait to meet the Filipinos at the datu's hideout. A few hours later, when we came on a large group of people clustered together in the forest, I had difficulty in recognizing the Filipino men right away because they were dressed like the natives. After Beth and I had rested, two Filipinos with visibly distended stomachs came toward us, addressing us in Visayan. I immediately asked them their names and why they were here with these people. I also wanted to know what caused their swollen bellies.

One of them answered that they were evacuees who had fled from the Japanese and that Datu Taylor had generously taken care of them. Their big stomachs, he explained, developed from suffering from malaria without any medicines to treat it, and he believed there was no cure for their malady. To me they looked like women in their ninth month of pregnancy. After conversing again with Filipinos, knowing they were indeed among the natives, I felt released from the anxiety that began when the two natives showed up at our hiding place. At last I believed that our lives were no longer in jeopardy. After my conversation with the two men, Beth and I were led to the datu's hut; once inside, to my surprise the chief asked if I was the daughter of the one-armed American.

This query made me nervous, but I had to find out if my dad had met the same tragedy as Jack, even though the knowledge might be painful for me. I admitted that I was his daughter and asked the datu if he knew where my dad was and whether or not he was all right. The chief smiled, displaying black teeth in the upper and lower parts of his mouth, and said the words I had prayed for: my dad was safe in the datu's other camp. If I wanted to hear from him, I could write a short note and a messenger would deliver it. I found a piece of paper in my pack, scribbled a few words, signed it, and a native courier left immediately with the note. Then, assured that this man was indeed Datu Taylor, I told him all about our tragic ambush in the jungle and how Beth had received her wounds. He appeared agitated and sad and explained to me that, without a doubt, Beth and I had been taken to Tigwa, deep in the forest, a place that his own people dreaded. He said that it was a miracle that Beth and I came out alive because the vicious Magahats made sure to kill all of their victims. The datu asked to see Beth's wounds, and I undressed them for him; when he saw the festering wound in her buttocks he squirmed with uneasiness. Then he mixed a new batch of betel nut, began chewing it, and as soon as he was ready, Beth turned over on her side and he commenced spitting on the wound. The moment the juices hit those maggots they dropped to the floor and died, leaving me marveling at the application of this native medicine because I had never seen it before. In a few days the datu's treatment began to heal Beth's wounds. What a miracle!

The first night Beth and I slept at Datu Taylor's campsite, a severe storm broke, and the rains came pouring down. When thunder and lightning struck with loud intensity, I watched in terror as all of the chief's men grabbed their spears and thrust them into the grass roofs of their open huts. I quickly reached for Jack's gun, fearing that the men intended to kill Beth and me, but as soon as the chief saw the terror in our faces, he calmed our fears by explaining what was happening. He told us not to be afraid, that his men would not harm us. On a stormy night like this one, their enemies the Magahats liked to roam the forest floor and attack them while they slept, killing the men and taking away the women and children for slaves. In preparation for such an attack, the datu's men kept an all-night fire burning and had their weapons ready for defense. With those reassuring words Beth and I settled in our corner of the hut and fell asleep; fortunately nothing bad happened that night, so I was very relieved. When I heard the sound of rice being pounded in a hollow log the next morning, I got up and stretched out. The women did not pay attention to their two visitors because of their busy chores, and they continued to separate the rice from the husk by pounding it out. Then they placed the crushed kernels in a semicircular flat basket and winnowed this against the wind so that the chaff separated from the grains of rice. Just before the men left to hunt for wild game in the forest, the chief approached me, asking if he could borrow Jack's gun to hunt with. I had to think fast for myself and for the chief because I could not bear to part with that gun, both for sentimental reasons and for safety reasons, and I could not afford to insult the chief. I told him that the gun belonged to my dead husband, that he made me swear never to part with it, and surely the chief would not want me to break a promise to a dead man. Whether he understood me or not, I was relieved that he did not insist on his way; instead, he turned around and ordered his men to bring back some good meat from the jungle.

At noontime the courier returned with a note for me, and when I opened it I immediately recognized my dad's handwriting. He wrote that he had heard about the tragedy of Jack's death and Beth's wounds. He advised me to stay where we were until she got better, and then we would come and join him at the other camp. After reassuring me that he was all right, he signed his name, with love. I wept with joy because next to Jack, my dad was the person I was closest to, and he was alive!

Beth and I passed the next four or five days living among Datu Taylor's people and although I appreciated their hospitality and protection, I became restless. I wanted to be reunited with my dad; I needed to see him, to hug him, to make sure that he was in fact all right. I also began to worry about the wording of his note because although he said he was fine, he mentioned nothing about my mom, and that left a cold feeling in the pit of my stomach. Two Filipino soldiers armed with rifles stumbled into the camp one day, and when they discovered I was leaving to meet up with my dad, they decided to come along and protect Beth and me on our way. I thanked the chief for all the kindness and hospitality he had shown us, shook his hands, and told him that someday his name would be known for helping Americans and Filipinos lost in his jungle during this awful war. This pleased him immensely, and he returned my thanks. When Beth and I left his hideout, he made sure that his son and one other native came along to show us the way; it was the best way for us to find my dad. The long hike took all day and we grew fatigued, so the men located an abandoned house in the forest where we stopped for a good night's rest. The chief's son and his companion offered to hunt for meat to go with our rice, and in a short time the chief's son reappeared with a dead monkey in his hands. While the fire was blazing, he tossed the animal into the hot coals to remove all its fur then placed the beast in the water boiling over the fire. When the meat was done and removed from the pot, the monkey's eyes were still open; it looked like a human being. But because hunger knows few bounds, one of the soldiers remarked that "It's either you or me, bud," and he ate the meat with gusto. I tasted a little but my stomach would not allow much more; I kept thinking about my own pet monkey.

We all slept in the house without any sides around it, but I felt safe because our Filipino guards stayed close. The following morning I awoke to discover that Beth was gone; frantic that something bad might have happened to her I interrogated the others, but no one knew anything. Then I called her name out loud from outside the house, and within a couple of minutes I saw Beth coming out of the woods with the chief's son behind her. Still upset about her sudden disappearance, I demanded to know where she had been, reminding her that we still had a long way to go to reach the datu's other camp and that we needed to leave as soon as possible.

Beth's rather blank expression suddenly changed to one of belligerence, and she announced that she was not going anywhere with me because she was staying behind with the chief's son. Then she stalked off into the house. Her abrupt tone and nasty behavior shocked me, but I tried to contain myself. I did not understand why she was no longer interested in going to stay with my dad, in finding the security of family. I followed her into the hut to get some answers from her, and when Beth continued to give me a hard time, I lost my senses: with my clenched fist I gave her a hard jab across her jaw and she fell to the floor. Then I jumped down on her, got her by the throat, and started yelling that she was an ungrateful witch. After I had nursed her and taken care of her all this time after the attack, now she was turning her back on me, and I just did not think that was right.

The soldiers witnessed my rage, so they quickly pulled me off Beth, and their physical restraint made me calm down and realize what I had done. I felt terrible. All of the emotions bottled up in me simply exploded at that time: I felt a delayed rage over Jack's death and took it out on the only other person who survived the attack. Was I so uncharitable as to be angry that Beth survived and Jack did not? It was a terrible thought but it may have contained some truth. I understood then that I could not convince Beth to leave with me, so she stayed with the chief's son and the other natives. That was the last time I saw her. Years later I found out that she had married the datu's son but she soon went out of her mind completely, which did not surprise me, considering what she had been through, and I felt guilty for a long time about leaving her behind. There is a superstitious belief among the Filipinos about the natives and a certain magic potion. When a drop of this liquid is mixed in with the water or food of the person they desire, the man or woman will go into a trance; they are hypnotized. There are also stories of Lom-ay, a kind of mind control. Sometimes I think that this is what happened to Beth, that one of the natives preyed on her weak mind, convincing her to leave me.

My guilt over leaving Beth was offset by my joy over seeing my dad again. Just as we spotted each other from a distance, we ran toward each other and hugged and cried. Then came the hard part: after we sat down my dad wanted me to tell him all about how our native guides viciously murdered Jack. I struggled through retelling that story, feeling like I relived it, and my dad had a hard time hearing it. After a few moments of silence, after I ended my story, he began to talk, telling me things that I did not want to hear. He said that after Jack, Beth, and I left him, some Filipino soldiers who had gotten away from the Japanese came on the platform where he rested. They told him that my mom had been caught at her resting-place when the Japanese surrounded the house, shooting at the civilians inside the house. My brother Philip, who had miraculously caught up with my mom, had been at the stream getting some water for her, and when he heard all the firing, he rushed back to her but fell into the hands of the Japanese who took them both prisoners. The Japanese brought them back to Mailag, stripped off their clothes, and tortured them. Then my mom and Philip were transferred to Malaybalay, where the Japanese put them in the stockade, anticipating that the knowledge of their capture would convince my dad and me to surrender.

I could not believe what I was hearing: my beloved mother and my wonderful baby brother were in the hands of the Japanese. Difficult as it was for my dad and me to know this, we decided not to surrender because we knew it would not help their situation, that it would mean certain death for us all. In our hearts we both believed that my mom would not want it any other way. For my dad and me to surrender when we had the freedom to live and carry on the fight would be closing the book on our lives—we might all be together again, but it would be the last time. The Japanese would kill us all. What I could not understand was why my mom had to be the sacrificial lamb for her only daughter and her husband. Despite my strong faith, it was too complex for me to comprehend.

My dad also related something else that happened while he sat on the platform high up in the big tree. After Jack, Beth, and I had gone, he filled his pipe and began smoking it. All of a sudden a beautiful woodpecker with a bright red beak appeared in front of him and began pecking away on the tree trunk across from where he was sitting. He took that as a bad omen because he felt spooky after the bird left the tree. To this day I have no idea where my dad got that superstitious belief about the woodpecker: it may have been from some of his travels around the world as a soldier in his youth, or it really may have been a premonition.

When all was said and done, after we had exchanged our devastating news, we had to decide what to do next. My dad thought we should get out of Malaybalay and head for Talakag, where his old friend Colonel James Grinstead, also a World War I veteran, presided over a guerrilla stronghold. I knew the trip would take days because several hundred miles of unfamiliar, treacherous mountains and jungles separated the two places. As my dad and I considered moving on, heavy night rains swelled the Pulangi River far above the waterline. The torrential downpour sent mud and all kinds of debris flowing with the speed of lightning, an awesome, terrifying sight.

Datu Taylor, sympathetic to our plight and our flight from the Japanese, came to visit my dad and me down at the river, and when he learned about our plan he suggested that we take a raft and follow the river downstream. He was positive that the Japanese would not be expecting anyone to travel by water because the river was so flooded. With some apprehension we agreed. Without wasting any precious time the datu ordered his men to build the sturdiest raft with the largest bamboo poles they could find in the forest, securing each pole with strong vines they gathered from the trees. The raft turned out to be a masterpiece, completed in just a few hours. As soon as it was ready, my dad and I thanked Datu Taylor for his help and loaded our few things on the raft, and then the chief ordered one of his best raftsmen to serve as navigator so that we would safely get over the dangerous waters. That man, carrying a long pole in both his hands, went on the raft first, then I seated myself in the middle part, and my dad settled on last. Our seating arrangements had to be just right in order to have a good balance on that raft. When everything was ready the chief gave a hard shove to the raft and the rapidly flowing current quickly picked us up, carrying us away on our precarious journey on that wild river.

At first we were off to a good start, as the raftsman maneuvered the raft with the bamboo pole in his skilled hands. But then the ride turned scary as large granite rocks suddenly appeared, so the man had to guide the raft around them in the fast flowing water so that we would not crash. Still he managed well until we came to a sharp bend in the river, and before the guide realized what was happening the raft bashed against a big rock then capsized, throwing us all into the water. I ended up under the raft with the knapsack still on my back, holding my breath, but my immediate concern was for my dad because he could not swim—his one arm would not allow him to last long in that turbulent water before he sank to the bottom. Remembering my swimming days at Silliman, I used both my hands under the bamboo poles, working my way around until I reached the edge of the raft. Finally, my head bobbed out of the water, I gulped down fresh air, at the same time looking beyond the edge of the raft where I saw my dad's campaign cap floating. Holding on to the tip of the raft I reached out to grab the hat with my right hand, lifted it up, and there under that hat was the face of my dad. It was a miracle! From then on every moment counted so I pulled his body over and helped him back on the raft before I got out of the water myself. As soon as we resettled on the raft and started on our way again, with no ill effects from our ordeal, the river became wider and more smoothly flowing. I felt relieved to have averted what might have been a terrible tragedy for my dad and me.

As we traveled more easily on the raft, I spotted a group of civilians on one side of the river who called for us to land, assuring us that it was safe. When we did, it felt good to be among the Filipino people again, especially when we found out that some of them were our friends from Mailag. They repeated the same sad story that the soldiers told my dad about the capture of my mom and brother, and they too became teary-eyed, expressing their hatred of the Japanese who showed no mercy to the civilian women and children they captured.

My dad and I lost most of our possessions when the raft capsized in the river; only the one knapsack remained, and I kept it strapped on my back. Our friends gave us clothing and blankets to replace the things we lost, a kindness I found overwhelming because I knew they did not have much to spare. My gratitude did not extend to telling them our intended destination, however, because the fear of collaborators remained my greatest concern. After eating a very welcomed hot meal, my dad and I left our old friends, headed northwest through cultivated farmlands and meadows, disguised with mud on our faces so that we would look more Filipino. Hiding behind the muddy clay did not do the trick for my dad, though, because the mud never completely covered his very white complexion, and his six-foot frame and blue eyes always gave him away. Even from a distance, people could observe the "Americano" traveling with his daughter, and some even recognized us as the Dore family. I was amazed to find out how well known we were on the island.

The first day of our land trek ended with our sleeping in an open field next to a farm. We situated ourselves next to a carabao wallow where, during the middle of the day, the beast rolled around in the muddy water to cool itself off. At night, however, the wallow became a breeding ground for millions of mosquitoes; still, we had to sleep next to it because my dad and I believed that the Japanese would not think anyone would be so foolish as to be out there—but we were. Spreading our mats on dry grass we tried to sleep, to rest up for the long journey ahead of us. The moon and the stars, our only light, reminded me of the beautiful universe God made for us, but my tranquil, peaceful moments did not last because of the "dive bombers," those mosquitoes that bit us everywhere. My biggest concern was for my dad: to think that he had to be subjected to a life like this when he had such a wonderful life before the Japanese army invaded the country we loved. It was sad indeed. Even though he suffered mightily through all of this, my dad did not complain; instead, he kept up my spirits by encouraging me to keep a stiff upper lip.

At dawn the next day we had to rise quickly and make use of the early hours when the Japanese patrols were not around. We still had to cross a major highway controlled by the enemy; their military convoys made frequent trips to and from Malaybalay on that road, so we had to make sure our timing was right. Having women, children, and old men along with us made the trip risky: a frightened child might suddenly panic and give away our position with his cry, or another child might stumble and fall and panic everyone in the group. Some families refused to leave their carabaos behind, animals that walk like turtles, taking their time and ignoring their master's whip, slowing everyone down. What still concerned me the most was the possibility that collaborators or spies could be among us, just waiting for the moment to alert the Japanese so that we could all be captured. However, I tried to focus on making a successful escape. I helped to brief each family we had collected along the way with proper instructions, encouraging them to be strong and focused as they made their dash across that highway. To convince them that there was nothing to it, my dad and I volunteered to make the first crossing. Miraculously, nothing bad did happen. Once we reached the other side safely, the rest followed in our footsteps, and we all rejoiced in our accomplishment.

We still had a long journey ahead of us as we continued up mountains and through valleys and jungles, heading toward Talakag, Bukidnon. The terrain was sometimes steep, and we struggled every inch of the way. When we arrived at the first mountain peak I saw the most beautiful valley below, populated with several deserted huts (at least I assumed they were abandoned because I saw no signs of active life). Before descending to the valley we decided to take a much-needed rest because the blazing sun had propelled temperatures to over one hundred degrees, sapping our already limited strength. For the first time I noticed a significant decline in my dad's health. Turning to one of the civilians who had brought some of his farm animals with him, I addressed him as "friend" and asked if he would mind lending me one of his carabaos because my poor father could no longer walk on account of his failing health. The good fellow, seeing the haggard and sickly condition of my dad, graciously agreed. Two men had to help my dad get on the carabao, but he kept losing his balance, so they finally had to tie him to the beast to keep him from falling off. Yes, it seemed like an undignified thing to do yet there was no other way, for my dad could not walk on his own, and the gradual downhill slope on those mountains was worse than some of the climbs we had on muddy trails. It was all very dangerous.

Once we reached the valley floor, each family, including my dad and me, headed for a hut so we could lay our tired bodies on the floor inside. I was confident we had distanced ourselves from the Japanese and believed a stay in that valley would help us recuperate from our ordeal. I untied my dad from the carabao, helping him into the hut where he could be sheltered from the blazing sun and lay his head on the cool bamboo. The sight of his body as just flesh and bones brought tears to my eyes, but I had to be strong for both of us; I had to suppress everything that had happened to my family and me in the past months, or I would break down and lose control. Like it or not I had to maintain my strength, even though I had never envisioned myself as a leader in the family.

Since hunger was our most constant companion (along with fatigue), I then scouted around to see what I could find to fill our stomachs. After I settled my dad comfortably inside the hut I heard a wonderful sound: a hen scratching around for food outside. I moved quietly to the area beneath the hut, grabbed a good piece of wood for a weapon, then took aim at the chicken's head. I hurled that wood with all my might, knocking the hen out cold. I went into the hut to get Jack's dagger so I could chop the hen's head off. The rest was easy because as a little girl I used to watch my mom and the maids prepare live chickens for scrumptious meals, and having a memory like an elephant, I remembered every step exactly as it was done. Just as the chicken was cooking nicely in the pot, I heard a loud warning call: "Japanese! The Japanese are coming down from the peak of the mountains!" I rushed outside where a group of people was pointing up to the very same place we had been a few hours before. Somehow the Japanese trackers managed to pick up our trail after all and followed us.

I dashed back in to the house to awaken my dad, and I got him tied to the carabao once more so that we could get away. Next I strapped Jack's gun belt around my waist because I could not leave behind the only weapon in my possession, but I did have to leave the boiling chicken as we fled to the jungle to find sanctuary. We had to keep going because we did not know how fast the Japanese could pursue us during the early afternoon hours. I do not even know how long we stayed on the run that afternoon; it seemed forever, but as long as we distanced ourselves from the Japanese we remained alive. By the time we reached the mountain village of Basak that day, I realized my dad was fading fast. The man I once knew as robust, warm, full of fun and laughter, with an outgoing personality, was a mere skeleton close to death. He suffered from malnutrition, beriberi, dehydration, and mounting depression. The thought that the Japanese had tortured and imprisoned his beloved wife caused him great guilt and remorse—he believed he should have been by her side. He regretted that he was not in her place so that she would be free to be with me.

To try and analyze why the Japanese committed such atrocities on the civilian population during World War II requires a deep look into their religious and military institutions. Such an analysis would only go a short way, however, in adequately explaining this utter absence of humanity. Although I mourned for everyone's losses, what concerned me the most was how the Japanese treated my mother and my brother. My mom held no real value as a prisoner because she knew nothing about what went on with the military: she was a housewife and loving mother her whole adult life. Her only real crime was being married to a white man—my dad. The Japanese hated all white men who sided with the Americans, especially if they helped the guerrillas. So my mom's guilt was by association and loyalty rather than by any overt action.

In addition to guilt over my mom's imprisonment my dad's health declined because he had received word, through the vast jungle grapevine, of the death of his youngest son, Philip. Neither of us could truly believe that this beautiful boy was dead. My dad could not accept the fact that in a very short time the Japanese worked Philip to death building an airstrip. When he had become ill with cerebral malaria and could no longer work, they beat him to death. The other prisoners wrapped Philip's body in a mat and buried him in the cemetery across the street from the Bethel Church; he did not even merit a coffin. I know about that grave because a few years after the war I returned to Malaybalay to visit the graveyard where my brother's body lay buried. The place was unkempt, with tall grass growing all over the cemetery; however, I managed to find the crude wooden cross with his name on it, and I wept as I prayed for him.

In addition to these psychological traumas, lice had invaded my dad's body, infesting his hair, his eyebrows, and every place in his clothing. They multiplied constantly, no matter how much I boiled his clothing. The native huts swarmed with these pests, and I wondered how those people lived with these vampire insects; and as long as we occupied some of those huts, the contamination and infiltration of the body lice continued. Nursing my dad proved a constant challenge for me because I had no medicine to help his condition. His eyes became sunken and his voice weakened, and even the sponge baths I gave him every day did not revive him. Every time I tried to help him, he responded to my efforts by simply looking at me with mounting tears in his eyes, tears that I believed were for me since he knew I would be alone after his death.

Sometime at the end of 1943 our group, finally a safe distance from the Japanese, received word that American submarines had successfully brought supplies to Mindanao from Australia. The subs dropped off guns, ammunition, medical supplies, food rations, and other equipment for the guerrilla units throughout the island. Even better, at least from my perspective, was the news that when all the cargo was unloaded, the submarines took American civilians and their families out of the country. Some of the deathly ill American soldiers also evacuated from the island for medical treatment in Australia. This information exhilarated me for two reasons. First, it meant that the Japanese were being driven out of the Philippines, and second, it meant that I could secure some help for my dad. Although he had been born in England, he served in the United States Army from 1901 to 1907, retiring with a veteran's pension. Furthermore, my dad had applied for citizenship in 1901 and by all accounts he had become an American citizen; therefore, I believed he was eligible to be taken out by submarine for treatment in a military hospital somewhere in Australia. With this in mind I struggled harder to keep him alive.

In February 1944 the opportunity for our evacuation arose. Once notified, I only had a day and a half to get my dad and me down to the coast where a submarine had surfaced in a secret rendezvous coordinated by the guerrillas. If I could have accomplished this, my dad would have had a fighting chance to survive. I know now that if we had taken one of the submarines to Australia, my destiny would have taken another turn with an entirely different ending. But that did not happen. I could not prepare my dad for that rendezvous or for any other subsequent one: he was simply too sick to be moved. On leap year day, February 29, 1944, my dad, the hero of my childhood, my mentor, and my inspiration for living, breathed his last and was gone. He was only 66 years old. His courage, fortitude, and zest for living had always been an inspiration to me, and he made me believe that I was as good a soldier as he was. Once again I did not even have the opportunity to cry because now that I was totally alone, I had to act quickly. Looking back, I believe I learned the toughness of a soldier from my dad, because he often said that real soldiers never cry—they just take things on the chin and keep their heads high. He also constantly reminded me that I was a chip off the old block and that I should never forget it. So I was still determined to survive, to make him proud of me.

Next to the hut my dad and I occupied lived a handful of civilian evacuees who felt sorry for me when they heard about my dad's death. Without a word they came and measured his body and built a coffin out of boards they found lying around on the ground. To this day I do not know how this wood just happened to be around because it was a valuable commodity during the war, but at least this meant that he would have a proper burial. As the coffin was being prepared, two of the natives who used to occupy the hut came in from the jungle. They heard about the dead American and were very concerned that his body and the coffin be taken out of the window rather than through the front door. They believed that by doing this, they would ensure that the spirit of the dead would not return to haunt them. Otherwise, if the body were taken through the doorway, his spirit would return in the same manner to dwell among them; the natives did not like this idea one bit. Whether American, Filipino, or native, they refused to have any spirit come back and live in their midst. What could I say? It seemed harmless enough, so I complied with their wishes. Careful not to drop my dad's body, the men gently lowered the coffin through the window, then followed a pathway leading to a meadow about four hundred feet away from the hut, where they dug a hole in the ground for final burial. When they reached a depth of six feet they lowered the coffin in the ground and covered it with dirt. After saying a prayer I asked to be left alone with my dad, so they returned to their huts. I knew my dad wished to be buried with military honors, with the firing of guns in the air as a last salute to a departed soldier, and I decided to give him that honor. My own version of honoring my dad differed slightly, but it was the best I could do. I removed the pistol from the holster on my waist, raised my right arm above my head and slowly fired one, two, three, four, five, six shots in the air, and it was all over. Yes, the old soldier never died, he just faded away—with grief and guilt.

When I returned to the hut, the civilians were glad to see me because when they heard those shots they feared I had taken my own life out of grief. I remained in the hut for one more night where I replaced the empty cartridge with bullets and slept with the gun in my hand. Everyone knew that I had this powerful weapon and after hearing the shots I fired, they understood I was no novice in using the weapon for my defense. Jack's automatic pistol was my last means of protection because I was alone in the world, without a father, mother, husband, or brothers to guard my life.

The next morning I joined a group of the civilians making an early start for Talakag. One of the families had taken me in temporarily because they felt sorry for me, and they even lent me their only horse so that I could ride with the wind. Although I never told them I once had a horse of my own that I had named Aspirin, they recognized that I had some knowledge about horses. Poor Aspirin, I had abandoned her in Mailag when the

Japanese made their surprise attack, and I knew that by now she had been butchered for food. Very often during the war people resorted to killing some of their pack animals so they could feed themselves and the soldiers. I discovered in the course of this war that carabao meat was about the toughest meat to cook; it never got tender and always tasted like dry leather. Horse meat and monkey meat, though, did not taste so bad, but I would not want either for everyday meals.

This group moved at a very slow pace because of all the animals and the various ages of the family members, so I asked my adopted family if I could ride ahead of the group. As soon as they agreed, my youthful vigor came back, my worries disappeared, and I galloped the horse along the trail. The animal picked up enough speed so that the wind on my face invigorated me; I felt like I was sixteen again and without a care in the world. The excitement of being on a horse even made me forget my grief over my dad's death. When I reached a bend where I could not see the road ahead, a large python slid silently across the trail, the horse saw the slithering creature and made a sudden stop, almost throwing me off the saddle. Holding tightly to the bridle and the thick hair behind the animal's head, I managed to keep myself from being thrown to the ground, but as I bent over hard from the waist down to keep myself from falling, I developed a terrible abdominal pain. The weeks had gone by very fast since my dad and I had first reached Basak, but even before he died I noticed that I had put on a lot of weight. Although I would not say I appeared fat, somehow I became uncharacteristically plump. The two Filipino men back in the jungles with Datu Taylor came to my mind, so I wondered if I had the malaria symptoms that they told me about. Their bellies protruded, and although mine was not that bad, it was getting big. I was too busy nursing my dad to think more about it, so I simply accepted that I had contracted malaria, and I thought my stomach pain that day was somehow connected to malaria. What a naive assumption! Luckily, when the pain hit I was just a short distance from Colonel James Grinstead's headquarters, where I knew I could get some help.

By the time I arrived at the post I had difficulty getting off the horse because of the severe pain. A couple of soldiers noticed my distress, came to help me alight from the horse, and took me inside the nearest building. They summoned the military doctor immediately and had me lie down on a cot while I waited for him; it felt so good to rest on something soft and comfortable. The doctor examined me right away and surprised me with his diagnosis: I was pregnant. This news stunned me into silence. Wow! How could it be that I was nurturing a child, Jack's child, in my body? During the months since Jack and I got married I did not recall experiencing any morning sickness, nausea, or cravings, nor did I feel any movement in my abdomen—absolutely nothing. Perhaps I simply never had the time to feel all those symptoms because of my preoccupation with murder, caring for the wounded, fleeing from the Japanese, and nursing my dad in his final months. With all of these stressful events happening in my young life (plus not really knowing the complexities of pregnancy) I never even suspected I could be pregnant. But after the medical examination and the doctor's diagnosis, I realized for the first time in my life that the intimate relationship Jack and I had was the beginning of the creation of our child in my body. At last this naive girl found out what the birds and the bees had to do with each other and how their little chicks were created.

When Colonel Grinstead heard about my arrival, he asked me to continue my services with the medical corps. He knew about my work as he was in touch with General Pendatun and Colonel Frank McGee, friends of his from before the war. I still had some time before my delivery, and Grinstead knew I was capable of working among the civilians and soldiers. Because the Colonel had no political ambitions to rise up in the ranks, he worried more about people's welfare than his image. Men of his caliber and insight, including Colonel McGee and my dad, were only interested in doing their part to end the bloody war and save lives. They wanted peace and freedom for the country and were not soldiers of fortune or fame.

In my private talk with Colonel Grinstead I revealed my marriage to Jack Grant, his murder by the Magahats, and my pregnancy. Like a sympathetic father he listened to my story of survival. He also noticed the gun belt around my waist and quickly realized the attachment I felt to it. Having heard about how the gun protected me and guessing how much Jack's last possessions meant to me, he did not attempt to take them away from me. The colonel knew that when the right time came, I would not hesitate to part with Jack's gun. That time came soon enough: just three weeks later when the Japanese escalated their drive to enter Talakag, Colonel Grinstead sent me a letter with his regrets, requesting that I hand over the gun belt to his courier. An officer needed a revolver for defense, and I had the only extra one available. At first it was difficult for me to part with something that had been my close companion since Jack's death. However, as the daughter of a military soldier and the widow of an American officer, I knew I had to obey an order. And since I worked for Colonel Grinstead's people I received food rations and other supplies in addition to the general protection they afforded me.

When the civilian evacuees finally learned of my connection with the military troops, they were exceptionally nice to me, offering me the only bed in a well-built house in the hills above Talakag. Somehow it gave me a sense of belonging to live within a circle of families again, even though it lasted only a short time. It felt wonderful to sleep in a real bed again! I had gotten used to sleeping on the ground, but this was like being home again: the rattan bed had a mat, blankets, and pillows with a mosquito net that hung over the bed. While sleeping on this bed, I had a series of dreams the moment I closed my eyes and allowed my exhausted body to relax. In my first dream I saw a figure standing on the floor looking down at me, and then it began lifting the mosquito net until it reached the top of the bed. The whole action was so real, yet I knew I was dreaming. When the lifted net exposed the image of the person, I opened my eyes and recognized my mom! When I said, "Mom," she dropped the net, ran out of the room, and I followed her in to the center of the living room. But when I embraced her, she fell to my feet dead. When I woke up, I pondered the dream because I had never had one like it before, but sleep quickly overtook me and I had a second dream. This time I saw my mom floating among the clouds in the sky, dressed in a long white robe, with her right arm stretched way down to her side. She had someone holding on to her hand: me. With her beautiful brown eyes my mom looked down saying, "Come with me, Dolly; come with me." But when I responded quickly, "Not yet Mom, not yet," she released her grip on my hand and let me go. She floated up to the sky and was gone; I floated downward, and when I actually opened my eyes, I was right in my own bed. The dreams bothered me because they occurred one after the other, and I did not understand what they were all about. But I worried that they signified something bad.

Late that morning a soldier arrived at the house bearing orders for me to come to Colonel Grinstead at his headquarters. Accustomed to speaking to high-ranking officers, I thought nothing unusual about the summons. When I arrived in the jeep, a soldier ushered me in to the office, and the colonel greeted me, asked how I was doing, whether or not I was comfortable where I was staying, and if I had enough supplies. After I assured him everything was just fine he advised me to brace myself because he had some bad news. Then he handed me a typewritten, signed affidavit by a civilian who had witnessed the dreadful execution of my mom. The man specified that Japanese soldiers took some government men, my mom, an American lady married to a Filipino teacher by the name of Ancheta, and their two children to the outskirts of Malaybalay, where they were stopped next to a very large hole in the ground. Just before the soldiers killed these people, the American lady pleaded with them to go ahead and kill both her and her husband but asked them to spare her children. The Japanese officer and his men laughed, then proceeded to execute every one of them with bayonets, pushing their bodies into a single grave. About ten prisoners died that day in that horrible way, including my beloved mother. The Japanese officer and his men who took part in this massacre were never brought to justice.

In the same affidavit the civilian witness told a story that I already knew: how the Japanese put my brother Philip to work at the airfield. When he contracted cerebral malaria and became very ill, they just beat him to death; then his friends wrapped his frail body in a mat and buried him across the street from the Bethel church in Malaybalay. The report was heart wrenching and painful, but instead of crying I went numb all over, and when the colonel saw that I did not react in a hysterical manner, he became really concerned. Usually this kind of news would make anyone go berserk, yet there I sat, a young pregnant girl reading the devastating report and showing no emotion. Even I could not understand why I did not cry because I loved my mom dearly, and now I knew she had been killed in a most horrible way. I sat there quietly counting my losses—the deaths of my husband, my mom, dad, and brother Philip—and I had no tears left just to show the whole world how devastated I really felt.

Colonel Grinstead then told me that he had offered ten thousand pesos to any of his soldiers who would go into Malaybalay to rescue my mother and brother, but that they did not succeed because the prisoners were heavily guarded at the stockade. He believed that the Japanese probably knew that someone might make the attempt to free them, causing them to put extra guards on to watch every move the prisoners made. Hearing those kind words from my dad's friend gave me some comfort in knowing that someone had at least tried to rescue my mom and my brother. When all was said and done I became mentally drained. Thanking the colonel for being so kind, I asked to be excused so that I might return to the house where I could be alone with my thoughts, and he ordered one of the soldiers to escort me back and remain with me as my bodyguard for the time being.

As the jeep left headquarters, I experienced a sudden flashback of both of my dreams from the night. I wondered if my mom's spirit had come to inform me that she had already died and that she wanted me to go and join her in her eternal home somewhere in heaven. But I remembered that when I told her that I was not ready, she released her grip on my hand. Did she purposely let go so that the bond between a mother and daughter would be finally broken and I could go on with my life here on earth? It was difficult for me to consider those questions. These dreams surely represented the close relationship between my mom and me.

Among the civilian evacuees living close to the house where I stayed was a male nurse named Vegas (not his true name for reasons that will follow). Vegas came to me one day after I learned of my mom's death, telling me that when my delivery time came, I should not hesitate to call him, that he would be glad to help me anytime of day or night. I thanked him for his concern and dismissed the conversation because I had no idea when the baby's birth would occur and I was preoccupied with other thoughts. Everyone had packed his or her things again in preparation for moving because the alert sounded. The Japanese were advancing toward Talakag, so we all moved further up toward the edge of the jungle for safety. About a hundred feet from the forest stood a corn shed (called a *kamalig*) where the owner stored his harvested corn. Although it had an upper level with a nipa roof to protect the corn from the rain, it had no sides except the bottom part for the storage. The civilians who looked after me decided that I should occupy the upper part of that shed when I was ready to deliver my child. Taking time away from their families, the men went searching for a bed, which they luckily found hidden in the bushes. They took this old single bed and mattress, placed them together up in the shed, and the women lent me four white bedsheets to tie on each post for my privacy. Each miracle was a blessing since I had none of my own family members with me. I sincerely thanked each one of those people.

At ten o'clock on the evening of August 8, 1944, I began to experience terrible pains in my stomach, but since they came and went, I just tried to endure them. At midnight the family of another pregnant woman who lived below the hill close to the corn shed called the male nurse Vegas to her house for help. When he arrived he discovered that the woman's baby was in the breech position, yet he continued to encourage her to push as the delivery progressed. It was a difficult labor, and Vegas obviously did not know how to handle it: he decided at some point to shove the unborn baby back into the woman's womb and try to turn it around so that it would be a normal, head-first delivery. By his attempting this maneuver, both mother and child died. While this was a tragedy for that woman and her family, fate was with me because with Vegas's attention directed somewhere else he did not attend me in childbirth. Had he done so, I would not be alive today to tell my story.

As I continued to bravely await the birth of my child, I could hear the wind outside gust into great blows and then die down. When this happened I turned my eyes toward the sky and saw the brilliant stars shining brightly over the shed and me. I thought surely that God must be watching out for me because there was nothing around me but His loving protection: all my family had been taken from me and there was nothing left for me to live for—except perhaps my baby. I had to believe that we were in His hands and that all would be well. While Vegas assisted the woman with the breech birth, my pains became more frequent and pronounced until, finally, after midnight I called out in the dark for someone to help me.

A middle-aged woman heard my voice and came to ask me what was the matter; did I think I was ready to have my baby? She told me that she was a midwife and that she would be glad to help me. It was a miraculous voice, especially when I realized that I did not know the woman. She told me not to be afraid, that she had to go and get a few things but that she would come back, and true to her word, she soon returned with a basin, a lantern, and some water in a bucket. Because of the excruciating pain I was experiencing I had no time to question her further as to who she really was. I remained on the rickety old bed and soiled mattress and I tried to cover myself with the only blanket I had, hoping the pain would go away.

Under normal conditions newborn babies have the privilege of being born in an immaculate hospital under the direction of professional doctors and nurses. They occupy comfortable beds with soft pillows and pure white sheets laundered to perfection and cleanliness; then one by one their families come and peek through the nursery windows to see their newborn beauty. In the meantime mothers receive bouquets of flowers and cards in their hospital rooms. My situation was nothing like that. However, on August 9, 1944, at about three or four in the morning I felt like I was in heaven with the angels: my beautiful platinum blonde baby girl was born, breech but without any complications, and she was all mine. Her first cry made me realize that the whole experience of childbirth had finally ended, and I felt the pain ebb away. When the midwife bundled her up and placed her in my arms I wanted to shout, "Hallelujah! Thank you God!" Her milky white skin, her blue eyes (they say all newborn babies are born with blue eyes), and her appearance—she was Jack Grant all over again. I thought that if he could only see her now he would be so proud and happy, but I knew he was gone forever from our lives, and it was up to me to pick up the pieces and go on. I had the perfect gift, our perfect baby girl. The midwife remarked that surely this child could not really be mine, that she was light-skinned and so beautiful that she must belong to the little fairies that live in the Baletti tree. This was a superstitious belief of some Filipinos, and when she found out that I used to walk back and forth under that tree where the little people supposedly lived, she claimed that they owned my child. Although I lived 26 years of my life in the Philippines I did not believe any of these superstitions, perhaps because of my Christian upbringing. Regardless of what the midwife said, I knew the child certainly was Jack's and mine, and without paying too much attention to her beliefs, I began to nurse my crying infant. Then the midwife changed the subject and asked me if I had ever seen a placenta before. When I said no, she raised this transparent sack filled with blood, so awful looking that I squirmed a little, and watching my reaction she said that she must leave me now to bury the placenta in the forest so that nothing bad would happen to me or my child. She picked up the lantern in her right hand, carried the placenta in her left, and made her way down the stairway of the corn shed. My eyes followed the light showing through the bed sheet until the trees and shrubs swallowed her up; then she was gone. I never saw that midwife again; I never knew who she was or where she disappeared. Was she an angel sent by God in my hour of need?

I now lay alone in the dark with my child. The baby had to be breast-fed, as was the custom in the Philippines; besides I could not have found any baby bottles even if I had wanted them. The purest milk comes from the mother anyway, as her milk includes natural immunities to protect her child from certain diseases. I believe that because I nursed my daughter she never became ill while we lived in the jungle. After nursing time was over and my baby slept in peace, I had to go to the john to empty my bladder, and I thought I would get up in my usual way, stretch out, and feel like my old self again. Wrong! Childbirth had drained me of my energy so that I had difficulty just getting out of bed. I literally bent over with the pain throughout my muscles and joints. With both hands, I clutched the bed-post and then crawled on my hands and knees to get to the bedpan underneath the bed. I felt like a 100-year-old woman, all crouched over; I shall never forget that experience. Fortunately, it never happened to me again, and I was glad—one experience like that was enough for me, yet it made me sympathetic to women who endured childbirth without medical assistance.

When the sun came up the next day, the baby started to cry because she was wet. As I dried her off and saw her distress change to comfort, I named her: Jean Louise Grant, the most beautiful name I could think of. The evacuees reacted with much elation when they saw this beautiful white baby that had been born in their midst. The women offered me some hot soup called *aroscaldo* (chicken soup with rice), believing this was nourishing food for a nursing mother, and even though they knew nothing about the other traumatic experiences I had been through, their kindness helped to ease some of my pain. Of course they wondered about my husband, the father of my child, and I am sure that they speculated about whether or not I was really married, but I still could not speak about Jack because he remained a painful subject for me. I could not share my mourning with others.

Three days after the breech birth of Jean Louise, another alarm sounded: the Japanese had broken through the lines and were heading our way. Their planes streaked over, dropping bombs on us, and they fired their machine guns from above so that we had to jump into foxholes where ten people crammed into a space fit for five. Picking up my baby with all the strength I could muster, I fled to the nearest foxhole and dug in with the rest of the civilians. As soon as the all clear sounded, we returned only to gather up all our things, and then we headed for the hills. Gunfire, including bazookas, still exploded close by, and we knew it came from the Japanese soldiers. As I got ready to leave the surroundings near the corn shed, the place I gave birth to Jean Louise, a family took pity on the two of us and offered me their horse and a raincoat to help us in our travels. Before mounting the horse, I made a sling from one of the bed sheets and placed it over my head, then I slipped my infant child into the sling that cradled her little body. While it was still light, the exodus of civilians and soldiers began to move out and hit the high country where the Japanese could not reach us.

My flight from the Japanese, with me and my child on horseback slowly moving along, reminded me of the Bible story about Mary and Joseph with the little infant Jesus. They fled from a wicked king who wanted to kill the child, but God would not allow this to happen. Although Mary was on a donkey and I was on a horse there seemed to be a parallel to our stories of suffering. Of course I envied her because she had had Joseph, her husband, to comfort her and console her anxieties and fears. He gave her his strength and encouragement when things went bad, but I had no one—except for Jean Louise—who provided incentive rather than strength. My little girl was a gift that was worth living for.

The invasion and occupation of the Japanese Imperial Army in the Philippines caused the horrible deaths of my mom and my brother Philip. My dad never forgave himself for their capture, even though he was powerless to prevent it, and he lost his will to live. An eyewitness identified my mom's remains by the dress she wore, the one I bought for her at Christmas time in 1942. Several years after the war, relatives of the murder victims dug up the bones of all those buried in that hole on the lonely hill. I was living and working in Manila at the time and received a brown envelope with two eight by eleven photographs and a letter inside. I chose to read the letter first; it was from someone I did not know, informing me that my mom's bones had been transferred to the Catholic cemetery in Malaybalay, Bukidnon, and were buried with the rest of those who died with her. The woman who wrote the letter had lost her husband in the massacre, and she explained that she and the other relatives believed that since their loved ones died en masse, they felt they should be buried together. She hoped this met with my approval.

Next I looked down at the two photographs, and when I saw them, my face went white and my body began to shake. My coworker turned to me and asked what was wrong. I wanted to scream at the top of my lungs but did not because I feared people in the office would think I had lost my mind and flipped out. Why? Because one of the photographs showed the skulls of those who were dug up, all lined up across a white coffin with a mark indicating which one belonged to my mom. The next photo was of a closed casket and a note indicating it was ready for burial. Although the second picture was not so bad, the first really traumatized me.

This terrible crime committed during World War II almost stripped me of my sanity. The trauma left me guilty, confused, and searching for answers as to "WHY?" I asked myself why my saintly mother had to die such a horrible death? Why did she make the last-minute choice to send me off, ultimately sparing my life while she died in my place? My dad and I had been unable to convince her to keep up with us in the jungle. She felt sick and tired of running for safety, and she could only endure so much of the unaccustomed rough surroundings. Above all my mom was confident that if she were captured, the Japanese would not harm an "old lady" like her. For ten long years the guilt and blame silently stayed in my mind; somehow I felt responsible for the death of my mom. There were times when I would look up toward the sky and question God, "Why did this happen to my mother, whom I dearly loved, God? My mother was taken, my youngest brother was beaten to death, my husband was killed, and my father died from suffering so long with tropical diseases and a broken heart. Now, I am left all alone." What followed all those years was dead silence from God, which I did not fully understand. Perhaps He was putting me through an obstacle course that He alone knew about. Maybe my faith was really being tested.

Later on, after I came to live in the United States, a Baptist minister analyzed my wartime experiences, and one day in his office he asked me if I knew why I had been chosen to go through what I did. When I replied no, that I did not understand, he assured me that it was because God knew that I could take it, that He knew I had a strong faith and a strong spirit that could not be broken, no matter what kind of trials I faced. I reminded the pastor that I was still hurting inside. He encouraged me to stay the course, and he gave me his blessing. Today I am finally free of any guilt or blame from the deaths of my family that took place during World War II in the Philippines, some ten thousand miles away from my new home in the United States. Like the eagle in the mountains I have been set free, and I have perfect peace, a peace that can never be taken away from me for as long as I live. It is God's ultimate gift within my soul.

11

A Steamboat Ride
to Manila

As Jean Louise and I traveled toward safety and freedom, passing through some small villages along the way to the coast of Mindanao, I heard people talking about some of the barrios we had just gone through: Manbuoyo, Lumitao, Initao, and Manticao. When our group of evacuees had arrived at some of these locations, a few left to remain and resettle their families. The grueling times were now behind us, and my nerves felt calmer as we moved toward Iligan, Lanao, where the guerrilla forces had driven out all the Japanese soldiers. About five kilometers outside Iligan the last family who kept me company on the highway bid me farewell as they went off in a different direction from Iligan, leaving me a lone night traveler with a little baby in my arms. I did not fear for my life because I was in friendly territory now, and I saw no threat of the Japanese along the way. I knew that American submarines had brought in new supplies of guns, ammunition, medical supplies, and good rations, making the guerrillas strong again, able to defeat the Japanese.

When I finally arrived in Iligan in the middle of the night, cradling Jean Louise as we both rode on the old horse, I inquired from two men who were outside their homes talking politics where I could stay for the night.

They gave me directions to the Red Cross center in town, which flooded me with relief because I had heard of the wonderful things that the organization did. Much later I discovered that this Red Cross was not like the one in the United States, and had no direct affiliation. As I neared the home that was called the Red Cross, I heard a woman screaming at her husband. Unsettled by this behavior, but deciding to ignore it, I called out, asking if anyone was at home. Silence followed, so I tried again, inquiring if the lady of the house was available.

From inside I heard the woman snap at her husband, "Now who the hell is that? Here it is midnight. No one in their right mind should be out this late." Even after all this time I can still remember that shrill voice, especially since I had expected a much more welcoming one. Then she ordered her husband to see who was at the door. When he saw me on horseback with an infant in my arms, he asked me what I wanted. I told him that I had been informed that this was the Red Cross and that my daughter and I needed a place to sleep for the night. By then the woman's curiosity had gotten the best of her, so she came to the door to see what was going on. She was drunk! Rudely she asked what the hell I wanted from them, but before I could respond, her henpecked husband related our dilemma. In her garbled, slurred voice she told me that they had no room for us, and she ordered her husband to take us somewhere else, a place I did not recognize since I was not from Iligan. She also instructed her poor husband, whom she called a bastard, to come back right away, or he would never hear the end of it. With those last words she bolted back into the house, silencing her cursing. Such an unwelcome experience with the Red Cross stunned me that night, but I said nothing; however, I did feel sorry for the woman's husband because he was so embarrassed over the whole episode. At a later date I learned that the woman was indeed an alcoholic. An American colonel had set her up with the Red Cross name because of their friendship, but when he moved out of the area, the woman was out of a job.

As the man guided my horse through a few streets he hardly spoke except to ask me where I came from. I told him that I was one of the evacuees hunted down by the Japanese, one who came out of the mountains of Bukidnon. Then he fell silent. Just a few blocks away from the Red Cross we finally came to a residential home obviously once owned by a well-to-do family, and at first I thought the family still occupied the house, but I was wrong. The man told me to wait until he found out if the woman in the home could take care of us for the night. He walked up to the door, knocking loudly a few times so that he could be heard, and finally a woman who looked to be about fifteen years older than I came to the door but did not open it. Instead, she asked who we were and what we wanted.

The man gave his name (I'll call him Bud), and, recognizing his voice, the woman opened the door. As she stood in the semidarkness, I could see a tall, attractive, friendly, and business-like woman. Bud asked her if she could take my baby and me in for the night, explaining that he could not accommodate us at his house because of his wife. Fortunately, the tall woman had three children of her own, so she felt sorry for Jean Louise and me, and she took us in. Bud left immediately, just as his wife had ordered him to do. The kind and generous woman asked me when was the last time I ate, and when I admitted that it had not been since lunch, she made me a cup of tea and a sandwich to fill my starving stomach. She then noticed how exhausted I was, so she led me to the vacant room in the back of the house; after putting Jean Louise in the middle of the double bed I crawled in and fell asleep. This was the most comfortable bed I had slept in since the war broke out, and it felt so great that I did not wake up until the middle of the next day. Since Jean Louise remained asleep, I had the time to enjoy the luxury of a hot shower—the feeling of being clean again was so invigorating. As I finished up, the lady of the house came in to talk to me. She finally introduced herself, and I will call her Mercy. She managed the building where I had spent the night, a transient officers' mess where hot meals were prepared and served in the well-furnished dining room. Officers came and went whenever they were in town, and even if they arrived at night they would be fed; however, they had to find sleeping quarters in one of the barracks close by, as this was strictly a mess hall.

Mercy told me that I could only spend a few days in that back room while I regained my strength because she feared she would lose her job if the commanding officer knew she harbored a mother and child in the back of the mess hall. But she promised to relocate Jean Louise and me to a more permanent place. Mercy not only allowed us to stay there night and day but gave us hot meals out of the kitchen as well. Even though the food was leftovers, it was considered property of the U.S. military, and it made her nervous to give this food to civilians; yet at the same time, her maternal instincts caused her to sympathize with our situation, and she wanted to help us. Mercy instructed me to lie low and to keep my infant from crying out so that we would not be discovered by any army officers. Fortunately little Jeannie, as I had come to call her, was such a good baby and slept most of the time. She only woke up when she was hungry or wet; then I took care of her immediately. Houseboys brought meals to my room, and when I was through, they took the empty plates back to the kitchen. With each passing day my friendship with Mercy strengthened, yet I remained silent about my horrifying experiences. She told me later that what impressed her about me was my intelligence, good upbringing, and friendliness. I do not know if she would have changed her opinion had she known about the fate of my family. I think it was really my baby she cared about most because of Jeannie's good nature and happy disposition.

My big break came after I had been at Mercy's establishment for the allotted three days: Mercy informed me that the military had opened up another transient officers' mess in Dansalan, almost a hundred miles from Iligan. Her employer asked her to take over the job because of her experience and told her to get a replacement for the mess hall in Iligan, so she asked me if I would be interested in managing this mess hall while she went up to the new facility. Mercy offered to train me to manage the place, assuring me that there was nothing to it. Since I needed a job to support my little girl and myself, I accepted the offer right away. Mercy trained me well, first writing down a set of instructions for me to carefully study. When she decided that I was ready to take the giant step of actually managing the mess hall, she spoke to the man in charge about me, and on her recommendation he hired me. He never even knew my age or about my lack of experience, and I wisely said nothing about it either because I wanted to be self-supporting. As long as no one bothered to ask, I did not volunteer information—I knew that much about survival.

Right after I took over the mess hall, an American sergeant was assigned to work with me. He had a jeep, and our joint job consisted of bartering canned foods for fresh vegetables, meat, and fruit. Because of my fluency with local dialects I found it easy to win the confidence of people and convince them to make the exchanges: I was a public relations person and an interpreter at the same time. The military was satisfied with my work because I secured needed items, and the local people remained happy because they knew that I would not cheat them.

Due to my heavy schedule in the officers' mess, I needed someone to take care of Jeannie when she was awake and needed her diapers changed. Breastfeeding her was not a problem because I fed her on a schedule that did not conflict with my work. When I told the Filipino cook about my need, he recommended his wife's relative who came from a family with 11 children and no father to support them. The mother earned a living by taking in laundry from the soldiers. The oldest girl, about 14 years old, could come and work for me. In exchange for taking care of Jeannie I offered to provide her with some money and to send some food home with her, and the mother eagerly consented. The girl came each morning and left in the afternoon after she finished her work and when I was able to wind down mine for the day.

One bright afternoon in the middle of a busy period in the dining room, I heard a very loud explosion from the back room, and I leaped out of my chair, making a dash for that room because that was where Jeannie and her baby-sitter were. When I arrived at the doorway, I was petrified to see my little girl covered with blood. I must have screamed because a visiting American officer rushed in just in time to prevent me from collapsing. When he saw Jeannie, he said that we had to get her to the hospital right away. He moved quickly toward my child, scooped her into his arms, and ran to the jeep outside, with me close at his heels. He drove to the emergency field hospital and had Jeannie examined, but when the doctors cleaned her up they found no evidence of any cuts or lacerations on her body. I was so relieved when they gave me the good news that only then did I think of the sitter. I had not even thought to look for her in the room because I was so concerned about Jeannie, and now I wondered if she had blood on her face and her clothing as well, if she had been injured from whatever had made that loud noise. I had to go back and find out.

Returning to the mess hall with the officer and a frightened but unhurt Jeannie, I went to the back room and, sure enough, the baby-sitter was still there, her clothing and face soaked with blood. She was in shock, silent, but able to move. I took her by the hand, and the officer and I drove back to the field hospital so that the doctors could examine her. When the medical officer cleaned up her face, he was horrified at what he saw: whatever caused the explosion left pellets on the girl's face, blinding her. Of course we had to report the incident to the military police so that an investigation could be launched, and the investigating team found a Japanese booby trap on the floor next to the double bed in my room. When the team questioned the baby-sitter, she said that she found a little gadget in the far corner of the window behind the wall. Thinking that it was some kind of a toy, she picked it up and brought it to the bedside, but when she knocked it on the wooden edge of the bed, the firing pin triggered the explosion. It was a miracle that the girl had not been killed and that Jeannie was not seriously injured. Although I felt so grateful that nothing had happened to my baby, I was distraught because there was nothing I could do for the baby-sitter except to send her back to her mother. I felt guilty about that for a long time.

The United States Army formally recognized the guerrilla forces in Iligan because of their mopping up operations in driving out the Japanese from that province. However the guerrillas did not remain there because other provinces needed help; and when they moved away, leaving behind just a small garrison of soldiers, the American mess hall closed down. In the meantime the U.S. Army established the PCAU (Philippine Civilian Army Unit) in Dansalan, Lanao, and they needed some dependable workers. Mercy, who also lost her job because of the closing of that mess hall, called me to work with her. The PCAU paid good wages, and we needed money to sustain ourselves. Mercy and I not only did inventory work, but we also distributed food supplies to displaced and hungry civilian evacuees, including the Moros who lived in the area. We helped give away tons of rice, flour, sugar, canned goods, powdered milk, and other dried goods. Each recipient had to fill out forms indicating a head of the household and how many were in the family, and as long as our employers approved their applications Mercy and I doled out the appropriate portion of supplies to them.

At first the distribution went smoothly, with people receiving their allotted provisions, but then I noticed that the Moro heads of household kept coming back, twice or even three times. Mercy and I prodded them with questions and were astonished at what we discovered: they listed all their dead relatives who were buried in the cemetery close by. As a result the PCAU ordered us not to give them any more than their allotted rations, and this made the Moros mad. They quietly left the building, so I did not expect them back until the next time they were eligible to legitimately pick up more foodstuffs. I was dead wrong. The Moros came back armed with machine guns and began firing at us from outside of the building. Mercy and I were in luck because the windows had bars on them, and we quickly bolted the warehouse from the inside, dodging bullets by hiding behind the mountain of supplies. After this incident the military had to be called in to prevent further trouble from the Moros, but despite any possible danger, Mercy and I remained with PCAU until their supplies ran out and they closed the distribution center.

Between these two jobs I managed to save enough money to take care of Jeannie and myself, and having even saved a little extra, I believed it was time for us to permanently leave the province of Lanao. While living there, I had repeatedly dreamed that we boarded a very large vessel that slowly sailed away from the Pacific Islands of the Philippines, where I was born and raised. I initially dismissed these dreams, but they came true in later years. For now, though, Jeannie and I boarded a local steamship in Mindanao in 1945 and left for the big city of Manila. I intended to make the capital city a springboard for us to travel to the United States, where I could find out more about my dad's citizenship papers and inquire about Jack's mother in Ohio. How I longed for a family again! In regard to my dad's papers, I believed they would help me acquire some of his back pension that accumulated from 1941 when the war started until 1944 when he died, money I counted on to get Jeannie and me established in our new home, wherever that might be. I never did get that pension money because I failed to file the claim within a year after my dad died. I could not convince the pension board that this was impossible because the Japanese were still

chasing me over mountains and through jungles in 1945, and there was no
pension board office in the province where I lived. The same thing happened to the entitlement of Jack's life insurance. His mother received it all
because I had trouble proving the legality of my marriage since all the original papers had been lost or destroyed. Jack's mother told the government
that her son did not have a wife and child, even though some of his army
buddies had told her of our existence. She was hurt and angry that Jack did
not marry the girl she chose for him—the one across the street from her—
and instead chose a Filipina American.

The steamboat ride from Mindanao to Manila took almost five days.
Although I had never been to such a large city in all my life, I felt Manila
would not be any more difficult to find my way in than the jungles in Bukidnon. When Jeannie and I disembarked from the ship, the *cargadors* (bag-
gage handlers) helped us a great deal. After I explained to them that I was
a displaced person, they told me about a refugee camp in Mandaluyong,
Rizal, where people like me could find food and a temporary shelter. Then
they summoned a jeepney, a salvaged military jeep converted into a passenger vehicle. Riding in one of those was an experience I will never forget because the driver zipped in and out of the heavy city traffic with his
foot heavy on the gas pedal. I was nineteen years old, wearing a bedraggled,
old-fashioned dress, carrying my one-year-old daughter in one arm and an
old suitcase in the other hand. Not knowing exactly where we were going
when I settled us in that jeepney, I kept my faith and a little prayer in my
heart.

Soon the driver stopped in front of a very large building then informed
me that this was the refugee camp, so I paid him. All kinds of people
swarmed around outside, and when I walked up the flight of stairs and
entered the place, it proved even worse, with hoards of people packed in like
sardines in a can. Before I could become a statistic, I had to fill out some
papers making me eligible to stay. My application was quickly approved,
and Jeannie and I were led to a far corner of the huge room where several
canvas cots and a blanket lay open and ready for occupants. Each day we
received simple meals at our cots because there was no room for a dining
table to seat the masses of refugees. The noise was tremendous, but I tol-
erated it because it came from the children, some of whom ran around while
others cried for attention. In spite of the bedlam Jeannie and I slept soundly
that first night after our exhausting journey at sea.

I awoke the next morning during the distribution of our breakfast
meal, sat up, and made ready to receive my tray of steamed rice and salted
fish. Two days went by in this way, giving me the opportunity to regain my
strength and spend some time with Jeannie, who was rapidly growing into

a very inquisitive child. Then I decided it was time for me to try to find my oldest brother Samuel. The last time I heard about him, the Japanese had him imprisoned in one of the camps in Luzon, so I did not know whether he was dead or alive, but I wanted to find out. I approached the man behind the desk at the refugee center, and I asked how I could make inquiries about my brother. In response he handed me the morning paper and told me to call the newspaper office about running an inquiry ad. The call proved emotional for me because I knew there was a good chance that I would hear bad news when what I wanted most of all was to hear that Samuel was alive. When the man at the newspaper came on the line, I slowly read him the words I wanted printed in his newspaper: "Mr. Samuel Dore, your only sister Dorothy (Dolly) Dore is in the refugee camp at Mandaluyong, Rizal. Please contact her if you are somewhere out there." Then the man on the phone instructed me to pay the fellow at the desk and get my receipt.

At about ten o'clock the next morning I heard my name called over the loudspeaker system, requesting that I come to the front desk. Having no idea what was wanted of me, I picked up my baby and timidly approached the desk. I saw a tall, slender, good-looking man standing close by; I would have recognized that face anywhere in the world because it belonged to my big brother Sam. In spite of the years of separation and hardship, we recognized each other immediately and with tears in our eyes we hugged each other. Then he turned aside to introduce his wife, Len, and I showed off Jeannie. It was indeed a great reunion for my brother and me—I felt as if I had been found. We did not stand around for long because once the introductions ended Sam said that he was taking us home with them. He told me to get my things so we could leave this terrible place. The sound of the word *home* brought back a flood of memories of our childhood when we had so much fun and felt so loved in the house we lived in at 88 Claveria Street in Davao City, Mindanao. I knew I could never recapture those good old days because they were gone forever, but I knew that now I had to concentrate on creating new memories.

Sam's rented house in Santa Mesa was just big enough for him, his wife, and their three children, and although they welcomed Jeannie and me, I quickly realized that our being there added a huge burden to my brother's family. However, I needed time to acquaint myself with the big city of Manila and to just relax a bit before Jeannie and I struck out on our own again. While waiting for that day to come I asked Sam how he managed to stumble on the ad I put in the newspaper. He told me that the day the paper came he was in a big hurry because he was running late for work, but for some strange reason, a strong force compelled him to pick up the newspaper and read it. When he turned the pages, they fell open to the advertisements and his eyes caught my ad. He called his boss, told him about his sister, and he allowed Sam to take the day off. Surely some divine intervention had been at work.

In the Philippines the oldest brother or sister in the family traditionally takes responsibility for the younger ones when their parents die. In my case I knew that my brother did not make enough money to sustain his family; therefore, I decided to get myself an apartment and a job so that I would be self-supporting. The war had changed tradition; I could not expect anyone to take care of me. Since he faced other problems with his family, Sam did not try to stop me from going out on my own.

During the short time I stayed with my brother and his family, Sam repeatedly asked for the details of my war experiences, especially information about how our mom and dad and youngest brother Philip had died. I reluctantly told him of the gruesome way the Japanese killed our mom and brother, and I also shared with him a little about Jack's death although I still could not speak too much about it. The trauma of that terrible murder continued to upset me, so I preferred to remain silent on the subject. I am glad that I did not share all those horrid experiences because Sam's were no better. He harbored a deep hatred for the Japanese because of his imprisonment at Cabanatuan, where prisoners of war, both American and Filipino soldiers, were incarcerated. He saw atrocities committed by the Japanese on our prisoners, and he experienced some of the cruelty himself. Hearing about the deaths of our family members did not soften his hatred for the Japanese, the communists, or any of their sympathizers. Sam carried this hostility to his grave, as I was unable to change his frame of mind. In part I believe his marriage of many years did not help his views because his domineering wife controlled his life, and she hated the Japanese as well. In his last years he became a very angry man with a disturbed personality. Sam was no longer the brother I knew. That brother used to be full of life, fun, and laughter, and with his good looks and personality he was popular with the girls wherever he went. Between the war and his marriage, he suppressed too many of his real emotions through the years until he developed lung cancer from being a heavy smoker. After surgeons removed half of one of his lungs, I helped him to bring out his anger as he began to recover, and he finally shared his feelings. This was how I found out about his imprisonment at the notorious Cabanatuan prison camp in Luzon. Those moments were precious to me because for a short time I had my brother back to his old self. Sam died in Manila at the age of 73.

The short weeks I stayed at Sam's place helped me appraise my situation. First I had to get an apartment so that Jeannie and I could have our own place. I had managed to save some money and had enough to pay for

Left to right: Sam, me, and George together in the fall of 1976.

one month's rent for a one-bedroom apartment that I found in the newspaper. The friends I met in Manila kindly offered me one or two items from their homes, and in time I had as much as I needed to get started on my own. Jeannie and I had a single bed, a table, two chairs, and a lamp. Fortunately, a refrigerator and a stove came with the apartment. Someone gave me an old record player, and I used it to listen to my collection of country western singers: Ernest Tubb, Eddy Arnold, Tex Ritter, Burl Ives, and Gene Autry. Some of their songs sounded sad, but they told a story of their own. I also knew it was time for me to get a job because my money would run out soon. I had no skills beyond my experiences with the medical corps and the officers' mess, but I was willing to work hard. My dad always told me never to be ashamed to do any hard work providing it was honest and respectable, easy advice for me to follow because I wanted it that way.

Although Japan surrendered on August 14, 1945, after the atomic bombings of Hiroshima and Nagasaki, the mopping up operations still continued in the city of Manila. The stench of dead Japanese bodies and civilians permeated the air around us. The contamination of food and water forced me to boil drinking water, and I continued breastfeeding my child until I could get some canned milk. I wanted to protect Jeannie from deadly diseases like typhoid, cholera, and dysentery that were so prevalent right after World War

II. Adults and children died of these sicknesses in near epidemic propor-
tions.

Soldiers could still be seen everywhere in the city of Manila. Members
of the United States Army, Navy, Air Force, and Marines arrived as occupation troops to replace those who had fought in the war. The Corps of
Engineers continued their work, bulldozing hundreds of dead Japanese
bodies, burying them in one hole in the ground on the outskirts of the city.
Some of the army men continued to pursue the Japanese in the hills, enemy
soldiers who either refused to surrender or would not believe that the Japanese Imperial Army had been defeated. Some Japanese soldiers who refused
to surrender committed hara-kiri. But as long as the fighting continued,
Filipino civilians remained restricted to certain areas in and around Manila
proper. About one hundred thousand Filipinos died on Luzon during the
fighting, and they continued to die even after peace had come. The Japanese
massacred some forty thousand civilians in Malaybalay, Mindanao, alone,
including members of my family.

Through some of my friends, who had access to the U.S. military newspaper *Stars and Stripes*, I read about a clerical job opening at one of the field
hospitals. I found a baby-sitter to look after Jeannie, put on some clothes
I had recently bought, fixed my hair, and inquired about the possibility of
getting hired. I traveled by jeepney to the 312th General Hospital located
in Mandaluyong, Rizal, where an American sergeant interviewed me, and
his first question was if I knew how to use a typewriter. I replied with a crisp
"Yes, sir," ever mindful of my military training, even though I knew nothing about a typewriter. The only thing I did with my fingers was to play the
piano, and I thought that surely the piano and the typewriter had something in common so it would not be too difficult to learn to type.

The sergeant then asked if I knew anything about a file system, and I
lied again, assuring him that I knew how to file, when in fact I knew nothing about any filing systems. Both responses were lies, but I was so desperate
for a job to support the baby and myself that I felt I had to tell some untruths,
God help me. But I knew that I was willing to work very hard, learn quickly,
and never make them sorry if they hired me. The sergeant told me to return
the next day since he had a few others to interview beside myself. He wanted
to be sure to pick the right person to work for him; there were many to
choose from.

When I showed up the next day, I was surprised that the sergeant hired
me on the spot, and at the same time I became a little nervous because I
had never done any office work in my life. After the sergeant showed me
around he told me he picked me for the job because my command of English
impressed him, adding that I was the best looking of all the applicants. I

thought, What flattery, but what if he finds out that I don't know anything about working in the office? I was not surprised or offended that he commented about my looks; I was used to that from soldiers, but I worried about being able to keep the job.

Later that morning, when the sergeant had me sit down behind the Underwood typewriter and asked me to type a short letter, he found me out. To my great relief he did not fire me. Being older and wiser he decided to take the time to teach me to use the machine and understand the alphabetical filing system he kept in the office. I listened intently to all his instructions, filed all the knowledge away in my brain, and after three days I knew all I had to know about filing and typing. In my triumph I reaffirmed that I was a quick learner: as long as someone instructed me with patience, in only a matter of days I could recall all the things taught to me.

My job with the 312th General Hospital proved short-lived due to the deactivation of the hospital units and their return to the United States. However, I managed to work long enough to learn all I needed to know about office procedures, so I was ready for anything. The sergeant, satisfied with my work, gave me a good typewritten recommendation so that I easily moved into my next job with the 31st Hospital. When that unit folded, I transferred to the 598th General Hospital. I gained a reputation for being dependable and reliable in my work, and my employers were very satisfied with my performance. During my employment with the American field hospitals I made many friends among the employees and my employers. When they heard bits and pieces of my story about how I survived the war, they generously gave me some canned milk for Jeannie and a few other supplies to improve our meals.

I worked with the U.S. military hospitals from mid–1945 to the summer of 1946, gradually relating more incidents about my life to key military personnel. I told them how I lost my parents and my husband and because the Japanese burned and destroyed all our homes and government buildings, I lost all my papers to prove who I really was. Lucky for me, they believed my story, which made them more sympathetic and helpful in directing me toward other assistance. When the American Graves Registration established itself in Manila, my friends told me to file my papers with them and have my dad's remains in the mountains of Basak transferred to a military cemetery in Manila. I followed their advice and submitted a map to the Registration service indicating the location of my dad's gravesite, and I included copies of my dad's discharge papers from the military. His body was found and transferred to the Clark Air Force Base Cemetery, where it remains today. All of these people were so very helpful to me, encouraging me not to give up, that the worst part of my life was behind me.

Gravesite of Sgt. Victor A. Dore at former Clark Air Force Base in Angeles, Pampanga, Philippines, my dad's final resting place.

As stores and shops reopened in Manila I began to do a little shopping for Jeannie and myself. After being frugal with my money for so long I now had enough to purchase incidentals and luxury items: a new dress for me and a new outfit for my little girl. During these shopping expeditions I ran into people that knew my parents and who were with me during the guerrilla days, and they helped me to get all the necessary papers I needed to establish myself again. I realized that I could not stay in Manila much longer. Seeing all of these people, even though it was a joy to see them alive, brought back painful memories, and I wanted to get away to the United States; but before Jeannie and I could even leave the Philippines, I had to assemble all my legal papers. I felt awful when I could not even prove that I was the legitimate child of Pauline and Victor Dore, residents of Davao City for over 25 years. The Japanese burned down all the municipal buildings that kept all records of marriages, births, and other similar documents. Because of Japanese hatred of the Americans and other whites, they looted and burned down their homes and confiscated their automobiles and household goods. Fortunately, the American and Philippine governments allowed affidavits with secondary evidence to be accepted in lieu of missing original documents. This meant that witnesses had to sign statements proving who Jeannie and I were, how old we were, and where we had been living. These papers had to be notarized to make the piece of paper legal and acceptable, steps that millions of people in the Philippines were forced to take after the war. I felt like an alien—a woman without a country, a family, or a home.

Fate smiled on us, though, as I began to run into people who migrated to Manila just like I did; the shock of finding each other after the war proved overwhelming because these people knew that my whole family had been killed. The amazing thing about such encounters, however, was that we even recognized one another—even though we had all aged in the course of hardship and trauma we looked remarkably the same. I spent many happy hours celebrating reunions with old acquaintances who kindly invited Jeannie and me to their new homes in Manila. Many of these people were my dad's age, and the war had taken a great deal out of them; but before they passed away, they signed affidavits acknowledging my parents' marriage, my birth, and the existence of my three brothers. As for my marriage in Mailag to Captain John William Grant, the judge who officiated at the marriage also turned up in Manila to start his own legal practice, and he gladly signed an affidavit attesting that he conducted the marriage that early morning of October 31, 1943. I also managed to find some of the civilian evacuees who were with me when my little girl was born in the corn shed. Some escaped the snare of the Japanese and survived, and after the war they too migrated to Manila. When I ran into them they were amazed to find that I came out of the jungles alive with Jeannie and were more than willing to sign affidavits about my giving birth on August 9, 1944.

Like many survivors of World War II in the Philippines, I placed a high priority on acquiring authorized verifications of my existence. In a way it seemed like a silly thing because I knew who I was. It was not my fault that the Japanese Imperial Army decided to be the tiger of Asia and gobble up the whole Pacific Rim. It was not my fault that they burned and destroyed my country and displaced millions of people from their homes. For innocent civilians like myself the war was a nightmare, a living hell from beginning to end. Sadly enough even today, the guilty parties who started the bloody war, the Japanese Imperial Army and their country, refuse to admit their part in that savage conflict. Like Pilate in the Bible they washed their hands of the blood of millions of people, yet those who survived sustained deep physical and psychological scars. How can the Japanese government justify the inhuman atrocities that were committed by their army? God will be the final judge.

Just before leaving my last job with the 598th General Hospital, I was granted a half day leave from my office work. I knew that my work could never be permanent with the military because it kept closing down its various establishments, so I decided to find a more permanent position. The U.S. Veterans Administration on Luzuriaga Street in Manila had just opened, and it was hiring office girls, so I applied for a clerk-typist job and was hired in the Contact Division working for an elderly man. Because I had good credentials from the military hospitals, the manager was convinced I was capable of working in his department. This division of the Veterans Administration dealt with applications for benefits for widows, orphans, and disabled veterans who survived World War II, who numbered in the thousands. As long as they could prove their relationship with their deceased spouse, the widows were eligible for a lifetime pension. My job involved preparing

Childhood photo of Jean Louise Grant (with me). (Photo c. 1950)

the affidavits and submitting them to the contact officers who had the applicants sign them prior to notarization. From our office the papers went to Washington, D.C., for final approval; upon approval, the government mailed the allocated monthly pensions directly to the widows.

When the volume of work grew steadily at the Luzuriaga office, the director decided we all needed a much larger office to work in and transferred operations to a high-rise office on Escolta in the heart of Manila. The newly appointed director was General R. Lovett, a good administrator. In addition to my work I continued to take care of Jeannie, with the help of a paid baby-sitter whom I trusted, and I saw my brother Sam and his family from time to time, but most of my free hours were spent playing with my daughter. It was a busy and happy time because of Jeannie, but I felt lonely. My civil service employment lasted from 1946 to 1951, when I finally resigned from my job to go to the United States with my daughter on the USS General Shanks. At long last I had enough money for us to get started there, and I longed to see the country my dad loved so well.

While living in my adopted country as a United States citizen for the last 48 years, I have been frequently asked how I feel toward the Japanese people now that the war is over, if I have any hatred for them after what the Japanese soldiers did to my family in World War II, if I hold any grudges. My response to all this is no. I cannot blame the Japanese people for their soldiers getting out of control and causing millions of people to lose their lives. As for holding any grudges or feelings of hatred, I refuse to be drawn into this type of emotion, either, because I know better: it would only destroy me. Instead, I prefer to leave the ultimate judgment to God, who sees all and knows all. Although the Japanese government denies that the atrocities ever happened or even that they started the war, they cannot deny themselves before God and escape His final judgment. In the meantime I am thankful that my parents never taught me how to hate or to be prejudiced against others because they are different from me in religion, race, or culture, and I intend to remain this way always. It was my saintly mother who taught me to forgive my enemies and those who despise and persecute me, leaving the ultimate judgment to Almighty God.

Several times I have attempted to get this story published, only to meet with rejection from people who were too uncomfortable with my unusual war story. But I believe that any and all war stories must be told, they cannot be swept under the rug, or wars will continue if their horrors are forgotten. With regard to my feelings about the war, I believe that there are no winners in the end. Both the aggressors and the liberators caused a great deal of destruction, after which the people of the Philippines have had to reconstruct their lives and their culture. Even though the Allies triumphed over the Axis powers, the countless dead are gone forever. In my own understanding and experiences about war I have come to realize that war is no solution to humanity's greed or pride. I often wonder about the adage "To the winner belong the spoils." Winners enjoy the spoils only until they themselves meet with death, and then they cannot take the spoils with them. When you sow hate, you reap hate. When you sow love, love comes back to you. So who are the true winners? I wish for humankind to learn from history, not to repeat it but to profit from the mistakes.

Looking back and remembering how I survived the insanity of World War II, I attribute my survival to my keeping my faith in God alive and reflecting on the wonderful memories of my childhood. I knew that my mom and dad truly wanted and loved me, and I knew my three brothers felt the same, all of which gave me a tremendous amount of security and confidence. Most of all, God must have really loved me because He made me worthy of undertaking a difficult path in life and surviving. He needed living witnesses of war's hell, and I am one. Thank God He never left me or forsook me because without Him I would have perished long ago.

My written life story is a legacy for my beloved children, my six grandsons, four granddaughters (one of whom is a youth minister), and ten great-grandchildren who have most of their lives to keep on going. I hope the story inspires them and gives them courage and hope as they forge ahead with their lives. I want them to know about their roots so they will be proud and so that no one can ever make them ashamed of where they came from. Their roots can be a source of strength from which to draw. We must never allow others to make us feel guilty or ashamed of our roots because we are who we are. Be proud of your culture, race, color, and creed, and remember that religious beliefs can be a bulwark to survival, as I well know. I journeyed through many unusual trials and tribulations beginning at the early age of fifteen and learned to trust in God for strength when the going got rough. I believe that history can teach us valuable lessons to live by.

I want my family to know that I have been blessed in having two different worlds to draw my resources from. From my mom's Philippine culture I inherited grace, religion, family unity, hospitality, warm friendships, and resilience to survive. She died that I might carry on where she left off in faith, hope, and love. From my dad's British and French background I learned much about discipline, duty, honor, and love of country. Most of all I learned horse sense or common sense, which I found so important in dealing with anything that happens in life.

Besides the family ties, love, tenderness, stability, and good sense that my parents gave me, my fond memories of attending a private Christian school in the Philippines remain dear to me. Silliman University High School, which my brothers Samuel and George and I had the privilege of attending for almost two years, solidified my belief in God. There, all preparations were made for me before World War II destroyed my country and its people. My athletic participation, religious training, and my association with several saints of God through our faculty members prepared me for the turbulent storms that unexpectedly hit our shores.

One of my biggest regrets is not having been able to recover my husband's body in the jungles of Tigwa. Even with the help of the American Graves Registration that tracked down and excavated all the remains of military personnel after the war, I could not find Jack's body. Because I had to leave his lifeless body lying on the ground in the jungle where the Magahats murdered him, the heavy floodwaters of the stream probably washed it away, never to be found. However, I had the consolation of finding his name etched on the upright marble column in the Manila Cemetery situated about six miles southeast of that city, within the limits of Fort Bonifacio, the former U.S. Army Fort McKinley. The 152-acre cemetery sits on a prominent plateau, visible at a distance from the east, south, and west, and it contains the largest number of graves of our military dead from World War II: 17,206. The chapel, a tall white masonry building enriched with sculpture and mosaic, stands near the center of the semicircle columns with rooms at each end. Twenty-five large mosaic maps in these rooms recall the achievements of the American Armed Forces in the Pacific, China, India, and Burma. Inscribed on the rectangular piers of the semicircle columns are the names of 36,280 of the missing who gave their lives in the service of their country and who sleep in unknown graves. Carved in the floors are the seals of the states and territories. John William Grant's name, along with thousands of others, is inscribed in alphabetical order in one of the upright columns there for all to see and remember.

One of the main reasons for my return to the Philippines in 1970, after living in the United States since September 21, 1951, was that my youngest daughter Sarah won a Miss Pearl of the Orient contest in San Francisco at the age of 16, and the main prize was an all-expense-paid trip to the country of her mother's birth. My husband, James Dowlen, Sarah, and myself were the guests of the Philippine government during the 35 days, and the tourist bureau planned our whole itinerary. It was a sentimental journey for Jim as well because his ship, the *Sangamon* CVE-26, assisted in General Douglas MacArthur's famous landing in Leyte, Philippines, in October 1944. Since we had many days to enjoy ourselves, we were pampered and dined in the best hotels and restaurants in the big cities we visited in the Philippines, including Davao, the city where I was born. The mayor and other diplomats invited us out to dinner; we also visited my dad's grave at Clark Air Force Base in Pampanga and went to Baguio City, located in the mountains of Luzon, the site of the equivalent of the Philippines' West Point Academy, Camp John Hay, which served as a civilian internment center during the war. Before returning to the United States we made one last stop: to the American cemetery where I found Jack's name. I wept for the fallen heroes, including my own, because I knew how great a sacrifice each one had made, including Jack, so that people like me would remain alive and free. They are the true heroes of the war.

Another regret I have was not being able to meet Kathryn Crave Grant, Jack's mother. Since I was the last person who was with her beloved son and I became his wife, I wanted to share with her all that I knew about the final months of his life: how Jack and I met and married and how our little girl, a carbon copy of the father she never met, was born in the mountains of Bukidnon. Kathryn had the opportunity to get to know us when Jeannie and I came to the United States in 1951 because those who knew Jack and me in the Philippines notified her of our arrival. But she bitterly resented me for being foreign born and for taking Jack away from the girl across the street. Kathryn died at the Crestview Nursing Home in Medina, Ohio, lonely and alone. She not only lost her son, but she missed seeing the most precious gift that her only boy, Jack, had given her: a granddaughter. Her prejudice and her blind pride sent her down to her sorrow, despair, and death. She robbed herself of the joy of living by not accepting the reality of her only son's marriage, his death, and his child.

As Jean Louise Grant grew up, she became a part of a loving, caring, and sharing Christian family—Jim's and mine. She remains intelligent, witty, and full of life. She often asked me about the mixture of nationalities that mingled in her blood. When I counted half a dozen of them, she said, "Do you mean I am like chop suey?" We always had a hearty laugh over this. Jeannie met and married a fine young man named Arthur Woodall, Jr., after graduating from Blackford High School in the Santa Clara Valley of California. The marriage took place on August 11, 1962, and they are still married today. Out of their marriage they have three sons: Mark Anthony, Kelly Edward, and Brien Kevin. The two older sons are married and have two daughters each. The youngest son, Brien, married Heather on June 21, 1997, and in time they will have some children of their own. Jeannie has always been a stable girl and a good wife to her husband. In spite of being born during the war, she has not suffered any aftereffects like I have; she was well nurtured, loved, and cared for during her infancy and never felt abandoned at any time. Most of all she was wanted and protected by me from the moment she was born to the time she grew up to be a fine young lady.

On July 25, 1999, I celebrated my 74th birthday, grateful and thankful to God that I have lived this long. Just before this birthday I finally received my college diploma; I am a graduate of a school of ministry, and I intend to go on to get a master's degree in counseling. It is never too late; you are never too old, to help others.

In the town of Talakag in the province of Bukidnon on Mindanao Island stands a building on a few hectares of property, built a few years after the war. The place is called Bethany Christian Home for Children, Inc. The executive field secretary is a 92-year-old American lady named G. Louise Lynip. I remember meeting Miss Lynip only once, when my family and I first entered Malaybalay after the surrender of our troops in May 1942. She was the missionary lady in charge of the Bethany Home, whose Christian Filipino friends took her to hide in the mountains of Bukidnon where the Japanese never found her, and she survived the war. In early 1994, while looking through some of my Christian newsletters and magazines, my eyes caught an advertisement for this Bethany Christian Home for Children, which took in orphaned, abused, and abandoned children. When I noted the Talakag address, my mind drifted back to those difficult times there during the war. Jim and I had recently lost our middle daughter, Mary Ellen "Niki" McCurry, from an aneurysm of the brain at the age of 37, and I decided we should sponsor one child in Talakag in Niki's memory. I chose a child who really needed help, a physically deformed and abused little girl. When I received my first letter from the Home, G. L. Lynip, the same missionary lady I met many years before, signed it, and she remembered me. Because I believe in the work of this lady and because I want to give back something positive to an area that took so much from me, I have decided to give all the proceeds of my book to the Bethany Christian Home for Children, Inc., because children are our future, the next generation that will improve upon our hard-earned triumphs, to keep us from using war as a solution to problems.

Index